Generational Wealth Begins with Generational Knowledge®

The Seven Stages of Financial Empowerment and a Legacy of Prosperity

—A roadmap for breaking cycles of poverty, building lasting wealth, and empowering future generations—

by Dr. Joaquin E. Wallace

Generational Wealth Begins with Generational Knowledge®:
The Seven Stages of Financial Empowerment and a Legacy of Prosperity

ISBN Paperback: 979-8-89576-096-3
ISBN Hardback: 979-8-89576-097-0

Published by:

Acknowledgments

When I created the **Seven-Stage Generational Wealth Model**©, I knew it had to reflect something deeper than financial theory. It had to tell the truth about how wealth—or the lack of it—is shaped across generations. We are influenced first as individuals, then by our families, our culture, our communities, and ultimately by society itself.

This work is personal for me. It's not just about financial education; it's about acknowledging where you come from and empowering you to build something greater. True generational wealth is not just about money; it's about shifting mindsets, healing old wounds, and creating new legacies rooted in both wisdom and action.

This journey wasn't taken alone.

First and foremost, I thank my wife, **Jamelle Wallace**. Your belief in me has been my anchor. Your patience, encouragement, and faith in the vision made the long nights and early mornings worthwhile. To my children, **Jameelah, Sasha, and Kendall**—you are the reason I remain committed to creating a better financial future, not just for our family, but for generations yet to come. To my granddaughter, **Quinn**—your light and laughter remind me daily why legacy matters.

To my **Mother** and **Father** and my **immediate family and friends**, your sacrifices and teachings have shaped the very foundation of this work. Every lesson, every conversation, every challenge along the way found its way into these pages.

A heartfelt thank you to each guest who participated in **The New Wealth Wave Podcast**. Your candid interviews, stories, and insights were instrumental in shaping the themes of this book. To **Rei**, who worked tirelessly and in lockstep with me to build the podcast, your creativity, diligence, and vision have been a gift to this mission.

To the team that helped bring this book to life—**Jo**, **Mike**, and my editor **Kathleen**—thank you for sharpening the vision, refining the message, and ensuring this story could reach those who need it most.

And to all of my **family, friends, and colleagues** who have walked with me, encouraged me, challenged me, and believed in me—you are part of this journey. I carry your voices with me on every page.

Also, a special shout out to all **NUPES**, representing excellence!

This is more than a book.

This is our collective legacy.

With gratitude,
Dr. Joaquin E. Wallace

Table of Contents

APPENDIX

Disclaimer

The information contained in this book is provided for educational and informational purposes only and is not intended as financial, investment, legal, or tax advice. While every effort has been made to ensure the accuracy and reliability of the content at the time of publication, the author and publisher make no guarantees of any specific outcome or result based on the information presented.

Investing involves risk, including the potential loss of principal. The strategies and opinions expressed are general in nature and may not be suitable for your individual circumstances. Before making any financial decisions or implementing any strategies discussed in this book, readers are strongly encouraged to consult with a qualified financial advisor, accountant, or legal professional who understands their unique situation.

The author and publisher disclaim any liability, loss, or risk incurred as a direct or indirect consequence of the use and application of any content in this book. Past performance is not indicative of future results.

By reading this book, you acknowledge that you are solely responsible for your own financial decisions.

Note: To protect the privacy of those involved, the names and identifying details of individuals have been changed throughout this book, except for podcast guests, who are identified with their permission.

How to Use This Book

This book is designed to be more than just something you read. It's a guide, a companion, and a practical tool to help you build lasting financial change and generational wealth. Each of the seven chapters represents a key step in your journey, carefully structured to build on the one before it. At the end of every chapter, you'll find reflection questions intended to help you personalize the lessons, dig deeper, and apply the principles to your real life. Take your time with these. The goal isn't speed—it's transformation.

Rather than reading this book cover to cover in a week, permit yourself to slow down and truly engage with each stage. Some steps may feel familiar, while others might challenge your mindset or habits. That's part of the process. Whether you spend a few days or a few weeks on a chapter, move at a pace that feels right for you. Come back to it often, revisit your answers, and let this book be a steady companion as you lay the foundation for a financially empowered future.

The questions at the end of each chapter can also be downloaded from my website: https://www.drjwallace.com/

Foreword

By Dr. Preston D. Cherry, CFP®, CFT™
Founder of Concurrent Wealth, Author of *Wealth in the Key of Life*

Some books educate. Some inspire. A few transform. This book is one of those few.

When I first crossed paths with Dr. Joaquin Wallace through our mutual mentor and financial therapy pioneer, Saundra Davis, I sensed a kindred spirit. Joaquin doesn't just speak about money; he speaks about life through the lens of money. And that's rare.

We connected instantly—not just as professionals in personal finance, but as two Black men deeply committed to using financial knowledge as a vehicle for healing, elevation, and intergenerational empowerment. We've both walked roads where wealth wasn't a given, but rather a discovery: of values, of self-worth, of vision. On his *The New Wealth Wave Podcast,* we unpacked those roads together, reflecting on the intersections of self-esteem, purpose, identity, and financial choices. That conversation still resonates with me, and I know it will with you.

Dr. Wallace's life is not a theory; it's a testimony. From building hope within correctional facilities to standing at the front of financial education classrooms, he has lived the transformation this book advocates. He knows that financial empowerment is not just about what's in your wallet; it's about what's in your history, your beliefs, and your spirit. His journey from athlete to coach to financial psychologist is itself a model of reinvention and legacy-building.

That legacy now lives in the Seven-Stage Generational Wealth Model, a behavioral, psychological, and strategic roadmap for building wealth with depth. Not just assets and accounts, but belief systems, emotional fluency, and future vision. From healing financial trauma to planting the seeds of long-term prosperity, Joaquin's model is as practical as it is profound.

In my own work, I often speak about Life Money Balance®, and how wealth, when aligned with identity, values, and life stages, creates true well-being. Joaquin and I each built "wheels" to represent our philosophies. Mine centers on Life-Centered, Lifestyle, and Money Psychology Utility. His begins with awareness and flows into financial dignity and legacy. Though the words differ, the harmony is the same: wealth must serve the whole person and the whole family, for the long haul.

That is where Joaquin's model shines. He doesn't start with a budget spreadsheet—he starts with understanding. He asks the reader to acknowledge Inherited Financial Narratives, name the invisible barriers, and activate their financial dignity. Only then does he move into more traditional financial planning, like investment or estate strategy.

That's the difference. That's the future of wealth-building.

What's more, this book doesn't talk at you—it walks with you. Dr. Wallace offers more than ideas. He provides actionable exercises, neuroscience-backed practices, and compassionate guidance. His words don't just inform; they equip. Whether you're a first-generation wealth builder, a parent hoping to pass down more than money, or a professional reexamining your own financial journey, this book will meet you where you are—and move you forward.

We live in a time where financial advice is everywhere, yet financial peace remains elusive for too many. That's because we've been taught money is math, when in fact, *money is meaning*. Joaquin knows this. He lives this. And now, through these pages, he teaches this.

Generational Wealth Begins with Generational Knowledge® isn't just the title of this book—it's a charge. It's a declaration that knowledge, healing, and action are the foundation for lasting change. True wealth isn't merely inherited; it's cultivated, consciously and collectively.

I wholeheartedly recommend this book—not just for your bookshelf but for your family table, your classroom, your boardroom, and your community gathering. It belongs wherever legacy is discussed and wherever transformation is needed.

Joaquin, thank you for offering us a model that speaks to our hearts as much as our minds. And thank you for showing us that the path to wealth is also a path to self-actualization, wholeness, and hope.

Let this book be your guide as you build not only assets, but also esteem.

Not just inheritance, but intention.

Not just success, but significance.

Because generational wealth doesn't start with money.

It starts with you.

Dr. Preston D. Cherry, CFP®, CFT™
Founder, Concurrent Wealth Director,
Financial Planning Program & Charles Schwab Foundation Center for Financial Wellness at UW–Green Bay
Author, *Wealth in the Key of Life*
Host, *Life Money Balance Podcast*

Seven-Stage Generational Wealth Model©

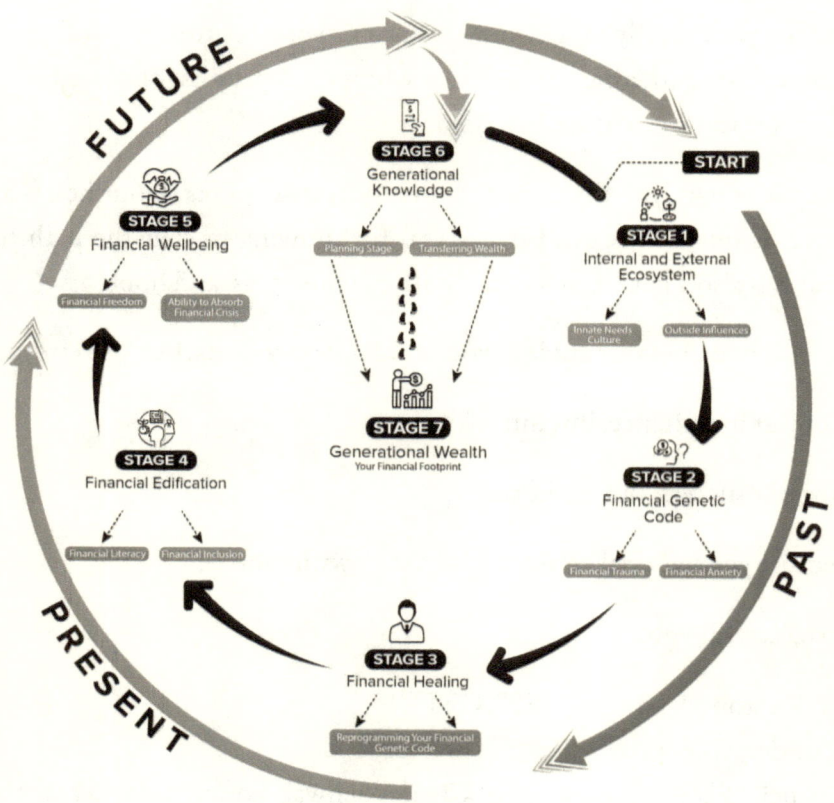

GENERATIONAL WEALTH BEGINS WITH GENERATIONAL KNOWLEDGE®
REG. COPYRIGHT © 2023 DR. JOAQUIN WALLACE.

Introduction:
The Financial Genetic Code Revolution

*"A tree's beauty lies in its branches, but its strength
lies in its roots."* —Matshona Dhliwayo

F ew things are as pervasive and influential in human experience as our relationship with money. It colors our decisions, shapes our opportunities, and often dictates the legacy we leave behind. Yet, for all its importance, our understanding of wealth—how to create it, nurture it, and pass it on—remains shrouded in myth, misconception, and, all too often, anxiety.

Throughout our lives, we've been told that money talks. However, for most of us, it speaks a language we were never taught to understand. We're raised to chase dollars, pinch pennies, and hope for a lucky break. Yet, despite our efforts, the results are stark: a nation drowning in debt, with 37% of Americans unable to cover a $400 emergency expense.[1] Clearly, something isn't adding up, and it's not just our bank balances.

Think back to the stories your grandparents used to tell about buying their first home for what now seems like pocket change or how one income was enough to support an entire family. That wasn't just nostalgia talking. The America of yesteryear painted a vastly different picture of wealth and opportunity.

Take the 1950s and 1960s, often considered the golden age of the American middle class. Iconic figures like Walt Disney and Sam Walton were building empires that would last generations, and the average American citizen wasn't doing too poorly either. In 1950, the median home value was just $7,354, approximately 2.2 times the median household income of $3,300.[2,3] Fast forward to 2025. The median home price has skyrocketed to $424,430, while the median household income stands at $74,580, resulting in a home price-to-income ratio of about 5.7:1.[4] Even when adjusted for inflation, this widening gap is staggering.

However, it's not just housing. Education, once a pillar of upward mobility, has been affected by inflation. The rising cost of pursuing a degree has made it increasingly unaffordable in today's climate, turning what was once a pathway to success into a financial burden for many.

Several factors have contributed to this shift, but three stand out as particularly noteworthy. First, the rising demand for higher education is driven by the need for advanced skills that require more specialized training. Second, the reduction of public funding for universities has shifted the financial burden onto students. Third, the administrative and operational costs of higher education have grown significantly, largely due to the technological advancements required to compete in a global marketplace.

In 1970, the average tuition cost at a public four-year college was $394 per year.[5] As of the 2024-2025 academic year, these costs have risen to an average of $9,750 for in-state students and $28,386 for out-of-state students.[6] That's before we even talk about the $1.75 trillion student debt crisis hanging over millennials and Gen Z like a storm cloud.[7]

The generational wealth gap is a critical issue in the U.S. today, and it is widening into a chasm. In 1989, Baby Boomers (then aged 25 to 43) owned 21% of the nation's wealth, amassed through investments in stocks, real estate, and pensions.[8] Leap ahead to 2023, and millennials (ages 27 to 42)—despite making up a growing share of the workforce— own a mere 6.4% of the national wealth.[9] The imbalance is stark and raises questions about why the wealth of previous generations hasn't been passed on or multiplied as expected in younger generations. It's like we're playing Monopoly®, but in this game, the previous generations have already bought up all the properties and hotels before we even rolled the dice. Now, this isn't about pointing fingers or reducing the conversation to generational blame games. The Warren Buffett's and Oprah Winfrey's of the world didn't create this system—they just mastered it. And let's be real: not every Baby Boomer is lounging in financial comfort. However, it is undeniable that the rules of the game have undergone significant changes.

The chance of earning more than one's parents has drastically diminished, a troubling sign that the American Dream of upward mobility is no longer a given for younger generations. For instance, if you were born in 1940, you had a 92% chance of earning more than your parents. Born in 1980? That chance drops to 50%.[10] It's as if we're running a race where the finish line keeps moving further away—and the track itself is crumbling beneath our feet.

It isn't just a problem of economic circumstance; it's also a matter of financial behaviors and the knowledge that's been passed down through generations—or rather, what hasn't. Over the years, the rules of wealth building have shifted, but traditional financial advice hasn't kept up with these shifts.

First and foremost, traditional financial advice emphasizes time-tested principles such as saving for retirement, investing in diversified portfolios, and managing risk through strategies like asset allocation. Furthermore, it highlights the importance of rational decision-making through long-term planning and reliance on historical data, all critical approaches for building generational wealth slowly and intentionally.

However, here's the catch: many people aren't introduced to these concepts until adulthood, if at all. By then, our financial habits have already been shaped by mental shortcuts and emotional biases, such as chasing short-term gains during market frenzies or panic-selling during downturns. As a result, our emotional and behavioral cognitive biases and heuristics (also known as mental shortcuts) continue to influence our decisions, indicating that traditional financial guidance hasn't kept pace with these changes. These cognitive quirks, amplified by today's 24/7 financial media cycle, render much of the traditional advice theoretical at best and irrelevant at worst. We're still being sold a blueprint for success that was drafted in a different economic era. "Save 10% of your income, buy a house as soon as you can, work for the same company for 40 years, and retire with a gold watch and a fat pension." Sound familiar? Yeah, good luck with that in today's employment environment, where job loyalty doesn't guarantee security, and avocado toast costs $18.

The disconnect is glaring. That 10% savings rule assumes wages outpace inflation—a fantasy for many millennials juggling student loans and rent. Also, the "stable career" playbook ignores today's AI-driven job churn, where skills expire faster than milk. Even homeownership, once a cornerstone of wealth-building, now locks younger buyers into mortgages that devour 40% of their income, leaving little room to invest or weather emergencies.

The traditional roadmap for success is indeed becoming increasingly out of sync with the realities of today's economy. Traditional guidance isn't wrong, but it's incomplete. It's like teaching someone to fish in a stocked pond while ignoring the hurricane offshore. To bridge the generational wealth gap, we need strategies that account for today's debt-laden starting lines, algorithmic market volatility, and the psychological traps baked into human nature. Millennials and Gen Xers, in particular, are rethinking many of these long-standing financial principles. Recent statistics show that these generations spend far less time working for a single employer compared to previous generations.

The Bureau of Labor Statistics found that the median tenure for workers aged 25 to 34 is currently about 2.8 years, while workers aged 35 to 44 average around 5 years with a single employer.[11] For Baby Boomers, staying with the same employer for two to three decades was once the norm, but younger generations are now prioritizing flexibility, growth opportunities, and work-life balance over long-term job security. This shift has compelled many to redefine success in terms of adaptability and continuous skill development, rather than long-term stability with a single employer.

As companies began phasing out full-time roles with comprehensive benefits and guaranteed pensions, a quiet but powerful shift occurred in the way Gen X and Millennials viewed work. The promise of staying with one employer for life, once seen as a reliable path to financial security, started to fade. In its place grew a mindset shaped by uncertainty and adaptability. These generations watched their parents face layoffs, downsizing, or reduced benefits, and many internalized the lesson that loyalty to a company no longer meant long-term security. As a result, they began to reimagine career paths, leaning into gig work, side businesses, and the idea of financial independence outside of traditional job structures.

Furthermore, the idea of purchasing a home, once seen as the quintessential marker of financial achievement, is also being reconsidered. Millennials are less likely to own homes than previous generations at the same age due to rising housing costs and economic instability. According to the U.S. Census Bureau, the homeownership rate for adults under 35 years old was 38.1% in the fourth quarter of 2023, compared to 43.1% in the fourth quarter of 2007.[12] The decline suggests that conventional wisdom around financial security and success is increasingly misaligned with economic realities.

The disconnect between the old playbook and new economic realities reveals an unsettling truth: our financial struggles are not merely about a lack of resources but are deeply rooted in our perceptions and behaviors surrounding money. Until we recognize this, we'll remain individuals bound by restraints, unable to break free from our past. Each time we reach for financial independence, the weight of our past struggles pulls us back. It reintroduces itself, reminding us that the barriers we confront and rise above to try to make a move toward financial independence are tethered to cycles we never chose. The traditional advice surrounding saving, investing, career trajectory, and wealth building no longer applies in today's employment economy and rapidly shifting workforce. To break free, we need to challenge our assumptions and develop new mindsets and strategies tailored to the modern landscape.

Generational Wealth Begins with Generational Knowledge®: The Seven Stages of Financial Empowerment and a Legacy of Prosperity is more than just a title; it's a rallying cry for a new era of financial empowerment. It's a bold declaration that the path to true wealth—wealth that sustains and grows across generations-is built not on quick fixes or get-rich-quick schemes but on deep knowledge that transforms.

I've been a financial planner since 2019, watching people from all walks of life grapple with this new reality. Let me be clear—it's rarely about the numbers alone. It's about the stories we tell ourselves, the behavioral biases we inherit, and the habits we were not aware we possessed.

Take Amber, a marketing whiz pulling in six figures. On paper, she should be living the dream. Instead, she's up at night, haunted by money stress. Or Alex, a brilliant engineer who feels a wave of guilt with every promotion. Their bank accounts might look different, but their struggles spring from the same well. Breaking free from financial restraints requires more than earning a higher income; it demands a profound mind shift, a deep understanding of financial knowledge, and the courage to rewrite our financial journey. We'll dive deeper into each of their stories later in the book.

Generational Wealth Begins with Generational Knowledge© is not just a slogan; it's also a solution rooted in the belief that true wealth isn't just financial but includes the behavioral characteristics, attitudes, and education surrounding it. Reframing our Inherited Financial Narratives unknowingly passed down through generations is essential, not only to teach the next generation effective financial management but also to confront the deep-rooted fears, traumas, and outdated beliefs that have shaped our financial behaviors.

Now, before you roll your eyes and think this is just another self-help spiel, please hear me out. It is not a case of positive thinking or manifesting wealth. It's a matter of understanding the deeply rooted factors that shape our financial lives, often without realizing it.

Over the years, I have seen countless individuals and families striving to achieve generational wealth. Time and again, I've seen how the absence of deep, ingrained financial knowledge creates an uphill battle, one that many fight valiantly, but few win. It is not due to a lack of effort; they are operating within an outdated financial framework.

That realization led me to develop the theory that financial empowerment and a legacy of prosperity are not so much about accumulating more money as they are about changing our relationship with it. That's why I developed the Seven-Stage Generational Wealth Model©—a proprietary framework that moves beyond surface-level tactics to confront the root causes of financial stagnation. Unlike traditional advice that focuses solely on what to do, this model reveals why we self-sabotage, how systemic traps derail even the disciplined, and which mindset shifts unlock exponential growth.

We'll unpack this blueprint in-depth, but here's the core truth it exposes: Wealth isn't built through spreadsheets alone. It's forged through the intersection of behavioral awareness, generational narratives, and strategies tailored to modern economic realities—three pillars most financial guides ignore. It is a framework for understanding and reprogramming your relationship with money. Because let's face it: you can't fix what you don't understand. Therefore, it provides practical insights on legacy building, wealth accumulation, preservation, and financial growth across generations. The model isn't just another set of tips and tricks; it's a roadmap for financial transformation. Consider it a GPS grounded in solid financial knowledge and behavioral science, refined through years of real-world application.

But why do we need such a radical approach? Why isn't traditional financial literacy enough? The hard truth is that financial literacy, as it's commonly taught, is little more than a Band-Aid® on a gaping wound. It's a surface-level solution that fails to address the deeper, often invisible forces that shape our financial lives. This self-perpetuating cycle, shaped by our internal environment, culture, trauma, and anxiety, becomes our Financial Genetic Code. Just as biological DNA determines our physical traits, this code influences every financial decision we make, often without conscious awareness.

Dr. Marcia Ruben, a guest on *The New Wealth Wave Podcast*, likens it to how we walk; we don't think about each step; we just do it. Similarly, our financial behaviors are often just as automatic and just as hard to change.[13] Financial advice often assumes a level playing field, prompting one to budget, save, and invest as if each of these suggestions is a simple choice, thus marginalizing our past or current circumstances. However, this mindset is categorically flawed. It's like imploring someone with a fractured leg to run faster. The suggestion to run faster isn't entirely wrong in context; however, one major truth is often overlooked and ignored.

NOT EVERYONE STARTS FROM THE SAME PLACE.

Therefore, understanding the hidden struggles individuals carry is essential and required before prescribing financial strategies. These may include, but are not limited to, their financial trauma, systemic barriers, or generational burdens, which shape their decisions both consciously and subconsciously. An example of this is the runner we referenced earlier, who appears fine yet hides their fracture. They may appear financially capable, yet carry invisible wounds that make progress difficult. Thus, ignoring these present realities sets people up for failure. True financial empowerment begins not just with numbers but with recognizing the weight people carry before expecting them to run. Saundra Davis, a highly respected financial therapist, educator, and coach, sheds light on this missing piece. In our conversation on the *New Wealth Wave Podcast*[14] she emphasized:

New Wealth Wave Podcast, EP 12: Saundra Davis

"Knowing better is essential, but knowing better doesn't mean doing better. So, how do we bridge the gap between what we know and what we do?"

The gap is where the real work begins. It's not enough to simply learn about budgeting or investment strategies. We need to understand why we make the financial decisions we do and how our past experiences and current environment shape those choices.

Davis pointed out that traditional literacy often ignores what people already know. "You've been surviving way before you met me," she noted, "so you've got some financial knowledge." The key, then, is not just to impart new information but also to help people identify gaps in their knowledge and, more importantly, understand how their existing behaviors are serving (or not serving) them. This approach aligns perfectly with the Seven-Stage Generational Wealth Model©, emphasizing how our internal and external ecosystems create our Financial Genetic Code. We must recognize that our financial behaviors are often automatic and shaped by years of experience and inherited beliefs. As Davis put it, "Our beliefs and those kinds of things come into play because I can know better yet still do things that are harmful."

In addition, Davis highlighted the emotional aspect of financial decision making, something that traditional financial advice often overlooks. She emphasized the need for "financial psychological safety" when discussing money matters. This safety allows people to be open and transparent about their financial situations without fear of judgment or shame. This perspective dovetails with Dr. Ruben's analogy of financial behaviors being as automatic as walking. Just as we don't think about each step when we walk, we often make financial decisions without conscious thought. Recognizing this automaticity is the first step towards change.

But change isn't just about knowledge; it's about action. As Davis pointed out, "Financial literacy is that transfer of information. The problem with that is you also have knowledge, and most financial literacy courses ignore what you already know." It is why the Seven-Stage Generational Wealth Model© doesn't stop at understanding our Financial Genetic Code. It moves us through the stages of financial healing, financial edification, financial well-being, generational knowledge, and ultimately, creating our financial footprints toward generational wealth.

But let's not get ahead of ourselves. We'll explore these missing pieces in later chapters. For now, consider for a moment the difference between being "rich" and building true wealth. Richness is transactional, a snapshot of financial abundance that can vanish as quickly as it appears. Wealth, on the other hand, is a legacy. It's the culmination of knowledge, habits, and strategies passed down and refined over generations. This distinction is at the heart of our journey through the Seven-Stage Generational Wealth Model©.

As we embark on this exploration, we'll challenge the status quo of financial education. In Part I, we'll delve into the past, examining the internal and external ecosystems that have shaped our financial behaviors. We'll confront the often-painful realities of financial trauma and anxiety in our Financial Genetic Code, recognizing that, for many of us, our relationship with money is colored by experiences of scarcity, loss, or exclusion.

However, we won't stop at diagnosis. Dealing with the past is not always easy, but ignoring these wounds is akin to building a house on a damaged foundation. I firmly believe that we begin this process by first engaging in our own personal self-reflection to heal internally before taking positive steps forward to grow.

In Part II, the Seven-Stage Generational Wealth Model© is, at its core, a path to healing, empowerment, and financial edification. The model forces us to self-assess our past, present, and future, exploring techniques for rewiring our financial mindset, building resilience, and accessing tools and knowledge that may have previously seemed out of reach.

This isn't your average high school economics class. We're discussing real-world, applicable knowledge that considers your unique situation and goals. From there, we'll learn to define and pursue true financial well-being, which extends far beyond the numbers in our bank accounts to include security, freedom, and joy. The goal is to help us avoid outliving our income while focusing on our financial health.

Part III looks to the future, where we'll focus on financial well-being, our "soft landing," and strategies to avoid outliving our income, because *Financial Health is Financial Wealth.* We'll also explore the importance of transferring assets and protecting resources through tools like estate planning, life insurance, long-term care, and other wealth protection strategies.

The goal is to guide and support you in creating lasting financial footprints. That means not only passing on assets, but also sharing financial wisdom with the next generation. After all, true generational wealth isn't just about leaving an inheritance; it's about equipping our children and grandchildren with the knowledge and skills to build on what we've created.

Throughout this book, you'll find insights drawn from my years of professional experience, as well as from the diverse voices featured on *The New Wealth Wave Podcast*. My podcast, available on platforms like Apple, Spotify, Amazon, YouTube *(@TheNewWealthWavePodcast)*, and through my website *(drjwallace.com/podcast)*, serves as a dynamic extension of the ideas presented in this book. Each episode dives deeply into various aspects of the Seven-Stage Generational Wealth Model©, featuring conversations with experts, thought leaders, and individuals on their own wealth-building journeys.

The podcast covers a wide range of topics, from tackling how our internal and external ecosystems are based around the notion of "Walls In" and "Walls Out" to understanding your Financial Genetic Code and strategies for building and preserving generational wealth. Guests share their personal stories, professional insights, and practical advice, offering listeners a multifaceted perspective on financial well-being and success. These stories and expert perspectives illustrate the universal nature of financial struggles and the transformative power of the Seven-Stage Generational Wealth Model©.

By integrating these podcast discussions into the book, a rich, multi-dimensional exploration of generational wealth is created. You'll hear from financial advisors, financial planners, behavioral financial therapists, successful entrepreneurs, and everyday people who have transformed their financial lives. Their experiences and wisdom complement the concepts presented in this book, offering real-world examples of how the Seven-Stage Generational Wealth Model© can be applied in various real-life situations.

I encourage you to not only read this book but also to tune into *The New Wealth Wave Podcast* as a complementary resource. The combination of written content and audio discussions will provide you with a comprehensive understanding of the path to generational wealth, helping you to internalize these concepts and apply them to your own financial journey.

You'll also encounter self-reflection exercises at the end of each chapter of this book. These aren't mere afterthoughts; they're integral aids for applying the model to your own life. While this book contains a wealth of information, its true power lies in how you internalize and act upon that knowledge.

Before diving deeper, let me share a bit about my journey.

For over 20 years, I've been an advocate for education and empowerment in my community. It all started with *Project Transition Incorporated*, a nonprofit I founded in 1997 in response to the Personal Responsibility and Work Opportunity Reconciliation Act of 1996, enacted by former President Bill Clinton. This passion project led to nominations for the Annie E. Casey Foundation and Ford Foundation fellowships and features in *Essence Magazine* and *Black MBA* magazine. In addition, I was recognized in *Contemporary Black Biography* as one of the most influential African Americans of the 21st century.

Today, I wear many hats. For eight years, I was a financial planner at Prudential Financial. During that time, I accumulated a briefcase full of licenses, including life and health, property, and casualty insurance. In addition, I have successfully passed the Series 6, 63, and 65 securities licenses, as well as the designations of Chartered Retirement Planning Counselor (CRPC™) and Accredited Behavioral Finance Professional (ABFP®).

Academically, I hold a Bachelor's degree in Economics, an MBA in Marketing, and a Doctorate in Business Administration with an emphasis in Public Policy.

I've authored a book titled *"Welfare to Work: A Practitioner's Perspective on How to Develop and Implement a Successful Welfare-to-Work Program."* I am an adjunct professor at Golden Gate University in the Financial Planning and Public Policy departments. These experiences have shaped my understanding of the intricate relationship between education, empowerment, and financial well-being.

I'm not just about talking; I'm about taking action. This book will provide you with the tools, knowledge, and insights to navigate your financial journey head-on, regardless of where you're starting. We're diving deep, questioning everything, and exploring new paths to achieve generational wealth.

As we progress through each stage of the model, you may recognize patterns in your financial life—moments of anxiety, self-sabotage, or learned helplessness that have been instrumental in your personal journey. This recognition, while sometimes uncomfortable, is the first step toward change. Remember, the goal isn't to achieve perfection overnight but to embark on a journey of continuous growth and improvement.

Each stage of the model will guide you toward the goal of generational wealth; however, it's essential to understand that this journey is unique for each individual. Financial literacy, as I've come to realize, is organic, not linear. Therefore, the Model acknowledges that we may oscillate between stages, particularly when faced with financial "flashpoints"— those moments of crisis or significant change that can trigger old patterns. Some may swiftly navigate through a stage, while others may take longer. That's perfectly fine; we navigate these stages throughout our adult lives constantly. However, armed with the knowledge and tools this book provides, you'll be equipped to handle these challenges with greater resilience and clarity.

Take Mayor Torrence Harvey of Newburgh, New York. He had the chance to look at the Seven-Stage Generational Wealth Model©, and his reaction was nothing short of profound. As a guest on *The New Wealth Wave Podcast*, Mayor Harvey's journey became a testament to the power of breaking generational financial cycles.[15] As the first in his immediate family to achieve numerous milestones (graduating high school, attending and graduating from college, and pursuing graduate studies), he found himself at a crossroads. He had broken barriers, yes, but the question of how to build and sustain generational wealth still loomed large.

New Wealth Wave Podcast, EP 21: Mayor Torrence Harvey

"I've been the first in my immediate family to do a lot of things. And one of the things that has been haunting me for a very long time was how to find generational wealth."

This question resonates with many who find themselves as the first in their families to achieve financial stability or success. The weight of being a trailblazer is often accompanied by the responsibility of ensuring that the trail doesn't end with you.

Mayor Harvey's experience underscores a critical aspect of the Seven-Stage Generational Wealth Model©: the importance of financial edification. Before encountering the model, he had toggled between Stages 3 and 4—Financial Healing and Financial Edification. This juggling act is familiar to many working to overcome financial traumas while simultaneously trying to educate themselves about sound financial practices.

The mayor's background growing up in the projects of Poughkeepsie, New York, had provided him with firsthand experience of the financial anxieties that can arise when confronting budgets, expenses, and the often-daunting task of putting real figures down on paper. His experience, coupled with his later education in economics and business, laid the groundwork for his understanding of financial literacy. However, it was the birth of his daughter that catalyzed a deeper dive into financial education and wealth-building strategies.

For Mayor Harvey, the recognition was obvious, as he was tasked with doubling down on his financial edification, thus focusing his attention on his personal financial literacy and financial inclusion, which culminated in purchasing his first home as a byproduct of his *"Aha!" moment*. This pivotal moment illustrates how personal milestones often serve as turning points in our financial journeys, pushing us to seek out knowledge and take concrete steps toward building wealth.

Mayor Harvey's story goes beyond personal achievement. It illustrates how financial education and wealth-building can create ripple effects that strengthen entire communities. As an educator and public servant, he sees himself as a bridge to financial knowledge, empowering his community to embrace financial literacy and pursue generational wealth.

His experience underscores the importance of understanding social structures and systemic barriers in motivating individuals to engage in financial education, thereby creating pathways for upward mobility and long-term prosperity.

We'll explore one of these hierarchies in the coming chapter. Remember, the true path of social mobility when starting from less is rooted in education, and this education includes insights into the rudimentary components of understanding money. For that reason, financial literacy isn't a luxury; it's a requirement, gifting you a lifeline.

This frame of reference aligns accurately with the Seven-Stage Generational Wealth Model's© emphasis on both internal reflection and external action. It's not enough to learn about financial concepts; one must also interpret how these principles interact with broader societal structures and personal histories.

Mayor Harvey's journey from the projects to public office, from financial uncertainty to actively working toward generational wealth, serves as a compelling example of the model in its true form. His story illustrates that while the path to financial well-being may not be linear, often requiring us to revisit earlier stages as we encounter new challenges, it is a journey worth undertaking.

New Wealth Wave Podcast, EP 21: Mayor Torrence Harvey

"Through the Seven-Stage Model, we're not just breaking chains—we're also forging new links of financial empowerment that have the potential to uplift entire communities. Remember that with the right tools and knowledge, we all have the power to rewrite our financial stories and create lasting change for generations to come."

As we continue to explore stories like Mayor Harvey's, it reminds us that it isn't just about numbers on a balance sheet. It's about breaking cycles, reimagining possibilities, and creating legacies that extend far beyond our individual lives. It involves understanding that true wealth isn't just about what's in our bank accounts but includes the knowledge, resilience, and opportunities we can pass on to future generations.

As we delve into each stage, from uncovering the roots of your Encoded Financial Behaviors to building a lasting financial legacy, call to mind that this process is as much about personal growth as it is about financial success. The two are inextricably linked, and true wealth cannot be achieved without addressing both.

Generational Wealth Begins with Generational Knowledge®: The Seven Stages of Financial Empowerment and a Legacy of Prosperity is more than a book; it's an invitation to participate in a revolution—a financial reformation that begins within you and ripples outward to touch your family, your community, and potentially generations to come. It's a call to break free from the limitations of your Financial Genetic Code and rewrite your financial future on your own terms.

The journey won't be easy, but I promise that it will be worth it. On the other side of this work is a life where money is a tool, not a tyrant; where financial decisions stem from a place of empowerment, not fear; and where wealth isn't just about dollars, but about creating a lasting legacy.

As you commit to transforming your understanding of money and wealth, be ready to overcome financial struggles and build a new legacy of prosperity and empowerment. Your path to true generational wealth begins here as you become empowered to build your future wealth.

PART I:

UNEARTHING YOUR FINANCIAL PAST

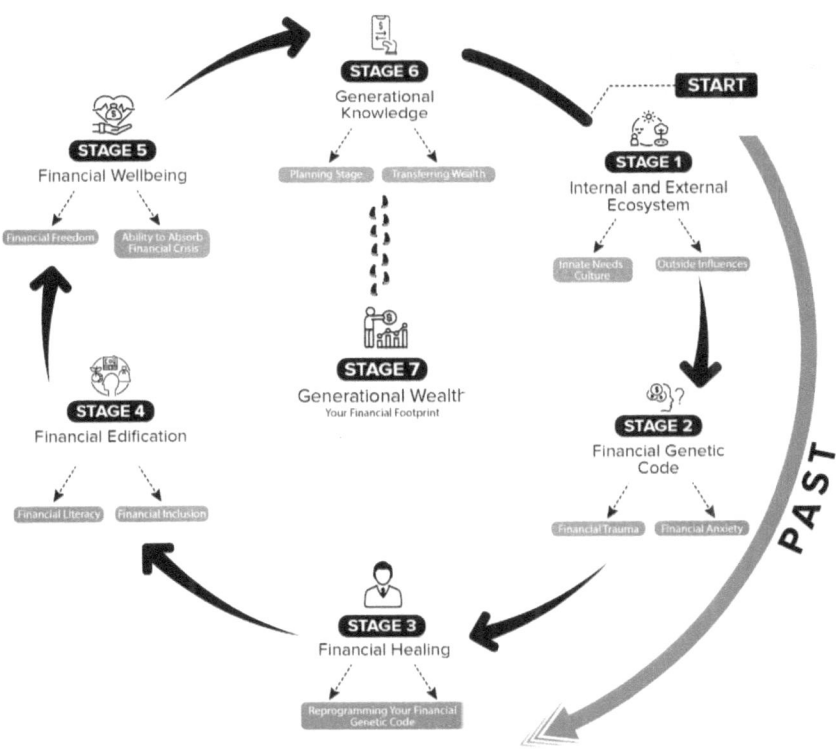

START

STAGE 1
Internal and External Ecosystem
- Innate Needs / Culture
- Outside Influences

STAGE 2
Financial Genetic Code
- Financial Trauma
- Financial Anxiety

STAGE 3
Financial Healing
- Reprogramming Your Financial Genetic Code

STAGE 4
Financial Edification
- Financial Literacy
- Financial Inclusion

STAGE 5
Financial Wellbeing
- Financial Freedom
- Ability to Absorb Financial Crisis

STAGE 6
Generational Knowledge
- Planning Stage
- Transferring Wealth

STAGE 7
Generational Wealth
Your Financial Footprint

PAST

GENERATIONAL WEALTH BEGINS WITH GENERATIONAL KNOWLEDGE®
REG. COPYRIGHT © 2023 DR. JOAQUIN WALLACE.

Chapter 1:
The Roots of Your Money Story

"Someone's sitting in the shade today because someone planted a tree a long time ago." —Warren Buffett

Money. It's just a simple tool for exchange and nothing more. At least, that's what we tell ourselves. However, if you've ever felt the sting of anxiety when monitoring your bank balance, or a rush of excitement at an unexpected financial bonus, you know there's more to the story. Money isn't just currency; it's a complex web of emotions, memories, and deeply ingrained beliefs that shape our financial lives in many ways.

Some people's earliest memories of money include the jingle of coins in a piggy bank or the familiar tension in their parents' voices when a toy was too expensive to bring home. For others, money was never scarce—birthdays came with wrapped gifts, "no" was rarely spoken, and needs were met without hesitation.

While these experiences appear worlds apart, both quietly shaped how each individual would come to view, use, and emotionally respond to money. One may carry anxiety around spending; the other, a sense of financial security, or even entitlement. Neither consciously chose these beliefs, yet both absorbed them.

These small, seemingly ordinary moments are more than just memories—they are the first threads in a larger financial story—a story written by repetition, reinforced by environment, and eventually embedded in what we now understand as the *Financial Genetic Code*.

As we embark on this journey of understanding our financial selves, we must recognize that our Encoded Financial Behaviors are shaped by two powerful forces that I call "Walls In" and "Walls Out." These concepts are fundamental to understanding why we make the financial decisions we do and how each forms the cornerstone of our exploration into generational wealth.

"Walls In" refers to the internal barriers we face—our limiting beliefs, ingrained financial habits, and the generational influences that have been passed down to us, often without our conscious awareness. These psychological obstacles shape our financial behaviors and decision-making processes.

"Walls Out," on the other hand, represents external barriers—the socioeconomic conditions, systemic inequalities, and financial pressures imposed by our environment. These broader societal challenges can hinder our ability to achieve financial independence and accumulate wealth for future generations.

Now, you may want to pause and consider the trajectory of your financial life. In the past, you perhaps found yourself grappling with the profound question: *Why do I make the financial decisions I do?* The answer lies buried deep within the fertile soil of your past, intertwined with the roots of the Inherited Financial Narratives handed down through the generations, your personal Encoded Financial Behaviors, and influenced by both your "Walls In" and "Walls Out".

Think of a mighty oak tree. Its sprawling canopy and sturdy trunk are visible to all, much like our current financial situation. However, what truly gives this tree its strength and resilience and ultimately determines its growth are the roots hidden beneath the surface. These roots, spreading far and wide and drawing nutrients from the surrounding soil, represent the foundation of our financial behaviors, attitudes, and beliefs. Just as the oak's roots are shaped by the soil in which they grow, our financial roots are profoundly influenced by the environment of our upbringing. The whispers of childhood, the cultural codes of our communities, and the *invisible hand* of our broader societal context all play significant roles in shaping our Encoded Financial Behaviors. These elements form our "Walls In" and "Walls Out," creating a complex ecosystem that influences every financial decision we make. Thus, the decisions we make in our relationship with money, rational or irrational, are a direct by-product of our internal and external ecosystems.

Stage 1: Internal and External Ecosystem (The Past)

Unlike the oak, we have the power to examine these roots, understand their origins, and, yes, even reshape them. This is where the journey to generational wealth truly begins—not with a get-rich-quick scheme or a magical investment strategy, but with a deep and honest exploration of the roots of our Inherited Financial Narratives and Encoded Financial Behaviors, including the "Walls In" and "Walls Out" that have shaped our financial lives.

You might be wondering, *Why start here? Why not jump straight into strategies for transferring wealth?* The answer is simple yet profound. I begin here because true, lasting generational wealth is built on a foundation of generational knowledge. In this case, it is self-awareness and understanding. Without this foundation, any wealth we might accumulate is built on shifting sands, vulnerable to the same patterns and pitfalls that have kept generational wealth out of reach for so many.

How many times have you heard stories of lottery winners who have lost their fortunes within a few years? Or professional athletes who, despite earning millions, found themselves in financial ruin after their careers ended? While these stories may be public, countless remain unheard. Entrepreneurs, professionals, blue-collar and white-collar workers, as well as executives, have faced financial hardship, unexpected losses, and setbacks that have had lasting ripple effects. Wealth can be built, but it can also be lost just as quickly, and sometimes even faster, due to economic downturns, unexpected misfortunes, or a lack of financial knowledge.

The untold stories of everyday people facing these challenges are often more relatable and realistic than those of entertainers, athletes, or individuals who inherited their wealth. These stories are powerful reminders that, without the right tools and understanding, anyone, regardless of race, gender, social status, or level of success, can fall into financial instability. These cautionary tales illustrate the truth that it's not just a matter of how much money you make, but your relationship with money itself, a relationship heavily influenced by your Inherited Financial Narratives.

This relationship is the lens through which you view every financial decision, from the mundane to the monumental. It influences whether you see money as a tool for freedom or a source of anxiety, whether you approach financial decisions with confidence or fear, and whether you view wealth as a possibility or an impossibility.

For many of us, these were written long before we even understood what money was. It was penned in the margins of our childhood experiences, the unspoken lessons of our family dynamics, and the cultural norms of our communities. Like invisible ink, these early Inherited Financial Narratives have often shaped our behaviors and beliefs without us realizing it.

Remember that piggy bank you had as a kid? The one with the chipped ear and the impossible-to-open bottom? For most of us, that was our first brush with the concept of money. However, long before you dropped your first penny into that ceramic pig, your Encoded Financial Behaviors were already being written, influenced by the "Walls In" of your family's financial habits and the "Walls Out" of your broader economic environment. That's why we need to unearth these roots before we can even begin to talk about building generational wealth. We need to shine a light on the hidden influences that have shaped our financial lives. Only then can we begin to break free from our past and chart a new course toward true financial empowerment.

The process of unearthing your financial past isn't always comfortable. It will require honesty, vulnerability, and a willingness to confront potentially painful truths. But I promise you, it will be worth it because on the other side of this exploration lies the potential for genuine transformation, not just in your bank account but in your entire relationship with money. Exploring our internal and external ecosystems is a vital first step in this journey toward generational wealth, as it allows us to understand the forces that have shaped our financial behaviors and beliefs.

As we work through this book together, I want you to keep in mind that your current financial situation is not your financial destiny. No matter where you're starting from or how deeply entrenched your financial habits might seem, change is possible. That change begins with awareness of both your "Walls In" and your "Walls Out." You can't change what you don't acknowledge, and you can't heal what you don't understand.

We're going to excavate the layers of your financial past. Each memory, lesson, and experience you'll uncover is a piece of the puzzle that makes up your Inherited Financial Narratives. Some pieces might be positive recollections, such as a treasured memory of your first allowance or the pride you felt with your first paycheck. Others might be rough and jagged, reminders of financial struggles or mistakes. However, each piece, whether positive or negative, has played a role in shaping your current financial reality and contributes to your Financial Genetic Code.

Childhood's Money Whispers

Imagine you're a five-year-old accompanying your mother to the grocery store. She reaches the checkout, and you watch her face tighten as she counts out the dollar bills and coins. Then, she speaks quietly but abruptly and sternly. "We can't afford that," she mutters, putting back the box of cookies you'd snuck into the cart. At that moment, a seed is planted in your young mind; a whisper that says that money is scarce, a source of stress, and something to be anxious about.

Your story may have gone differently. Perhaps you grew up hearing your parents confidently discuss investments over dinner, tossing around terms like "diversification" and "compound interest" as casually as they passed the salt. The seed planted in your mind might have been one of abundance and money as a tool to be mastered rather than a tyrant to be feared.

These early experiences are money whispers; they're not mere childhood memories. They're the first lines of code in your Financial Genetic Code. And like computer code, this early programming runs silently in the background, influencing every financial decision you make. To authenticate this, let's look at the numbers. A study by the University of Cambridge found that children's money habits are formed by age seven.[1] Seven! That's before most of us have even held our first dollar bill. By the time we're adults, making rational or irrational financial decisions, we're just acting out behavior transcripts written in our childhood.

It's important to understand that these whispers affect everyone, regardless of their upbringing. Whether you grew up in a wealthy household or a struggling family, you received Inherited Financial Narratives about money. These messages might have been explicit, like being told, "Money doesn't grow on trees," or implicit, gleaned from observing the financial behaviors and attitudes of those around you.

Do you know that your first financial advisors weren't certified professionals or Wall Street gurus? They were your parents, guardians, or other influential figures in your early life. Whether they realized it or not, these individuals served as your financial fiduciaries, shaping your initial understanding of what money is, how it works, and your relationship to it. It's essential to understand what a fiduciary is in the financial context. A fiduciary is a person or entity with a legal and ethical obligation to act in the best interest of another party. According to the U.S. Securities and Exchange Commission (SEC), *"A fiduciary duty is the highest standard of care imposed by law. As an investment adviser, you are a 'fiduciary' to your advisory clients."*[2] While your parents or guardians didn't have a legal fiduciary duty, they often assumed an informal fiduciary role in shaping your financial mindset.

Some of us learned about money through scarcity, where every "no" carried weight and taught us what we couldn't have. Others learned through quiet abundance, where needs were met without hesitation and money was simply expected to be there. Either way, those early experiences didn't just fade—they settled deep within us, quietly shaping how we think, feel, and make money decisions. It is the root of the Financial Genetic Code, formed long before we knew we had one.

This concept was powerfully illustrated in Episode 20 of *The New Wealth Wave Podcast*, where I interviewed Tony Award-winning actress LaChanze. This remarkable talent has graced Broadway for 38 seasons, earning a combined 8 Tony Award nominations and 4 Tony Award wins, including Best Revival of a Musical and Best Actress in a Musical, respectively.[3]

New Wealth Wave Podcast, EP 20: LaChanze

"Despite her illustrious career, LaChanze shared how her early experiences with financial instability continue to influence her mindset. She described growing up in a working-class family that later faced financial struggles after her parents separated. LaChanze recalled, "My mom worked three jobs, and I was the eldest. Her help was my support."

These early experiences instilled in LaChanze a strong work ethic but also a persistent anxiety about financial security. Even as a highly accomplished actress, she constantly thinks about work and income. As she put it, "The more money I earn, the more money I spend. Therefore, I'm constantly in this position of what the external ecosystem is providing for me."

Thus, early experiences often teach the importance of hard work while also instilling anxiety about financial security. Even after reaching success, this lingering worry can cause individuals to focus narrowly on their jobs and income. As the saying goes, "The more money you make, the more you spend," fueling a cycle of dependence on external financial conditions.

On the other hand, someone who grew up in a household where money was plentiful but never discussed might develop anxiety around financial decisions, feeling ill-equipped to manage money as an adult. This scenario illustrates how "Walls In" can manifest even in seemingly privileged circumstances. In my work with clients, I've encountered numerous individuals who exemplify this paradox. These are people who, from the outside, appear to have every financial advantage. Yet, they are trapped in a gilded cage of financial anxiety and resentment. Their "Walls In" are built not from a lack of resources but from a surplus of unspoken expectations and conditions. Parents in these situations often use money as a tool for control, creating a complex web of financial and emotional dependencies. Children raised in such environments may grow up to view money not as a neutral tool but as a source of stress and obligation. This can result in two seemingly opposing behaviors: 1- impulsive spending as a form of rebellion, or 2- a complete aversion to financial matters.

I recall one client who came from a wealthy family but struggled with severe financial anxiety. Her parents had always provided generously, but with strings attached. Every financial decision was scrutinized, and every purchase was questioned. As an adult, she found herself paralyzed when it came to making financial choices. To say the least, she was a "financial hostage." She'd either spend impulsively as if to assert her independence or avoid financial decisions altogether, overwhelmed by the weight of her parents' expectations. This type of financial entrapment creates its own "Walls In." The individual may have access to resources but lack the confidence and skills to manage them effectively. They're held hostage not by a lack of money but by the emotional baggage attached. At the same time, they may face "Walls Out" in the form of societal expectations about how someone from their background should behave financially.

These experiences underscore the complexity of our financial relationships and the deep-rooted nature of our Inherited Financial Narratives. They remind us that financial well-being isn't just about the numbers in our bank accounts but also our emotional relationship with money. Whether we grow up with too little or too much, how money is discussed (or not discussed) in our formative years shapes our financial behaviors far into adulthood.

Recognizing these patterns is necessary as we work toward building generational wealth. The focus isn't on accumulating resources; rather, it's on promoting a healthy, balanced relationship with money that we can pass on to future generations. That is why understanding and addressing our Inherited Financial Narratives is vital. We can begin to break free from the cycles of financial anxiety and entrapment by creating a new narrative around money for ourselves and those who come after us, which we address in Stage 3.

These whispers don't just affect our financial behaviors. They can also have far-reaching consequences, influencing our career choices, relationships, and even our ability to build and maintain wealth over time. It is why breaking free from negative financial mindsets is a key focus of my Seven-Stage Generational Wealth Model©. The process begins with the first part of Stage 1, which encompasses identifying and unearthing our internal ecosystem.

Once we become aware of these whispers and the mindsets they've created, we can begin to challenge and change them. We can rewrite our Inherited Financial Narratives, creating a new narrative that supports our goals for financial growth and generational wealth.

As we move forward, I encourage you to listen closely to the money whispers from your childhood. What messages did you receive? How have they shaped your current relationship with money? Remember, awareness is the first step towards change.

The sum of these is what your internal ecosystem, or your "Walls In," refers to as the personal experiences, emotions, and beliefs that you've developed around money. It's the voice in your head that whispers, "You can't afford that," or "You deserve this splurge." It's the knot in your stomach when you check your bank balance and the rush of excitement when you imagine financial freedom.

Your external ecosystem, or "Walls Out," on the other hand, encompasses all the outside influences that have shaped your financial worldview. That includes your family's attitude towards money, your cultural background, education, neighborhood, healthcare and broader societal factors like economic conditions and government policies.

Understanding both these influences helps to create your overall financial views, which I refer to as your Inherited Financial Narratives. This awareness is crucial in navigating and potentially overcoming the barriers to your financial growth and building generational wealth.

Inherited Financial Narratives

"Before you fix your finances, you must fix your financial inheritance - the unspoken rules, fears, and limits passed down without consent."

Our culture and the very air we breathe are thick with messages about money. And these messages can vary wildly depending on where and how we grew up. For instance, in many Asian cultures, saving is not just a financial strategy; it's also a cultural priority. Take the Japanese concept of "kakeibo," which is a structured method for household budgeting and saving, and embodies this practice as a form of discipline and responsibility.[4] This deep-seated belief is reflected in Japan's high savings rates over the years. However, recent data indicate a shift; Japan's household saving rates declined to 1.5% in 2023, marking three consecutive years of decrease.[5] In contrast, China's cultural emphasis on filial piety continues to influence financial expectations within families. A study revealed that 49% of urban and 73% of rural elderly residents in China received financial support from their children, underscoring the enduring belief that wealth and financial responsibility are familial obligations passed down through generations.[6]

Comparatively, in the United States, the expectation for children to provide financial support to their parents in retirement is considerably lower. A survey found that only 8% of American parents anticipate receiving any financial assistance from their children during retirement.[7] This stark difference highlights more than just a gap in retirement planning. It reveals a fundamentally different perception of the role of money within family dynamics. In the United States, there's a long-standing belief that financial independence is something each person must earn for themselves. This often means planning ahead—putting money into savings, investing in real estate, or finding ways to earn income beyond a 9-to-5 job. Whether it's building equity in a property or creating passive income streams, the expectation is clear: your financial future is your responsibility.

These cultural contrasts highlight the profound connection between our views on money, family, responsibility, and the long-term distribution of wealth. The Latino community provides another compelling example where the concept of "*familismo*" (prioritizing family over individual needs) often extends to financial matters. A 2021 survey by Bank of America's Better Money Habits found that 72% of Hispanic millennials provide financial support to family members, compared to 53% of non-Hispanic millennials. This support includes assisting with daily expenses, housing costs, and other financial needs.[8] This isn't just generosity; it's a cultural value encoded into financial behavior.

Throughout history, people's financial habits have been influenced by various Inherited Financial Narratives forged by tradition, trauma, and systemic forces. These invisible codes dictate everything from how we save to whom we trust with our wealth. In Middle Eastern cultures, the Islamic principle of "*zakat*" requires individuals to give a portion of their wealth to charity each year. Beyond its spiritual purpose, this practice shapes attitudes toward wealth accumulation and social responsibility.

In many African cultures, the concept of "*ubuntu,*" or the communal sharing of resources, influences attitudes toward individual wealth accumulation versus community support. Wealth isn't measured in bank statements but in how many lives you sustain. Similarly, in some European cultures, particularly in Scandinavian countries, there is a strong emphasis on social welfare and high taxation, which fosters a cultural belief that personal wealth is secondary to collective security. These codes aren't "right" or "wrong"—they're survival strategies refined over centuries.

In the African American community, our Inherited Financial Narratives are uniquely shaped by a history of systemic discrimination and financial exclusion. Years of being denied access to fair banking, housing, and credit have bred a deep-seated mistrust of financial institutions. Some of these biases are rooted in painful truths; others have been amplified by generational storytelling. In some homes, where the grandparents were denied home loans because their skin color made a ZIP code "hazardous" due to redlining, or when one's parents watched their savings vanish in predatory lending schemes, or the parents lost their car to a repossession scheme masked as an "easy payment plan," wariness becomes survival instinct. Those experiences weren't just financial setbacks—they were traumas. And like all traumas, they left scars. These scars manifest as anxieties, biases, and wariness passed down through generations, creating a cycle that's hard to break. They become your Inherited Financial Narratives.

The "Scar Tissue Narrative" originates from past financial wounds—moments of hardship, loss, or instability that leave a lasting imprint on how we perceive and manage money. Like emotional scar tissue, these beliefs form as a way to protect us from future harm. For instance, someone whose family lost their home during a financial crisis may grow up with an intense fear of debt, avoiding even healthy financial tools like mortgages or business loans. Another example might be an individual who grew up with very little and, as a result, feels guilty spending money on themselves, even when it's well within their means.

This narrative can quietly shape generations, teaching children to avoid risks or distrust financial systems without ever questioning why. While it's born from a desire for safety, the scar tissue narrative often limits financial potential. Healing requires not just financial literacy but also emotional awareness—recognizing that the fears driving our decisions may be outdated and learning to make choices based on current realities rather than past pain.

This wariness isn't just anecdotal; it's also reflected in the data. According to the FDIC, 10% of Black households are fully banked, compared to 70.6% of White households.[9] That's not because Black folks don't understand the value of banking; it's because our Inherited Financial Narratives include a flashing warning sign that says, "Banks: Approach with Caution."

In marginalized communities, particularly within the African American community, the prevalence of check-cashing stores is also a clear reflection of the historical and systemic barriers that have shaped our Inherited Financial Narratives. These businesses often serve as a lifeline for those who are unbanked or underbanked, but they also reflect more profound inequities in access to traditional financial services. According to data from the Center for Responsible Lending, check-cashing and payday loan outlets are disproportionately concentrated in low-income and minority communities. You'll find more check-cashing stores in many urban areas than traditional banks. These outlets provide quick access to cash but with fees ranging from 1% to 10% of the check's value. For families living paycheck to paycheck, these fees quickly add up, compounding the financial challenges they already face.[10]

The reliance on check-cashing stores stems from the fact that communities of color are often excluded from traditional banking systems. Historical redlining practices, discriminatory lending policies, and predatory financial products have fostered a lasting distrust. When trust is broken, people seek alternatives, even if those alternatives come with high fees and fewer protections. These Inherited Financial Narratives aren't just abstract concepts; they have real, tangible effects on financial behaviors and outcomes. Cultural attitudes towards debt can significantly influence individuals' willingness to take on student loans for higher education, potentially impacting long-term earning potential and wealth accumulation. For instance, a study conducted by the Brookings Institution revealed that cultural beliefs and financial socialization play a significant role in shaping decisions related to borrowing for college, and these decisions can have long-term implications for wealth accumulation.[11]

Understanding your Inherited Financial Narratives is vital because they often operate on a subconscious level, influencing your financial decisions in a subtle yet significant way. They can affect everything from saving and spending habits to attitudes toward investing, entrepreneurship, and wealth display. Moreover, in our increasingly globalized world, many of us are juggling multiple sets of Inherited Financial Narratives. You might have grown up in one culture, be living in another, and be working in a corporate culture with its own set of financial norms. This cultural complexity can create both challenges and opportunities in your financial life. By becoming aware of these Inherited Financial Narratives, you gain the power to examine them critically. You can choose which aspects of your cultural financial heritage you want to maintain and which you might want to adapt or change as you work towards building generational wealth.

Such insights reveal that learning from the various Inherited Financial Narratives isn't just about changing how we manage finances. It's also about reevaluating those Encoded Financial Behaviors we've inherited about money and family, allowing us to unlearn generations of financial beliefs—good, bad, or indifferent—and create new, empowered financial habits.

In today's world, financial struggles encompass not only income inequality and market volatility but also broader issues. They are also a matter of the stories we carry about money. Breaking free from these inherited and practiced financial hardships will require a shift not only in our financial actions but also in our mindset.

This shift in mindset aligns with Charles Lindblom's theory of incremental change. Although originally developed to understand policymaking in government, Lindblom's ideas can be powerfully applied to personal financial transformation. Lindblom argued that significant change often occurs through a series of small, incremental steps rather than dramatic overhauls. He stated, "Making policy is at best a very rough process. Neither social scientists, nor politicians, nor public administrators yet know enough about the social world to avoid repeated error in predicting the consequences of policy moves."[12]

In the context of personal finance, this theory suggests that eliminating generational financial hardship is most effectively achieved through small, manageable changes focused on realistic expectations. Rather than attempting a complete financial overhaul overnight, individuals can make steady progress by implementing gradual shifts in their financial behaviors and thought patterns. This incremental approach allows for learning, adaptation, and sustainable change over time, ultimately leading to a more robust and lasting transformation in one's financial mindset and circumstances.

Therefore, shifting our mindset, we will begin the healing process to incrementally embrace the idea that Generational Wealth Begins with Generational Knowledge®. Understanding these different perspectives will help us take the first steps in preparation to overcome the influence of the external forces identified in Stage 1 of the Model. In doing so, we will be prepared to create a financial legacy rooted in informed choices, shared responsibility, and sustainable growth.

The Invisible Hand of Your Environment

Now, let's zoom out even further as we explore the external factors that shape our financial lives. Beyond your family and culture, there is the broader environment you grew up in, known as the *Invisible Hand,* which subtly shapes your financial worldview. It includes elements like healthcare systems, educational institutions, political landscapes, and economic policies. While they might seem removed from your day-to-day financial decisions, they create the backdrop against which all your financial choices play out. In the United States, for instance, a study in the *American Journal of Public Health* showed that medical debt is a leading cause of bankruptcy.[13] The high cost of healthcare can influence decisions about employment, savings, and even family planning. In countries with universal healthcare, citizens might have different financial priorities and less anxiety about potential medical expenses.

Let's not forget the role of education. In response to growing concerns over financial instability, California Governor Gavin Newsom signed Assembly Bill 2927 into law in June 2024, mandating that high school students complete a semester-long personal finance course to graduate, starting with the 2030–31 academic year. This initiative aims to equip students with essential financial skills, including budgeting, saving, credit management, and investing, by the time they graduate. The legislation requires public schools, including charter schools, to begin offering this course during the 2027–28 school year.[14]

With financial knowledge becoming increasingly important in a complex economy, this educational requirement reflects a broader national shift toward preparing young people for the financial challenges they will face. Yet in many schools, financial literacy is treated as an afterthought, if taught at all. Only 35 states require high school students to take a course in personal finance to graduate.[15] Just 57% of American adults are considered financially literate.[16] Even if you did receive some financial education in school, likely, it didn't account for your unique Financial Genetic Code. The reality is that a cookie-cutter approach to financial literacy doesn't work. It isn't practical or efficient. It's like expecting everyone to play the piano using the same sheet music, without first asking if they can even sight read, let alone if they're naturally rhythmic or tone-deaf. You have to know the person in front of you before prescribing solutions that may do more harm than good.

To be effective, financial education needs to reflect the diversity of experiences, mindsets, and cultural backgrounds that shape our relationship with money. A one-size-fits-all curriculum might teach the basics, but it often falls short in addressing the specific financial challenges or strengths that individuals inherit from their upbringing or community. Real financial empowerment comes from education tailored to these unique circumstances, not a broad brush.

The impact of education on our financial lives cannot be overstated. The quality and type of education we receive can significantly influence our earning potential, financial literacy, and overall approach to money management. In many countries, the rising cost of higher education has created a generation burdened by student debt. This debt can delay major life milestones, such as homeownership or starting a family, and impact long-term wealth building. In the United States, student loan debt has surpassed $1.7 trillion, affecting over 45 million borrowers.[17] Moreover, disparities in educational access and resources between affluent and underserved communities perpetuate cycles of poverty and wealth and reinforce Inherited Financial Narratives. Schools in wealthier districts often offer more advanced courses, better college preparation, and even financial literacy classes, giving their students a head start in the financial race of life. In contrast, marginalized youth face systemic barriers that limit their access to generational knowledge and upward mobility. The difference in how these experiences affect their Inherited Financial Narratives and financial genetic code is stark.

The state of the economy also plays a significant role. Did you grow up during an economic boom or a recession? In a thriving urban center or a struggling rural town? These factors don't just affect your bank account; they can also influence your perspective on money itself. Consider the Great Recession of 2008 and its impact on attitudes toward debt and investments in stocks. If you came of age during this time, you might have developed a deep-seated fear of debt just by watching foreclosure signs pop up like weeds in your neighborhood. A study by the Federal Reserve found that people who experienced high unemployment rates between the ages of 18 and 25 were less likely to own stocks even decades later.[18] That's the Invisible Hand at work.

Additionally, consider the impact of where you grew up. A groundbreaking study by Raj Chetty and his team at Harvard found that the neighborhood you grow up in can change your lifetime earnings by up to 20%.[19] Twenty percent! That's not just about having more or less money. It's about the opportunities you see (or don't see), the financial behaviors you observe, and the very idea of what's possible for someone "like you."

Examining the political realm more closely, we observe that local, state, and federal policy decisions have far-reaching consequences for individual financial well-being. Take, for example, tax policies. The structure of income tax brackets, capital gains taxes, and estate taxes directly impacts wealth accumulation and transfer. A change in these policies can significantly alter financial planning strategies for individuals and families across generations. Also, government spending priorities shape the economic landscape in which we operate. Infrastructure investments can create job opportunities and boost local economies, while cuts to social programs might increase the financial strain on certain populations. The Federal Reserve's monetary policy decisions, such as setting interest rates, have a ripple effect throughout the economy, influencing everything from mortgage rates to the return on savings accounts.

Housing policies also shape financial outcomes. Zoning laws, subsidized housing programs, and mortgage regulations can either facilitate or hinder wealth building through homeownership. The legacy of discriminatory practices like redlining continues to impact wealth distribution along racial lines, highlighting how past political decisions can have long-lasting financial consequences.

Trade policies set at the national level can affect job markets and consumer prices, potentially altering the financial landscape for entire communities. A shift towards protectionism or free trade can lead to industry booms or busts, changing the economic prospects for workers in various sectors. Even environmental policies have financial implications. Regulations on industries can affect job markets and local economies, while investment in green technology can create new economic opportunities. Climate change policies (or lack thereof) can impact everything from insurance rates in flood-prone areas to the long-term viability of certain industries.

The interplay between these policy areas creates a complex ecosystem that shapes our financial lives in both obvious and subtle ways. For instance, a community with strong public schools might attract more businesses, creating a virtuous cycle of economic growth and increased property values. Conversely, cuts to education funding could lead to a less skilled workforce, potentially deterring business investment and stunting economic growth.

Understanding these political and policy dynamics is important for successfully managing our financial lives. It helps us anticipate potential changes, adapt our financial strategies, and even engage in the political process to advocate for policies that align with our financial interests and values. As we continue to explore the roots of our Encoded Financial

Behaviors, it's important to recognize how these broader systemic factors interact with our personal experiences and cultural backgrounds to shape our financial realities.

The interaction between these and the broader ecosystems often reveals aspects of your financial decision-making that need refinement. For instance, your internal belief in frugality inherited from your parents "Walls In" might clash with an external cultural emphasis on conspicuous consumption "Walls Out", creating internal conflict and financial stress.

Recognizing External Influences on Your Financial Behavior

Understanding these connections helps us recognize how our individual financial struggles or successes are often intertwined with larger systemic issues. It reminds us that while personal responsibility is crucial, our financial lives are also shaped by forces beyond our immediate control.

These environmental factors interact with personal circumstances, often creating what psychologists refer to as "ecological systems." This concept, developed by Urie Bronfenbrenner, helps us understand how different levels of the environment (from your immediate family to the broader societal structures) interact to influence individual development and behavior.[20]

In the context of financial behavior, these ecological systems are creating a financial ecosystem, with the *roots of influence* that influence your financial beliefs and behaviors. These influences are visualized in the image below. At the center is you, with your personal experiences and beliefs about money. Surrounding you are concentric circles that are your roots of influence, including your family, culture, community and the broader societal structures we have discussed.

The Roots of Influence

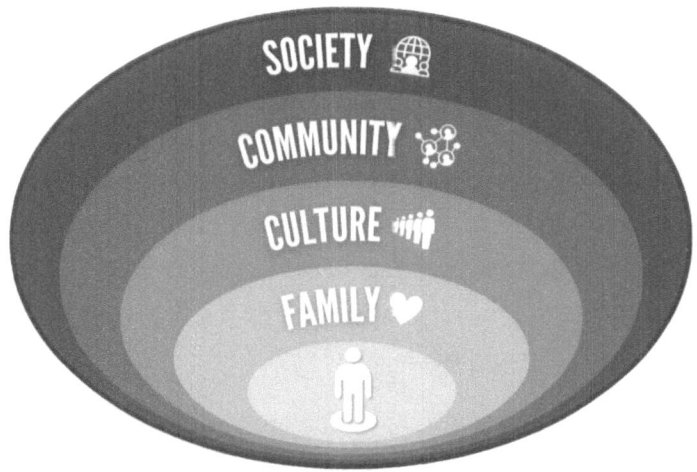

Figure 1

This ecosystem concept helps explain why simply pulling yourself up is often easier said than done when it comes to financial success. Your financial choices and opportunities are shaped not just by your individual efforts but by the entire ecosystem in which you operate.

The work of theorists like William Julius Wilson on structural inequalities offers crucial insights into how these larger societal structures and economic conditions impact financial opportunities. Wilson's research suggests that factors such as race, class, and geographic location can create significant barriers to financial success.[21] These structural inequalities often result in disparate access to financial education, resources, and opportunities, profoundly influencing an individual's ability to build and sustain wealth.

Understanding the relationship between your internal and external ecosystem is crucial for advancing toward financial healing and altering the Financial Genetic Code. We'll explore this more deeply in Stage 3 of our framework.

To truly understand your financial behaviors, we need to examine the psychological forces that drive your decisions. Maslow's Hierarchy of Needs provides a useful framework for understanding how your financial priorities shift as you move from basic survival to self-actualization.[22]

Maslow's hierarchy begins with basic physiological necessities: food, water, and shelter. When these essential needs go unfulfilled, financial choices become predominantly survival-oriented. I term this the *"CDC cycle"—Choice, Decision, and Consequences.* In these circumstances, individuals may say, "I'm not in a position to save or invest. I'm focusing instead on meeting my immediate needs."

At the ***innate and safety levels***, financial decisions often center on survival: securing food, shelter, and stability. It reveals a strong focus on saving, paying bills on time, or holding onto reliable employment, even when growth opportunities are limited.

At the ***social level***, money often becomes a tool for connection and acceptance. People may spend to fit in, attend events, or keep up with peer expectations—sometimes at the expense of long-term goals.

As we reach the ***self-esteem stage***, financial choices begin to reflect personal accomplishment. We might pursue homeownership, launch a business, or invest in self-image, not just for status, but to affirm our worth.

Finally, at ***self-actualization***, money becomes a vehicle for purpose. The focus shifts from accumulation to impact—giving back, building a legacy, and aligning finances with deeply held values.

Understanding your current position on Maslow's Hierarchy of Needs is crucial to understanding your financial behaviors and setting realistic goals. I encourage you to take a moment to rank each level of the hierarchy based on its current importance in your life and then list items that fulfill each of these needs. This exercise will provide you with a personal roadmap for your financial journey.

Intertwined with this hierarchy is the modern phenomenon of FOMO—Fear of Missing Out. In our hyper-connected, always-on world, we constantly scroll through curated Snapchats of others' highlight reels, fueling a relentless pressure to match their experiences. It's no wonder that the *keeping up with the Joneses* mentality has found new life in this digital age.

Although FOMO is the buzzword among Gen Alpha, Gen Z, and Millennials, Gen X and Baby Boomers have been grappling with similar concepts for decades. The difference now is that, instead of comparing ourselves to our neighbors down the street, we are up against the entire online world, where every click can trigger a sense of falling behind.

Social media has played a crucial role in amplifying these sentiments. Platforms like Instagram and Facebook are designed to showcase the best moments of others' lives—vacations, luxury purchases, new homes—while rarely showing the financial realities behind the scenes. This constant exposure to others' seemingly glamorous lifestyles can lead people to spend beyond their means, chasing fleeting moments of status and satisfaction at the expense of long-term financial security.

Another important concept in understanding our financial behaviors can also be attributed to "learned helplessness," a psychological condition first coined by Martin Seligman in the 1960s.[23] Learned helplessness develops when people face repeated failures or negative outcomes and begin to believe they have no control over their situation, even when opportunities for change exist. Over time, this mindset fosters resignation and passivity.

In the context of finances, learned helplessness can manifest as a belief that poverty is inevitable, that wealth is out of reach, or that factors like family background or socioeconomic status predetermine one's financial situation. This mindset can be particularly pernicious because it becomes a self-fulfilling prophecy. If you believe you can't improve your financial situation, you're less likely to take steps that could lead to improvement, reinforcing the belief. Over time, it can lead to a passive approach to money management, such as avoiding budgeting or financial planning, stemming from the belief that one's actions have little impact on financial well-being. In extreme cases, it can lead to neglect of financial health, such as ignoring debts or failing to save for the future.

Now that we've explored these various influences—ranging from childhood whispers to Inherited Financial Narratives and from healthcare systems to political landscapes—we begin to see the complexities that form the roots of our Encoded Financial Behaviors.

What does all this mean for you? It means that your financial behaviors —the good, the bad, and the ugly—aren't just a result of your choices. They're also the product of a complex interplay between your childhood experiences, cultural background, and the broader economic environment you grew up in. We aren't trying to make excuses. We're trying to understand and become empowered with the right knowledge, because once you understand the roots of your Inherited Financial Narratives, you can start to rewrite them.

Consider Amber, our stressed marketing executive from the introduction. With further analysis, we see that her money anxiety was not just about her current bank balance. It was rooted in watching her parents struggle, growing up in a culture that equates spending with self-worth, and coming of age during an economic downturn.

Remember Alex, who felt guilty about his success? His discomfort wasn't just modesty. It resulted from growing up in a community where financial success was rare and standing out could be dangerous. This behavior is common in places where an Invisible Hand always seems to be pushing people down rather than lifting them up. This behavior further leads to *Imposter Syndrome*, a psychological pattern where individuals doubt their accomplishments, skills, or abilities, often feeling like a fraud or being unable to justify their success.

Understanding these roots doesn't magically solve their problems. However, it does shine a light on the path forward. It allows them—and you—to start separating the financial facts from the financial fiction written into your narrative.

As we move forward in this book, we'll look more deeply into each aspect of your unique Financial Genetic Code. We'll explore how to recognize the whispers of your childhood, decode your Inherited Financial Narratives, and see the workings of the Invisible Hand in your life.

But for now, I want you to start thinking about your own Inherited Financial Narratives. What were the money messages you heard growing up? How has your culture shaped your view of wealth? What economic forces have played a role in your financial journey?

Below, you will find a self-reflection exercise to take a self-inventory, which will help you map your money roots and identify key influences in your financial upbringing. Go through every section, as it will prepare you for Stage 2 of the Seven-Stage Generational Wealth Model©.

Remember, this isn't about judgment. It's about awareness, because awareness is the first step towards change. And change, future wealth builder, is what this journey is all about. As you recall, this is an incremental process. We are not attempting to change our lives overnight; we are taking a long view to achieve our realistic goals.

Escaping these constraints requires recognizing these patterns and understanding their origins. My goal is to challenge the notion that the past dictates the future and to realize that financial control can be regained through knowledge, support, and proactive strategies. This process involves both unlearning harmful beliefs and engaging in positive financial behaviors, a key focus of Stage 3 in our model.

In the next chapter, we'll start to unpack the emotional baggage that comes with our Financial Genetic Code. We'll look at financial trauma and anxiety; heavy stuff, I know, but vital for understanding why we do what we do with money. So, take a deep breath. We're just getting started on this journey of financial self-discovery. And trust me, while it might get a little uncomfortable at times, it's going to be one hell of a ride.

Mapping Your Money Roots: A Self-Reflection Guide

This guide is designed to help you unearth the roots of your Encoded Financial Behaviors. Take your time with each section, be honest with yourself, and remember, there are no right or wrong answers. The goal is self-awareness and understanding.

Section 1: Childhood Money Whispers

1. What's your earliest memory involving money? How did it make you feel?

2. What phrases about money did you often hear growing up? (e.g., "Money doesn't grow on trees." "We can't afford that!")

3. How did your parents or guardians handle money? What did their behavior teach you?

4. Was money a source of conflict in your household? If so, how?

5. Did you receive an allowance? If yes, what were the rules around it?

Section 2: Inherited Financial Narratives

1. What cultural background do you come from? How does your culture typically view money?

2. Have there been any cultural traditions or beliefs about money that have influenced you?

3. In your culture, is discussing money openly encouraged or discouraged?

4. How does your culture view debt? Saving? Investing?

5. Are there any cultural expectations about financial support for family members?

Section 3: The Invisible Hand

1. How would you describe the economic environment you grew up in?

2. What major economic events (recessions, booms) occurred during your formative years? How did they affect you or your family?

3. How did the healthcare system in your country influence your family's financial decisions?

4. How did the education system impact your financial journey?

5. Can you identify any government policies that have significantly affected your financial life?

Section 4: Psychological Factors

1. Looking at Maslow's Hierarchy of Needs, where do most of your financial concerns fall?

2. Have you ever made a financial decision due to FOMO (Fear of Missing Out)? Describe the situation.

3. Do you ever feel helpless about your financial situation? If so, where do you think this feeling originates?

4. How do you define financial success? Where does this definition come from?

5. What's your biggest fear when it comes to money?

Section 5: Current Financial Behavior

1. How would you describe your current relationship with money?

2. What financial habits do you suspect might be rooted in your past experiences?

3. Do you make certain financial choices over and over without fully understanding the reason behind them?

4. How do you feel when discussing money or making major financial decisions?

5. What's one thing about your financial behavior you'd like to change? Why do you think you haven't changed it yet?

Reflection

After completing this guide, take some time to reflect on your answers. What patterns do you see? What surprises you? Are there any connections between your past experiences and current behaviors that you hadn't noticed before?

Remember, awareness is the first step towards change. By understanding the roots of your Inherited Financial Narratives, you gain the power to rewrite them. Use these insights as a starting point for your journey toward financial empowerment and building generational wealth.

Keep this guide handy and revisit it periodically. As you progress on your financial journey, you may uncover new insights or notice changes in your perspective.

Chapter 2:
Decoding Your Financial Genetic Code

"When you know better, you do better."
—Maya Angelou

Financial trauma's silent echoes are often passed down through generations, much like unspoken family heirlooms. These echoes manifest in the smallest of moments—a parent's strained sigh over bills, the uneasy shuffle through a grocery line with food stamps, or the unspoken shame that lingers in every purchase. In the African American community, these whispers carry the weight of centuries-old struggles, evolving into what modern psychology now recognizes as intergenerational financial anxiety.

For me, these money whispers weren't abstract ideas; they were woven into the fabric of my childhood. I grew up in the company of "funny money" moments, standing alongside my mother as she pulled out those vibrant-colored food stamps that carried more than just financial aid. They carried a sense of deep-seated shame, a complex signal of survival and struggle.

My mother, a single parent and a relentless force of nature, juggled three jobs simultaneously, navigating the complex, often unspoken rules of survival economics. Money was tight, like a ghost that hovered around every corner of our household, never directly acknowledged but ever-present in every decision we made. In our home, we didn't discuss finances openly; we lived with them.

We were far from the top of the financial ladder; we were at the bottom. Every grocery trip, every decision to delay a bill payment, and every calculated choice to stretch resources became a testament to survival. The colorful food stamps we relied on to "make groceries," as many African American families say, were both a blessing and a burden. They represented a way out of hunger but also a stamp of financial struggle, a stigma that quietly took residence in our hearts.

Looking back, it strikes me how we, as children, turned that shared struggle into a weapon of mockery. Even in our tight-knit community, where nearly every family was dealing with similar challenges, we teased one another for using the very assistance that kept food on the table. We didn't realize it at the time, but that teasing reflected something much more profound. It was what researchers in financial psychology refer to (either directly or indirectly) as a form of *shame displacement*. While not always explicitly labeled, this behavior is evident in empirical findings, such as those documented by Gladstone et al.[1] Other studies have also shown that this can function as a psychological defense mechanism and a way communities process financial stigma by internalizing it and redirecting the pain outward.[2]

This paradox, the denial of our shared struggles in childhood, wasn't just about cruelty or childhood ignorance. It was the defense mechanism we used to cope with the collective wounds left by years of financial trauma. Angela Davis, a scholar who has written extensively on the intersections of race, class, and justice, helps us understand these economic realities in their historical context. Her work brings clarity to the denial and mockery I witnessed during my childhood.[3] While the shame that poverty brings to the African American community often obscures the more profound reality of economic exclusion and a lack of financial education, it went beyond ignoring our poverty to coping with the overwhelming sense of helplessness it sometimes brought.

These insights resonate with a reality I have come to understand in adulthood: that what we experienced wasn't just poverty but the inheritance of historical disenfranchisement that has reached back through generations. Financial anxiety in communities of color often has deep roots in childhood experiences, creating complex relationships with money. For African Americans, financial matters are uniquely complicated, influenced not only by personal choices but by historical obstacles to building wealth and persistent systemic inequalities that continue to shape economic opportunities and outcomes.

Yet, recognizing these patterns doesn't mean we have to dwell on the pain of the past. Instead, we need to understand them because this is the next vital step toward breaking them. As Maya Angelou wisely wrote, "When you know better, you do better."[4] The financial habits we inherit, including shame, fear, and avoidance, are not our destiny. They are simply part of our Encoded Financial Behaviors, a genetic code that shapes our starting point but doesn't have to define our future.

Stage 2: Anxiety and Trauma

New Wealth Wave Podcast, EP 12: Dr. Michael Thomas, Jr.

"This recognition of trauma's role in financial behavior represents an important shift from blame to understanding. When someone exhibits anxious financial behaviors, such as hoarding money despite financial security, avoiding financial decisions altogether, or engaging in compulsive spending, these aren't simply bad habits. They're often trauma responses rooted in neurological patterns."

In Chapter 1, we began unearthing the roots of your Encoded Financial Behaviors. We explored the whispers of childhood, decoded Inherited Financial Narratives, and recognized the Invisible Hand that shaped your financial worldview. We also mapped and identified the forces that have influenced your financial journey—your "Walls In" and "Walls Out." These components comprise what we define as your internal and external ecosystem, the first stage in understanding your financial self.

Now, it's time to go deeper. We move beyond the surface of what shaped us and venture into how these influences have become encoded into our very being, your Financial Genetic Code. Think of it as your financial DNA: a sequence of experiences, beliefs, and behaviors that unconsciously steer your money decisions. This code is built from the thousands of financial flashpoints in our lives, such as moments of anxiety, triumph, confusion, or clarity that leave lasting imprints on our minds.

However, unlike our biological DNA, which is fixed from birth, our Financial Genetic Code is something we can decode and ultimately reprogram. That's the heart of Stage 3 in our journey, where we will be dealing with the transforming process of reprogramming our Financial Genetic Code through financial healing. To illustrate this concept, let me revisit a story shared by Dr. Marcia Ruben, a seasoned expert in leadership and neuroscience.[5]

Dr. Ruben's personal experience is also backed by neuroscience. I first met her in a doctoral-level leadership course at Golden Gate University. In 2023, she was awarded the title of Emerita. She developed the "NeuroStroll®," an innovative process that helps leaders achieve their goals by understanding how to access specific parts of their brains, especially those connected to the emotions that influence their present-day decision-making. Much like her work, our exploration into decoding the Financial Genetic Code involves retracing those emotional pathways, understanding the roots of our financial fears, and reshaping the narrative.

Dr. Ruben's financial journey resonates with so many of us who have experienced financial uncertainty in our formative years. She recalled growing up in a household where money was scarce. Her father, a refugee, struggled to keep their house and also put food on the table. One day, Dr. Ruben, then just a young girl, saw her family's budget posted on the pantry door. She learned as an adult that her father faced a financial crisis.

As a child, her allowance was a small part of the household's expenses, but she vividly remembers the day when she didn't see her name on that list. She picked up her parents' fear, and that seemingly trivial absence left an imprint of fear in her young mind. That moment became etched into her hippocampus, the part of the brain responsible for memories associated with emotions. And so, without realizing it at the time, that experience of fear became a part of her Financial Genetic Code.

This fear followed her into adulthood. Despite starting her career with idealistic dreams of teaching, Dr. Ruben recognized by her late twenties that a career in education would not generate the financial security she longed for. The earlier financial anxiety she had internalized began to steer her decisions. Determined to rewrite her story, she shifted gears, diverging from the world of teaching into business, where she would learn to invest, save, and grow her wealth. She even started an investment club, collaborating with women to deepen her understanding of the stock market and create the financial resilience she had lacked as a child. Over time, she began to rewrite her Inherited Financial Narratives and reprogram her Financial Genetic Code, turning fear into empowerment and uncertainty into knowledge.

Dr. Ruben's journey, like that of so many, underscores a profound truth about our financial lives: the Financial Genetic Code we inherit may shape our present, but it doesn't have to define our future.

The first step in reprogramming it is to recognize the moments, such as Dr. Ruben's encounter with her family's budget, that have become flashpoints in our financial story. These moments, encoded in our memories, shape our financial behaviors, often without us even realizing it. For some, these flashpoints may be the struggles of living paycheck to paycheck, the pain of a parent losing a job, or even the fear of scarcity when unexpected bills arrive. For others, it may be the pressure of having to appear financially stable in front of peers or community members, even when the reality is far from it.

However, before we look more closely at how you can begin to decode and reprogram your Financial Genetic Code, let's briefly revisit the foundations we laid in Chapter 1. Remember the self-reflection exercises from Chapter 1? They helped you map the factors that shaped your Inherited Financial Narratives. We talked about your internal and external ecosystems—how the forces of family, culture, and society create "Walls In" and "Walls Out" that either fortify or hinder your financial journey. Now, we'll build on that foundation, looking at how those factors have become internalized, creating patterns of anxiety and trauma. This exploration might feel uncomfortable at times. After all, we're venturing into territory that many prefer to avoid. However, understanding your Financial Genetic Code is vital for any meaningful financial transformation.

Just as our biological DNA carries instructions that determine our physical traits, our Financial Genetic Code carries the instructions for our financial behaviors—habits of spending, saving, investing, or avoiding money altogether. Whether you grew up in an environment of scarcity or abundance, these early experiences are coded into your brain, creating patterns that persist into adulthood. The challenge is that many of us aren't fully aware of how deeply ingrained these patterns are, nor how they subtly influence our approach to handling money.

Here is where the concept of financial flashpoints comes into play. Flashpoints are those high-intensity emotional experiences that shape our perception and interaction with money. Remember Dr. Ruben's story about seeing her name missing from the family budget? That's a classic example of a financial flashpoint that shaped her financial narrative for years to come. Psychologist Dr. Brad Klontz has written extensively about how financial flashpoints, often rooted in trauma or loss, can lead to harmful financial behaviors, like excessive saving due to fear of future scarcity or compulsive spending to cope with emotional pain.[6] These flashpoints create imprints on our Financial Genetic Code, but are not insurmountable.

As you begin to decode and identify the patterns that have shaped your financial life, you may discover, for instance, that your tendency to avoid looking at your bank account or to live paycheck to paycheck is tied to the financial flashpoints of your childhood. Perhaps your fear of investing stems from a moment you witnessed your parents lose money in a business deal or financial crash.

"You didn't just inherit eye color or blood type - you inherited financial fears, silence, and survival mechanisms. Now, it's your turn to rewrite the code."

The key is to understand that these Encoded Financial Behaviors are not just random choices—they reflect the Financial Genetic Code passed down to you through generations of shared experiences, culture, and family dynamics. They are the result of centuries of systemic barriers and personal experiences that we discussed in Stage 1. Your Financial Genetic Code is a byproduct of your internal and external ecosystems. However, the most empowering truth is that your Financial Genetic Code is not set in stone. It can be decoded, examined, and rewritten.

With awareness comes power; the power to break the chains of generational financial trauma and rewrite the Inherited Financial Narratives we pass on to future generations. This journey is about more than just money; it's about reclaiming your power, reshaping your relationship with wealth, and ensuring that the Financial Genetic Code we pass on to our children is one rooted in empowerment, not limitation.

This code manifests itself most visibly through two powerful forces: financial anxiety and trauma. These aren't just temporary states of worry or financial stress. They're deep-seated psychological responses that can create what I called in Chapter 1, the "Walls In"–invisible barriers that keep us trapped in negative financial patterns, even when we consciously want to break free.

As we continue with this chapter, we'll explore how these "Walls" form, why they persist, and most importantly, how to recognize them in your life. We'll examine how your brain processes financial information, why certain money situations trigger intense emotional responses, and how past experiences create present-day financial flashpoints.

Understanding your Financial Genetic Code isn't just identifying past influences. It's recognizing how those influences have become encoded into your financial narratives and behaviors. It's seeing the connection between that time your parents argued about money when you were seven and your current reluctance to discuss finances with your partner.

Remember, you can't rewrite a story if you don't understand the language it's written in. So, let's explore the science behind the Financial Genetic Code.

The Science Behind Your Money Behavior

When it comes to financial decisions, we often like to believe that we make choices based purely on logic. However, as we uncovered in Stage 1 of the Seven-Stage Generational Wealth Model©, our relationship with money is deeply influenced by factors beyond conscious thought. To fully grasp our Financial Genetic Code, it's essential to understand the powerful neuroscience that shapes our financial behavior.

At the heart of this science lies the principle of survival. The brain's primary function is to minimize danger and maximize rewards—essentially, to keep us safe. Our brains are wired to be extremely sensitive to threats, with more neural circuits dedicated to anticipating and avoiding threats than seeking and experiencing rewards.[7]

This insight sheds light on our approach to money. Our brains constantly scan for potential risks and react with remarkable speed. Within a fraction of a second, the brain's threat detection system activates, assessing any situation that might threaten our sense of security. Research supports this concept. A study published by Nobel Prize winner Daniel Kahneman showed that people are more likely to recall adverse financial events, such as a debt crisis, than positive ones, suggesting that our brains are wired to prioritize negative experiences in financial contexts.[8] This tendency to focus on potential losses rather than gains can lead to a cycle of financial anxiety, making it difficult for individuals to adopt a more balanced financial perspective.

This survival-driven wiring explains a critical cognitive bias known as loss aversion. In this phenomenon, the fear of losing money exerts twice the psychological weight as the prospect of gaining the same amount.[9] Rooted in our brain's threat detection machinery, loss aversion causes irrational financial decisions by prioritizing avoidance of perceived losses over pursuit of potential gains. For example, someone might cling to underperforming investments to sidestep the pain of realizing a loss, even if reallocating funds could yield long-term growth. This instinct isn't merely cautious; it is counterproductive, as studies show it can lead to lower portfolio returns over time by amplifying opportunity costs.[10]

The paradox of loss aversion lies in its self-reinforcing nature. Every financial setback, whether a market crash, an unexpected expense, or even childhood memories of scarcity, strengthens neural pathways that equate risk with danger. Over time, these pathways calcify into automatic mental shortcuts, overriding rational analysis. A person might avoid opening retirement statements during volatile markets or delay starting a business despite favorable conditions, all to evade the biochemical "threat" response triggered by uncertainty. Yet this avoidance often exacerbates financial instability, thereby trapping individuals in cycles of anxiety and inaction.

This phenomenon bridges directly to the brain's two key financial architects—the amygdala and hippocampus. The amygdala, often referred to as our emotional control center, serves as our financial alarm system. When we encounter a money-related situation that triggers past trauma or anxiety, our amygdala springs into action, initiating what neuroscientists call the "fight, flight, or freeze" response. This reaction isn't just psychological; it's biochemical. Our bodies release stress hormones like *cortisol*, our heart rate increases, and our thinking becomes narrowed and focused on perceived threats. In financial terms, this might manifest as panic-selling investments during market downturns, freezing when faced with important financial decisions, or aggressively avoiding financial planning altogether.

In small doses, cortisol helps us respond to short-term threats, giving us the energy to act quickly. However, in today's world, where financial stress is constant and ongoing, this response can become problematic. Chronic elevation of cortisol levels can impair sleep, decision-making, and overall well-being. According to Dr. Ruben, prolonged exposure to stress hormones can lead to significant health issues, including heart disease, anxiety, digestive problems, headaches, sleep problems, weight gain, memory and concentration impairment, and depression. If we experience prolonged financial difficulties, this stress response becomes a constant companion, making it difficult to think clearly about long-term financial planning.

It's important to note that many people get stuck in this stage of financial anxiety and trauma due to negative thinking and self-talk. These negative thoughts can create a feedback loop, reinforcing the stress response and making it difficult to move forward.

Dr. Ruben further highlights how this biochemical response influences our behaviors:

New Wealth Wave Podcast, EP 5: Dr. Marcia Ruben

"This negative self-talk activates our brain's threat response system, further increasing cortisol levels and deepening our sense of financial insecurity. The anxiety cycle reinforces itself, creating a barrier to effective financial decision-making, which can lead to further underlying health conditions as cortisol continues to be secreted in the body."

A rather striking fact is that the body flags these financial threats subconsciously, much like how we automatically know how to write. This subconscious response means that we may not even realize we're in a heightened state of stress when making decisions. Meanwhile, our hippocampus, the brain's memory center, stores and recalls both positive and negative financial experiences. It's why the memory of bounced checks from years ago might still make your stomach churn, or why the sight of past-due bills might trigger intense anxiety, even if your current financial situation is stable.

One of the most fascinating aspects of our brain is how it develops automatic habits to conserve energy. An example is when we learn how to drive. Initially, every action requires deliberate thought, but over time, we begin to drive on autopilot without thinking about the mechanics. The same applies to our financial behaviors. Many of our decisions are based on ingrained habits, shaped by early experiences, Inherited Financial Narratives, and our Financial Genetic Code, rather than active choices. Each negative financial experience reinforces our brain's neural pathways, making them stronger and more automatic.

Financial Trauma in Your Wallet

This neurological understanding of financial behavior and the relationship between financial trauma, anxiety, and our brain's response patterns become clearer when we consider what Dr. Michael Thomas, Jr., an accredited financial counselor and lecturer at the University of Georgia, describes as the "indelible mark" left by financial experiences.[11] In Episode 16 of the podcast, he explained:

New Wealth Wave Podcast, EP 12: Dr. Michael Thomas, Jr.

"This insight is important because it helps explain why many of our financial behaviors seem automatic or unexplainable. We might not remember the specific childhood incident where we witnessed our parents arguing about money, but our brain formed neural pathways that continue to influence our financial decisions decades later."

It also helps to explain why financial trauma can have such lasting effects on our behavior. Whether it's witnessing foreclosure as a child, experiencing periods of severe poverty, or dealing with chronic financial instability, these traumatic experiences create neural pathways that trigger anxiety responses long after the initial event has passed. The anxiety becomes a protective mechanism, albeit one that often hinders rather than helps our financial progress.

Understanding this neurological foundation helps explain why traditional financial advice often falls short. When I work with clients, I frequently observe how their brain's threat response system can override logical financial planning. As I've observed through years of counseling diverse clients, particularly within the African American community, our financial behaviors are rooted in complex neurological patterns shaped by our internal and external ecosystems and generational experiences. This relationship with money runs deeper than the surface of conscious decision-making.

As Brian Thomas eloquently stated in Episode 13 of the podcast, children are the "financial passengers" in their parents' lives, absorbing and becoming byproducts of the internal environment they witness.[12]

The financial knowledge, behaviors, and trauma that children experience growing up profoundly shape their later relationship with money, often unconsciously. The financial services industry has historically misunderstood these neurological and psychological aspects of our relationship with money and the resulting trauma response.

The anxiety-trauma cycle becomes even more complex when we consider what Tiffany Grant describes through the socio-ecological model. Financial trauma isn't just individual; it can be communal and generational. As she explained in Episode 7, "The individual is at the center, but then after the individual, there are relationships. Then, after that, there are organizations; then after that, there are communities; after that, there are policies, and after that, society. All of these different things play into how the individual operates."[13] She further explained:

New Wealth Wave Podcast, EP 7: Tiffany Grant

"This systemic trauma creates layers of anxiety that manifest in various ways. For instance, the anxiety about engaging with financial institutions might stem not just from personal experiences but also from witnessed or inherited trauma passed down through generations. This anxiety can then reinforce patterns of financial avoidance or defensive financial behaviors."

This multilayered approach helps us understand that simply telling someone to "save more" or "invest wisely" fails to address the complex web of neurological, emotional, and social factors influencing their financial decisions. The impact of these systemic influences becomes particularly evident when we examine learned helplessness in financial behavior. Grant's observations about learned helplessness further illuminate how trauma and anxiety can become self-perpetuating:

"It happens to a lot of people... we can just get really comfortable. When I say 'comfortable,' I'm looking at, for instance, government programs...

it was perpetuated through the generations. I even have friends whose grandmothers were on government assistance, and their mothers were on government assistance. Now, they're on government assistance. They don't have to be, but they choose to be because that's what they know."

This "comfort" she describes isn't truly comfort at all—it's often a trauma response, a way of coping with deep-seated financial anxiety by staying within familiar, albeit limiting, patterns. The brain, seeking to protect us from perceived financial threats, can keep us locked in these patterns through constant anxiety responses.

Understanding these trauma responses and anxiety triggers is important because they directly impact our ability to make sound financial decisions. When we're in an anxious state, our brain's threat-response system overrides our logical decision-making capabilities.

This pattern of learned behavior shows how our Financial Genetic Code can be shaped not only by personal experiences but also by family patterns and systemic influences. The neural pathways created by these experiences form what Dr. Thomas calls "adaptive behaviors"— automatic responses that may have been useful in the past but may no longer align with our current financial goals.

He notes, "This insight is particularly relevant when dealing with financial anxiety and trauma. We can't simply 'logic' our way out of trauma responses. The anxiety we feel about money isn't a character flaw—it's a neurological response to past experiences, both personal and collective."

The brain's response to financial stress is particularly relevant when we consider the unique financial challenges and historical context faced by African Americans. Research by the American Psychological Association reveals that African Americans experience disproportionate levels of financial stress, with 67% reporting money as a significant source of anxiety compared to the national average of 36%.[14]

The complexity of our brain's financial processing becomes even more apparent when we consider relationships. Drawing on my extensive experience counseling couples, I have observed how two individuals bring their unique neural patterns, shaped by past experiences, family dynamics, and, in many cases, unresolved financial trauma, into their partnership. These patterns influence their financial behaviors, emotional triggers, and decision-making processes, often without their realizing it. For instance, someone who grew up in a financially unstable household might have developed heightened sensitivity to financial risk, which could manifest as anxiety over spending, extreme caution with investments, or even hoarding behaviors. Meanwhile, their partner might have experienced financial abundance but learned unhealthy spending habits, making them more prone to impulsive financial decisions. When these patterns collide, it creates tension, often not rooted in the finances themselves but in the unspoken fears and emotional baggage each person carries.

Recent neuroscience research, particularly in social baseline theory[15], provides fascinating insights into how social connections influence our financial stress response. A study cited by Dr. Ruben during the podcast session demonstrated how physical contact with a trusted individual could significantly reduce stress responses, which has profound implications for how we approach financial counseling and support systems.

Understanding these neurological underpinnings is important when you are seeking to improve your financial well-being. While essential for survival, your brain's threat detection system can sometimes work against your modern financial goals. By recognizing these patterns and understanding their origins, you can begin to develop more effective strategies for managing your Financial Genetic Code. This neurological perspective on financial behavior represents a significant advancement in how we approach financial education and counseling. Remember, this understanding isn't just academic; it's practical knowledge that can transform your approach to your financial journey. In my practice, I've observed how this awareness enables clients to transition from unconscious financial reactions to conscious financial responses, laying the groundwork for more informed financial decision-making and sustainable wealth-building.

Identifying Your Inherited Financial Narratives and Their Influence on Your Financial Behavioral Patterns

To understand how these ingrained narratives shape our financial behaviors, let's briefly return to the learned helplessness concept we covered in Chapter 1. As we explored, learned helplessness manifests itself particularly strongly in our financial behaviors. When generations of families face systemic barriers to wealth creation, it creates a form of "financial surrender," a deeply ingrained belief that financial security remains out of reach, regardless of the actions taken. This thinking pattern becomes encoded in our Financial Genetic Code, passed down through families like an invisible inheritance.

I remember sitting with Mrs. Jane, a retired schoolteacher whose story exemplifies this pattern. Growing up in a household where her parents had been repeatedly denied mortgages in the 1960s, she'd internalized a belief that homeownership was not for "people like them." Despite having a stable career and a good credit score, she had never even considered buying a home until our sessions together. "It just wasn't something we did," she told me, her voice carrying the weight of generations of similar thoughts.

This learned helplessness creates the fertile ground where our Inherited Financial Narratives take root. *Money Scripts®*, a term coined by financial psychologist Dr. Bradley Klontz, are the unconscious beliefs about money that guide our financial behaviors.[16] In my model, we need to dig even deeper to understand the Inherited Financial Narratives that have been unconsciously handed down over generations and that continue to shape our behaviors in the present. In the African American community, these narratives often carry additional layers of historical and cultural significance.[17]

When we examine Inherited Financial Narratives in African American households, we often find they're intertwined with historical trauma. The pressure to 'make it' financially isn't just personal, it's communal. Additionally, we see African American professionals report feeling an obligation to support extended family members, creating what can be best described as a "financial caretaker responsibility or black tax."[18] This term refers to the financial support that Black professionals often provide to their extended families, stemming from cultural expectations and historical socioeconomic disparities. This dynamic can contribute to financial instability and stress, affecting both individuals and families.

Upon closer examination of these Inherited Financial Narratives, several dominant patterns emerge that influence our community's financial behaviors. The first, and possibly most widespread, is what we call the "Inherited Scarcity Loop." This belief runs deep in our community, and let me be real with you: It's that voice in your head saying, "Better hold onto every dime 'cause you don't know when the next check is coming." It's that anxiety that has you checking your account three times a day, even when you know the money is there. I see it all the time in my practice: successful professionals earning six figures, still behaving like they're one paycheck away from being broke.

Take my client Jerome, a tech executive earning $ 200,000 a year, who still keeps his "struggle stash"–a hidden cache of money not in a bank account nor invested. "My grandma always said to keep something for a rainy day," he told me during one of our sessions, "but Doc, I'm living like every day is gonna be a hurricane." That's the scarcity narrative talking, keeping us in a state of survival mode even when we're thriving.

Financial insecurity among middle-class African Americans is a persistent issue. Despite achieving middle-class status, many families struggle to accumulate wealth and maintain stability. A study by the Boston Federal Reserve revealed that these families often face challenges in maintaining their socioeconomic position, leading to heightened financial stress.[19] Regardless of their actual financial status, the stress they experience is not just about having money but believing they deserve to keep it. This mindset, often rooted in past experiences of financial hardship or shaped by societal pressures, can create a constant state of anxiety about not having enough. It can manifest in various ways, from excessive frugality to the opposite extreme of "hustle culture"–the belief that one must be constantly working and thriving to avoid financial ruin. It can be particularly damaging because it often leads to short-term thinking and decision-making. When continually worrying about not having enough, it becomes challenging to plan for the future or make strategic financial decisions. That worry can trap us in a circle of financial anxiety, preventing us from achieving true financial well-being.

It is worth noting that most of the financial advice circulating on social media and from trendy financial influencers can exacerbate this anxiety. Many of these sources offer oversimplified solutions or "get-rich-quick" schemes that are, at best, half-truths and, at worst, potentially misleading and harmful information.

During my conversation with Rahkim Sabre in Episode 11 of the *New Wealth Wave Podcast*[20], I mentioned the following:

> "However, it's important to understand that financial literacy, while important, is not the ultimate goal. I like to view financial literacy as a mere band-aid to a larger, underlying problem. The real goal should be financial well-being and, ultimately, generational wealth, which encompasses not just knowledge but also emotional and psychological comfort with one's financial situation."

Apart from the scarcity narrative, there's the "Flex Narrative," and y'all know exactly what we're talking about. It's that pressure to show out and prove we've "made it." A study published in the Journal of International Consumer Marketing found that African Americans scored higher in materialism and conspicuous consumption compared to non-African Americans.[21] For many in our community, the flex narrative isn't just about showing off, it's a way of saying 'I survived, I overcame.' This display of wealth, even when it strains their finances, serves as a psychological counter to generations of economic marginalization.

However, here's where it gets tricky. The "Provider Narrative" often collides with these other patterns. That deep-seated responsibility to take care of everybody: Mama, cousins, and the whole church congregation, if you can. I had a client, Michelle, a corporate lawyer who was the first in her family to graduate from college. "Every time my phone rings," she told me, "I know somebody needs something. And how can I say *no* when I'm the one who 'made it'?"

This issue becomes even more pronounced in the entertainment and professional sports world, where sudden wealth amplifies the provider script to new heights. Seasoned financial planner Louis Barajas, one of our guests in Episode 19 of the podcast, shared with me how he witnessed this pattern play out dramatically with his high-net-worth clients. Imagine a 16-year-old athlete suddenly becoming a millionaire. It's not just immediate family anymore, but an entire entourage expecting support! The weight of being "the one who made it" multiplies exponentially.

The Provider Narrative transforms into what can be called a "prosperity ripple," where success generates an ever-expanding circle of financial responsibilities. It's no longer just the constant ringing of the phone; it becomes an unending chorus of needs and expectations. Many clients describe feeling overwhelmed by a sea of responsibility, where saying "no" seems like betraying their roots. In the Black community, the duties linked to the provider narrative often go beyond the traditional "sandwich generation" idea of supporting both children and parents.

"It becomes more like a club sandwich, which begins with mothers, fathers, sisters, brothers, and is sprinkled with layers of aunties, uncles, cousins, church members, and childhood friends, all looking for help."

What makes this especially challenging is how deeply it's woven into our Inherited Financial Narratives. When you're the first to break through, there's often an unspoken expectation to lower a ladder for others. This ongoing financial caregiving creates a dangerous cycle: the more successful you become, the heavier the burden grows. It's like running a marathon while carrying more people with every mile. Eventually, something has to give.

This is exemplified in the Financial Martyrdom Narrative, which refers to the deeply ingrained belief that personal financial sacrifice—often to the point of self-neglect—is a necessary expression of love, duty, or resilience. In many African American households, this narrative has roots in historical and generational patterns where surviving economic hardship meant prioritizing everyone else's needs above one's own. Parents may forgo retirement savings to help adult children, grandparents may drain limited resources to support extended family, and individuals may work multiple jobs not for personal advancement, but to carry others financially. These sacrifices are often praised as noble, even heroic—but they can quietly perpetuate cycles of financial instability.

While rooted in care and communal responsibility, this Inherited Financial Narrative can have unintended consequences. The burden of always being the provider or the "strong one" often prevents individuals from building personal wealth, establishing boundaries, or investing in their own futures. Shifting away from financial martyrdom doesn't mean abandoning support for family or community—it means creating a healthier balance where generosity is paired with sustainability, and self-care is recognized as a financial priority, not a luxury.

These dynamics do more than drain bank accounts; they can cripple wealth-building potential across generations. The harsh reality is that many successful professionals end up depleting their resources trying to be everyone's financial savior, leaving them vulnerable when their rainy day arrives. The key lies in learning to put on your oxygen mask first—a lesson many clients struggle to accept, but one that's essential for creating sustainable success that can truly lift others. This pressure to be the family's financial savior often creates a complex web of guilt, responsibility, and sometimes, resentment.

Then there's the "Education-Equals-Salvation Narrative," that bone-deep belief that if we just get enough degrees, financial security will follow. Now, don't get me wrong, education is crucial. However, the blind pursuit of educational credentials without financial literacy often leads to devastating student loan debt in our community.

Let's talk about the "Investment Avoidance Narrative," and I know some of y'all are feeling this one. It's that voice saying, "The stock market is not for us," and that real estate is the only safe bet. The 2022 Ariel-

Schwab Black Investor Survey provides a comprehensive examination of investment behaviors among African Americans, revealing that while a significant portion of professionals express interest in investing, only 23% actively participate in the stock market beyond their employer-sponsored retirement plans.[22] The historical exclusion from financial markets has created a generational hesitancy that persists even when access is available.

Dr. Brad Klontz's four core Money Scripts®—a concept we touched on earlier—are found across all communities but show notable differences in African American households. These two concepts—Inherited Financial Narratives and Money Scripts®—are not mutually exclusive but rather deeply complementary. While Inherited Financial Narratives reflect the broader historical and communal experiences shaping financial attitudes, Money Scripts® offers a more personal, psychological lens through which individuals internalize and act on those beliefs. Together, they provide a more comprehensive understanding of how financial behaviors are formed and transmitted across generations. You might have inherited your Financial Genetic Code, but your financial destiny is yours to choose. Below is a more detailed look at 20 Inherited Financial Narratives that make up our Financial Genetic Code. This is not an exhaustive list, but rather a selection of the most common ones I have encountered in my work and personal experience.

20 Essential Inherited Financial Narratives

Narrative Name	Description	Behavioral Impact	Healing Thought
Scar Tissue Narrative	Fear rooted in past financial pain or betrayal.	Avoidance of growth opportunities, skepticism of financial tools.	I am not my past. I can build new outcomes.
No One Taught Me Narrative	Lack of financial literacy is passed down generationally.	Shame, trial-and-error financial habits, and disorganization.	I can learn what I was never taught.
Financial First-Gen Narrative	Being the first in your family to build wealth.	Pressure, fear of failure, and decision paralysis.	I'm pioneering with purpose and grace.
Invisible Retirement Narrative	Belief that retirement isn't possible or relevant.	Lack of planning, delay in retirement savings.	I deserve a secure and joyful future.
Financial Shame Narrative	Guilt or embarrassment from past money mistakes.	Financial self-sabotage, secrecy, and helplessness.	I can reset, reflect, and rise.
All or Nothing Narrative	Belief that small efforts aren't worth it.	Perfectionism, financial extremism, and under-saving.	Small steps create lasting wealth.
Don't Talk About It Narrative	Cultural silence around money conversations.	Poor planning, family tension, and estate confusion.	Talking about money is love in action.
Anchor Guilt Narrative	Guilt from surpassing the family financially.	Self-sabotage, over-giving, under-saving.	I can grow and still honor where I came from.
Financial Martyrdom Narrative	Self-neglect in favor of others' financial well-being.	Burnout, delayed goals, and poor boundaries.	My financial health matters too.
Inherited Scarcity Loop Narrative	Generational fear of running out of money.	Hoarding, underspending, and anxiety with abundance.	There is enough. I am safe to thrive.

Narrative Name	Description	Behavioral Impact	Healing Thought
Self-Insurance Superiority Narrative	Distrust in institutional protection plans.	Underinsured, financially vulnerable.	Protection is a wise and empowering act.
Just Survive, Don't Build Narrative	Mindset focused on survival over legacy.	Low ambition for investment or growth.	I am worthy of building, not just surviving.
Estate Planning is for the Rich Narrative	A belief that planning legacies is for the wealthy.	No will, trust, or clarity in asset transfer.	My family deserves security and a legacy.
Budgeting Means You're Broke Narrative	Stigma that budgeting reflects lack.	Overspending, shame around structure.	Budgeting gives me peace and power.
Success Means Isolation Narrative	Fear that success will create distance from others.	Minimizing achievement, guilt, and hiding wealth.	I can rise and stay connected.
Money Will Always Run Out Narrative	Belief that financial security is temporary.	Overworking, over-saving, scarcity anxiety.	I can rest knowing I am secure.
You Have to Work Twice as Hard Narrative	Cultural pressure to overperform to succeed.	Burnout, fear of slowing down.	I am worthy without proving myself.
Debt is Evil Narrative	Taught that all debt is harmful.	Avoidance of strategic credit use or growth.	I can use debt wisely and confidently.
We Don't Deserve Wealth Narrative	Internalized belief that wealth is for others.	Wealth rejection, undercharging, and underinvesting.	Wealth is my birthright and responsibility.
Money Changes People Narrative	Belief that financial gain corrupts values.	Avoidance of growth, income limits, and self-sabotage.	Money reflects who I already am.

Figure 2

My presentation at the San Francisco Economic Roundtable proved this point to be incredibly impactful. The audience consisted of affluent individuals with significant assets, yet many still grappled with financial anxieties stemming from deeply ingrained beliefs about money. Their struggle was perfectly illustrated by one attendee's remarkable transformation journey, as captured in her testimonial letter (see Appendix A). Here was an accomplished individual who, despite her education and resources, had spent years constrained by limiting beliefs about wealth creation. She was fixated on real estate as the sole path to financial security, becoming a landlord and spending her most productive years managing properties instead of pursuing her true passion for filmmaking.

Her story reflects the deeply personal impact that Inherited Financial Narratives can have, even for individuals who have achieved educational and professional milestones. At 80 years old, she chose to re-engage with her financial life in a new way, approaching long-held beliefs with curiosity and a willingness to learn.

After engaging with the Seven-Stage Generational Wealth Model©, she reported gaining a more profound sense of financial clarity and self-awareness. While outcomes vary from person to person, what stood out in her case was a shift in mindset—away from fear, avoidance, and outdated wealth-building expectations, and toward a more intentional, values-based approach to managing money.

Her journey doesn't guarantee a specific outcome. However, it highlights the potential for change at any stage of life when people are encouraged to reflect on and redefine their relationship with money. Her experience emphasizes the importance of financial education that respects both history and healing.

Whether you're 25 or 80, the ability to rewrite your financial story is within your grasp. These Inherited Financial Narratives, passed down through generations, were often written for survival in a different time. However, they may no longer serve us in the pursuit of building generational wealth today. Just as our ancestors adapted and survived through impossible circumstances, we also have the power to evolve our relationship with money.

This experience at the Economic Round Table solidified my conviction that the Seven-Stage Generational Wealth Model© transcends race, socioeconomic background and age—offering a universal framework for the pursuit of financial well-being. When we understand and consciously work to reprogram our Financial Genetic Code, we open ourselves to new possibilities for wealth creation and, more importantly, financial self-actualization.

As we wrap up Stage 2 of the model, remember that awareness is the first step toward transformation. Whether you're just starting your career, rethinking your financial path in your forties, or nearing retirement and wondering if change is still possible, know that it is possible at any point. You hold the power to reshape your relationship with money. The model is not limited by race or background; it's a roadmap that everyone, regardless of their financial starting point or age, can use to build a legacy of wealth. The neural pathways that guided your financial behaviors in the past were carved through years of experience. However, neuroscience shows us that our brains remain plastic and are capable of forming new connections and patterns throughout our entire lives.

Your generational wealth doesn't begin with money; it begins with this knowledge.

Understanding where you come from, the financial habits you've inherited, the "Walls In" and "Walls Out" that have kept you stuck, and the mindset you've built over time is the foundation of real wealth. The decisions made by your initial financial fiduciaries, such as parents, cousins, friends, neighbors, and those who provide you with unsolicited information, have shaped your financial landscape, but that doesn't mean they bind you. This fresh knowledge, if embraced, can be used to create new patterns, new behaviors, and a new legacy.

What you choose to do with this knowledge is where true power lies. Generational knowledge equips you to break generational cycles, build healthier financial habits, and teach those who come after you. It becomes the cornerstone of creating a sustainable financial future, not just for yourself but also for the generations to follow. With each financial decision, you are either continuing old patterns or creating new ones that will reverberate through time.

Now, before we begin the journey toward financial healing, let's create your personal Financial Trauma/Anxiety Timeline. This exercise will help you identify critical moments that shaped your Financial Genetic Code.

Your Financial Trauma/Anxiety Timeline Activity

Instructions:

1. Draw a horizontal line across a blank page, representing a timeline of your life from your earliest memories to the present.

2. Mark significant financial events in your life, and the age you were when they took place. These can be positive or negative. Include:
   - Earliest money memory
   - First experience with financial stress
   - Major financial decisions
   - Money-related family events
   - Career/income changes
   - Financial victories and setbacks

3. Record your emotional responses to each event:
   - What feelings surfaced? (fear, shame, pride, anxiety, relief)
   - How intense was the emotion? (Rate 1-10)
   - What beliefs were formed from this experience?
   - How does this event still influence you today?

Reflection Questions:

After completing your timeline, consider:

- Pattern Recognition:
  - What beliefs were formed from this experience?
  - How does this event still influence you today?
  - What recurring emotional themes do you notice?
  - Are there specific triggers that consistently provoke financial anxiety?
  - How have past experiences influenced your current money habits?

- Intergenerational Patterns:
  - Which financial behaviors mirror those of your parents or grandparents?
  - What financial messages were passed down to you?
  - Which patterns do you want to break or maintain?

- Impact Assessment:
  - How have these experiences shaped your current financial decision-making?
  - Which emotional responses still feel fresh and active?
  - What financial behaviors do you now recognize as responses to trauma?

Moving Forward:

Remember that awareness is the first step toward transformation. As you review your timeline:

- Acknowledge the pain without judgment
- Celebrate the resilience that got you through difficult times
- Identify patterns you're ready to change
- Note the strengths you've developed from these experiences

Your Financial Genetic Code is not your destiny; it's simply your starting point. You have the power to reshape your financial future, regardless of age, background, or current circumstances. The patterns we've discussed—whether they're cultural scripts, family patterns, or personal trauma responses—can be recognized, understood, and ultimately transformed.

As we move forward to Part II of this book, Reprogramming Your Present: Inherited Financial Narratives and Your Financial Genetic Code, we'll build on this understanding to begin the actual work of financial healing. You'll learn specific techniques to create new neural pathways and healthier financial behaviors. For now, sit with your timeline. Let it tell you its story. Understanding where you've been is necessary to charting where you're going.

Remember, you're not alone in this journey. The very fact that you're doing this work—facing your financial past with courage and honesty—is already changing your Financial Genetic Code. You're proving that transformation is possible, that healing is within reach, and that your financial future remains unwritten, ready for you to author a new chapter.

PART II:

REPROGRAMMING YOUR PRESENT: INHERITED FINANCIAL NARRATIVES AND YOUR FINANCIAL GENETIC CODE

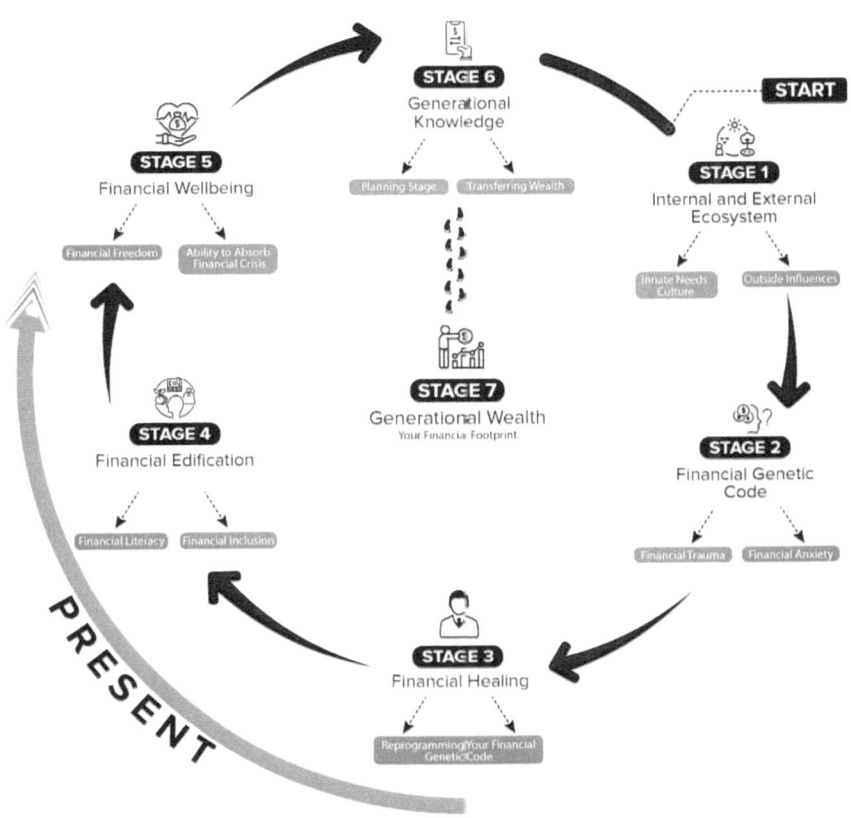

GENERATIONAL WEALTH BEGINS WITH GENERATIONAL KNOWLEDGE®
REG. COPYRIGHT © 2023 DR. JOAQUIN WALLACE.

Chapter 3:
The Path to Financial Healing

"Healing takes courage, even if we have to dig a little to find it." —Tori Amos

I n the journey toward generational wealth, progress is rarely linear. Instead, it often feels like traversing a winding road filled with unexpected detours, setbacks, and moments where we must pause and re-evaluate. At some point, we all encounter barriers that hinder our ability to build and preserve wealth. That is where financial healing becomes essential. Yet, the question begs, can we fully achieve financial well-being while creating our financial footprints toward generational wealth?

Those who have been fortunate enough may be in a position to suggest, "Absolutely!" However, for most of the population, I would say, "You may be able to achieve it. But, at what cost?" For that reason, healing is not just a destination but a continual process. Financial healing goes beyond increasing income or accumulating assets. At its core, it means unearthing and transforming our emotional and psychological relationship with money.

This healing process requires us to confront the emotional baggage associated with our financial decisions and how those emotions can unconsciously influence our behavior. As we saw previously, recent research in behavioral economics by Nobel laureates Daniel Kahneman and Amos Tversky has shown that we feel losses approximately twice as strongly as equivalent gains, a phenomenon known as loss aversion.[1] It helps explain why those who have experienced financial trauma often develop extremely cautious or even avoidant behaviors around money, even after their circumstances have improved.

For many, moving forward financially means addressing past wounds—those moments of financial trauma, anxiety, or scarcity that have shaped our money beliefs. Dr. Rachel Yehuda's groundbreaking research on transgenerational trauma provides fascinating insight into how these financial wounds can be passed down through generations. Her studies on epigenetic inheritance demonstrate that traumatic experiences can affect gene expression across generations, lending scientific weight to what we observe as the Financial Genetic Code being passed down in families.[2]

Whether it's the stress of living paycheck to paycheck, the fear of accumulating debt, or the burden of supporting others while feeling financially insecure, there is a need for healing. It involves identifying and addressing the hidden triggers. Only then can we begin reprogramming our Financial Genetic Code.

Stage 3 of the Seven-Stage Generational Wealth Model© focuses on this healing. It requires recognizing the financial flashpoints—those emotional scars that have caused you to stumble—and reframing them in a way that helps you move forward. The ultimate goal is to shift from a mindset of mere survival to one of thriving. This shift involves altering your financial habits and acknowledging and transforming the psychological and emotional patterns you've inherited.

Stage 3: Financial Healing (Present)

As we examine the concept of financial healing more closely, it's essential to acknowledge that this stage is not one you complete and then leave behind forever. Financial healing is an ongoing process. Life's unpredictable twists—whether personal or economic—can sometimes reopen old wounds. The difference is that with healing, you now have the resources to handle these challenges without being held back by past fears and anxieties.

The Seven-Stage Generational Wealth Model© we've been exploring isn't a straight path; it is one we are constantly moving through and evolving with as our circumstances change. For example, landing a new job may trigger financial anxiety, sending you back to Stage 2, where the emotional toll of financial trauma is often revisited. Even those who seem to be advancing through the model may find themselves circling back. Recently, during a consultation with a potential client, a woman shared how simply looking at numbers made her anxious. Despite significant strides in her career, the emotional baggage associated with her finances continued to pull her back into old patterns.

In my experience consulting with both incumbent and potential clients, I've observed that many individuals' lack of participation in their company's retirement plan is a direct byproduct of their internal and external ecosystems. These influences, rooted in financial anxieties and past traumas, are often embedded within their Financial Genetic Code.

Understanding and addressing these foundational issues is crucial, as they significantly influence financial behaviors and decisions. Once individuals heal from these underlying constraints, they can approach financial edification with the confidence and clarity needed to build a secure future.

Part of this financial healing process is learning to forgive yourself for past financial mistakes. Maybe you accumulated debt, missed investment opportunities, or didn't know better. The beauty of Stage 3 is that it allows you to let go of those past mistakes and instead focus on the future. Forgiving yourself frees up mental and emotional energy that can be channeled into building wealth and creating a better financial legacy for future generations.

As you go through this stage, the healing process serves as the bridge between where you've been and where you're headed. It's the process of moving beyond the emotional weight of financial trauma, and it's a vital part of building generational wealth. It is the stage where you rewrite your financial narrative and step into the life you've envisioned—one where financial freedom, not fear, dictates your decisions.

Financial Flashpoints and Rewriting the Code

In Stage 2 of the model, we explored financial anxiety. At the core of that stage is what we call "financial flashpoints." Remember, these flashpoints were pivotal moments in your financial journey—moments of stress, hardship, or revelation that became embedded in your subconscious and shaped your relationship with money. Perhaps it was the first time you watched a parent or caregiver struggle to pay bills, or that eye-opening moment when the weight of your debt became undeniable. These memories leave lasting emotional imprints. They act as pieces of data that are deeply embedded and have become an active participant in your Financial Genetic Code, quietly influencing how you make decisions, manage stress, and respond to money matters.

We often celebrate the rare, high-profile family success stories—the relative who rises to fame as an athlete or entertainer. However, these cases are less common than those of family members who have quietly achieved financial success by other means. More frequently, family pride stems from the relative who, after graduating from college, enters a high-earning career in fields such as medicine, law, or education. Just behind them are the entrepreneurial relatives—electricians, plumbers, general contractors—who, through skill and hard work, have built thriving businesses.

Yet, with this success often comes profound responsibility. The expectation to support loved ones financially can add intense pressure, creating a subtle yet heavy emotional toll. This quiet strain is part of the journey for many who find financial success, where the demands of uplifting others can be both rewarding and deeply exhausting.

The challenge with these experiences or financial flashpoints is that they often act like blind spots in our financial lives. You may not consciously connect a formative experience from your childhood to your present financial habits, but the underlying programming is still there, influencing your decisions. Whatever your flashpoint, these moments become part of the Inherited Financial Narratives that govern your life. They dictate how you react to money, how you feel about wealth, and even how you perceive your worth in relation to financial success. Unexamined, these narratives can hold you back, trapping you in cycles of financial stress, avoidance, or even fear.

However, just like you can rewrite a movie script, you can flip the Inherited Financial Narratives that have become part of your Financial Genetic Code. This is where financial healing becomes transformative. The real work begins when you confront those old beliefs and transform them into tools for building generational wealth. Financial healing entails taking the power away from those flashpoints and turning them into lessons, not limitations.

"To rewrite your Financial Genetic Code, you must first identify the beliefs and behaviors that stem from your flashpoints. For example, if your flashpoint was growing up in an environment of financial scarcity, you might have developed an avoidant relationship with money, where you shy away from making decisions or taking calculated risks. Healing involves challenging that belief - reprogramming your mindset to embrace abundance and possibility rather than fear and scarcity."

This process doesn't involve erasing your past; rather, you're reframing it. You're acknowledging the financial strategies and survival mechanisms you inherited while choosing not to let them define your future. Whether it's escaping the cycle of paycheck-to-paycheck living, learning to invest, or simply cultivating a healthier mindset around wealth, rewriting your Financial Genetic Code is an ongoing growth journey.

The "Aha!" Moment: The Turning Point in Financial Healing

Nearly everyone who embarks on this journey reaches a turning point—a moment of clarity that shifts their financial perspective. It is the *"Aha!" moment* when you realize that your financial past doesn't have to dictate your financial future. It's the moment when the fog lifts, and you start to see the possibility of financial freedom, not as a distant dream but as an attainable reality. All the guests on *The New Wealth Wave Podcast* have shared stories of their *"Aha!" moment.* Let's set the stage for the question that I asked all of them:

"What was your '*Aha!' moment?*"

I felt that this question was necessary in setting the tone with the guest and the listeners. The question allows the guest to become vulnerable to the listeners and tell their story in their own words. In most cases, the moment of their awakening emerged after years of financial struggle or hardship, marked by a profound shift in their thinking. For some, the turning point came when they began to see money not as something to be feared but as a tool for growth and empowerment.

Take Rahkim Sabree's story, for example. He spoke candidly on the podcast about growing up in a financially challenging environment.[3] His journey began when he was born to teenage parents who later separated. His early life unfolded in a world where financial survival was a daily battle. Raised by a single mother who relied on Section 8 housing and food stamps to get by, Rahkim was no stranger to the struggle that many African American families face, where every dollar is stretched to its breaking point. Financial stability feels like a distant dream. His mother, like many, became a master of making ends meet, but the stress of keeping their heads above water left a mark on Rahkim that would shape his relationship with money for years to come.

Imagine being a teenager at 15, sitting at the kitchen table, not to do homework, but to help your mom figure out which bills could wait another week and which couldn't. The weight of financial stress didn't just belong to his mom; Rahkim carried it too. He grew up learning that money was scarce, that survival was the priority, and that wealth—real, lasting wealth—was for other people, people far removed from his reality.

 New Wealth Wave Podcast, EP 11: Rahkim Sabree

"I became very central to managing the household finances. My mom taught me how to price out the name brand versus the store brand. We'd sit at the kitchen table, going through the bills, figuring out what we could afford. I didn't know it at the time, but all of these observations were forming the basis of how I would think about money."

These were lessons in resourcefulness, but they were also lessons in scarcity. Rahkim didn't realize it at the time, but these experiences were shaping his financial mindset, creating what he would later come to understand as an Avoidant Financial Narrative. And in this way, his Encoded Financial Behaviors began with struggle, anxiety, and avoidance.

Many individuals learn early to focus on getting through the present, setting aside thoughts of future wealth or financial stability. It's not always a lack of ambition, but rather an environment that leaves little space for dreaming beyond immediate survival. Families may pass down strength and resilience, yet often alongside deeply ingrained beliefs that money brings stress, tension, or even danger.

The challenge with financial trauma is that it doesn't simply disappear with higher income. It lingers, quietly embedded in spending habits, financial fears, and deeply held beliefs about what is possible. True financial healing often begins only when exposure to new financial environments challenges these inherited narratives, offering a different vision of what wealth can mean.

Initially, Rahkim was searching for a job, hoping for a steady paycheck that could help him break free from the cycle of financial struggle he had experienced all his life. Instead, he discovered a world he'd never encountered before; a world where people openly discuss credit scores, investments, 401(k)s, and retirement plans. It was a realm of opportunities he hadn't even known existed.

For Rahkim, the pivotal *"Aha!" moment* didn't come all at once. It was gradual, the way healing often is. Day by day, he realized that the narrative he'd inherited—one of scarcity, stress, and survival—didn't have to be his story forever. He didn't have to carry the weight of his past into his future. The more he learned about financial empowerment, the more he saw that his upbringing, though filled with love and resilience, had not equipped him to build wealth. He wasn't alone. Rahkim's story resonates deeply with many African Americans who grew up in similar circumstances, where the focus was on survival rather than prosperity.

Rahkim speaks candidly about the turning point in his journey. "I started working at a bank, but the whole idea of credit and savings accounts was foreign to me. I was like, 'Wait, people plan for retirement? They don't just live paycheck to paycheck?' It was mind-blowing. And then I realized—I can do this too."

That moment was the beginning of Rahkim's financial healing. For many, this moment of realization is key to overcoming generational poverty. We don't have to merely survive; we can thrive! But to get there, you must first confront the emotional baggage tied to your Inherited

Financial Narrative(s). The scarcity mindset, learned helplessness, fear of losing everything, and anxiety around bills are all deeply ingrained beliefs that must be unlearned.

Financial healing begins with allowing yourself to see money through a new lens.

It means recognizing the sacrifices made by those who first managed your financial well-being—whether they were guardians, parents, or mentors—and acknowledging the unsolicited financial narratives you may have received along the way. But it also means not letting their financial struggles or anxieties shape your own future. As you start to explore and understand financial tools, you will gradually begin to heal from the emotional wounds left by growing up in an environment—both within yourself and around you—where money was a constant source of stress.

Entering the structured world of banking and financial literacy can highlight gaps in personal knowledge, but it also brings a deeper awareness of financial traumas rooted in past experiences. This journey of discovery extends beyond individual healing, revealing the broader, generational impact of financial hardship, especially within marginalized communities. Through this lens, financial healing becomes not only a means of personal growth but also a step toward breaking broader cycles of generational trauma.

Financial trauma in African Americans is a subset of larger generational trauma, rooted in systemic barriers, lack of access to financial resources, and the cultural silence around money. Growing up, discussions about money were almost taboo. In many African American families, talking about finances was considered rude or inappropriate, leading to generations of people who, despite their resilience, were left unprepared for the complexities of wealth building, not to mention creating generational wealth.

Yet, a certain power unfolds when we start having open conversations about money. As these discussions evolve, financial anxiety gradually begins to lose its grip. Rahkim refers to this exchange as "socialized financial education"—a continuous flow of financial insights within the community, where sharing becomes the norm. These aren't just surface-level conversations aimed at flaunting account balances or probing insecurities; they are practical discussions, grounded in real strategies.

Tremendous strength comes from comparing credit scores, sharing ideas on credit management, debating the benefits of various financial products, and trading tips on maximizing retirement contributions. This healthy exchange shifts the focus from isolation and secrecy to collective empowerment, creating a foundation where financial literacy becomes a community effort and a pathway toward breaking cycles of financial trauma.

Having peers who openly share financial insights, experiences, and networks can feel like a lifeline, offering a new understanding of financial possibilities. Rather than feeling overwhelmed by the unknown, you can leverage this community's knowledge, gradually building your understanding of credit, savings, investments, and the specific benefits offered by employers. In this environment, you'll begin to see finances not as a source of stress but as a puzzle with solutions—a challenge that can be mastered with the right tools and mindset. This mental shift is critical in the process of financial healing, which often starts with something as simple as an open conversation.

Engaging in shared learning can shift your focus from financial survival to financial growth. It can help you rewrite your Inherited Financial Narratives for the present and the next generation.

Many people spend their lives shackled by financial trauma, even when help is within arm's reach. They go through life on "management missions," constantly putting out fires rather than addressing the root cause of their money problems. They continue to struggle, unaware that financial healing could be right around the corner. The power of having financially literate peers who are willing to share their experiences cannot be overstated. Such exposure provides an education that might not be available through traditional channels. Time and again, I've seen how this kind of community support leads to significant milestones, whether it's purchasing a first home, starting a successful business, or building generational wealth. These achievements symbolize financial progress and the tangible results of financial healing, made possible through community support.

As Dr. Wendy Ashley explains in Episode 26 of *The New Wealth Wave Podcast*, our financial behavior is deeply rooted in what she calls "the soil that builds people."[4] Drawing from research on adverse childhood experiences (ACEs), she highlights how early trauma, whether physical, emotional, or financial, fundamentally shapes how we interact with the world, including our relationship with money. In other words:

 New Wealth Wave Podcast, EP 26: Dr. Wendy Ashley

This trauma literally alters our brain chemistry and narrows our vision, affecting how receptive we are to learning and growth. What's particularly striking is her observation that while the original ACEs study focused on predominantly White, middle-class communities, these impacts would likely be "triple" in communities of color, where historical and intergenerational trauma add additional layers to financial behavior patterns.

See, you can't plan for the future if you're unwilling to face your past and deal with it. It is a fundamental truth that many people struggle with, especially when it comes to their financial healing. There's often resistance to adopting a healing mindset because of the illusion that "there's nothing wrong" or "I'm making a lot of money, so I must be doing fine. I don't need anyone." However, wealth is not just about the size of your paycheck; it's about your relationship with money. Many high-income earners are trapped in the same financial spirals as those earning much less, and the only difference is that their wealth masks the underlying issues.

The Power of Community and the Resistance to Financial Healing

The pushback often comes from a place of anxiety and shame, especially if someone's lived experience has been one of not having enough. Money, however, is emotionally charged, and for this set of individuals, it represents security, status, and success. If you've grown up feeling the strain of financial instability, there's a natural desire to distance yourself from that reality as quickly and as far as possible. This survival instinct—this need to push forward without looking back—often creates resistance to seeking help. Admitting that you need help can feel like admitting that you're failing, even if you're making a lot of money. For such individuals, it's easier to set aside their past financial trauma and continue believing they're doing fine, as their income allows them to maintain a great lifestyle and *keep up with the Joneses.*

The power of community in financial healing cannot be overstated. When you set out to heal your financial past, it's essential to surround yourself with people who understand the importance of this process and who can support you in meaningful ways. This aligns with Albert Bandura's Social Learning Theory, which demonstrates how people learn behaviors primarily through observation and modeling.[5]

Therefore, when we surround ourselves with financially literate peers, we receive advice. Still, more importantly, we engage in a powerful form of social learning that can fundamentally transform our financial behaviors. A positive, financially aware community can provide resources, knowledge, and the emotional reinforcement needed to challenge old beliefs and adopt new, healthier behaviors. This also contributes to transforming negative or unhelpful Inherited Financial Narratives and Encoded Financial Behaviors into more positive ones moving forward.

However, it's important to recognize that not all communities are conducive to financial healing. Being part of a community that doesn't value financial growth or that perpetuates harmful money habits can hinder your progress, no matter how much you want to change.

Many people hesitate to admit they need help, even when their financial situation isn't ideal. This reluctance is compounded when their previous experiences with financial professionals or systems have been negative. Someone who has had a negative experience with a financial professional may carry that distrust into future interactions, believing that all financial professionals are primarily motivated by selling products or taking advantage of their clients. As a result, they may avoid seeking financial guidance altogether, perpetuating a cycle of avoidance and financial distress.

Resistance to financial healing is quite common, particularly when people have experienced financial trauma or developed negative Inherited Financial Narratives. For example, some people might avoid dealing with money altogether because they believe that *money is the root of all evil* or that they don't deserve financial success. Others might engage in financial vigilance, constantly hoarding their resources out of fear that they will lose everything. Both avoidance and vigilance are rooted in past experiences that shape our views and handling of money.

Another form of resistance comes from those who, despite earning enough, still struggle with financial boundaries. These individuals often experience the Survivor's Remorse Narrative—guilt for having financial success while their family or friends struggle. As a result, they feel obligated to help others, even at the expense of their own financial well-being. The inability to set clear financial boundaries can lead to a cycle of debt and stress, even among high earners.

Louis Barajas, a financial advisor known for his work with entertainers and athletes, shed light on this dynamic in Episode 19 of *The New Wealth Wave Podcast*. He described how Survivor's Remorse is compounded by an "entourage effect"—the often-unspoken pressure to maintain and support an ever-expanding circle of dependents who accompany a successful individual throughout their career.[6] For many high-profile clients, particularly athletes, the "entourage" becomes a financial drain that can persist long after their peak earning years.

Barajas explained that this phenomenon is rooted in guilt and cultural expectations within communities where resources are historically limited. These individuals feel compelled to share their success, even when it risks undermining their long-term financial security. He recounts how, when he advises clients to set firmer boundaries, the entourage may resist, going so far as to disparage him to maintain access to the client's resources. The effect, Barajas notes, is a pervasive cycle that slowly depletes the wealth of even the highest earners, as they continually fund the needs and wants of their social circle.

LaChanze, a highly accomplished theater actress, also shared her personal experiences in Episode 20 of the podcast, which we explored earlier in the book. Her story echoes what I've heard from countless other successful Black professionals: there's a moment when you realize you've unconsciously become responsible for your immediate and distant relatives. What's fascinating is how this Provider Narrative evolves through different stages of financial success. At first, it feels like a badge of honor, finally being able to help those who supported your dreams. Then it morphs into something more complex, what LaChanze describes as a *crushing weight of obligation*, where your success becomes everyone else's safety net. It's no longer just about sharing resources; you must also manage the emotional manipulation that often comes with saying "no."

Listen, you know the lines: "Oh, you think you're better than us now?" or "You've forgotten where you came from." These aren't just words; they're emotional arrows aimed at our deepest insecurities about success and belonging. They make the path to financial healing even more challenging. The guilt becomes almost tangible. It's a constant presence with every paycheck. Many clients report feeling relief when giving money away, not because it feels good to help, but because it temporarily silences the chorus of guilt and obligation. It's like paying an emotional tax on success.

But here's where it gets even more complicated. It doesn't just involve money. It involves the psychological toll of carrying everyone's financial hopes and dreams on your shoulders while trying to build your foundation. LaChanze learned that there comes a critical turning point (Stage 5) where you have to rewrite this narrative fundamentally. You recognize that true financial healing isn't just making more money; it's breaking free from these Inherited Financial Narratives, particularly patterns of financial martyrdom.

It's essential to recognize that financial healing isn't just an individual process, but also has a socio-economic and racial context. As we've seen, in communities of color, particularly among Black Americans, there is often a deep-seated distrust of financial systems. This distrust is not irrational—it's rooted in systemic racism, historical financial abuses, and generational trauma. For many, capitalism itself is associated with exploitation and inequality, making it challenging to embrace financial systems that people feel have worked against them and their families for generations.

This distrust manifests in real and tangible ways, such as the non-participation of many Black and Latino communities in formal banking systems. When financial institutions have historically excluded or exploited these groups, it's understandable that there is hesitation to engage fully in those systems. For some, it goes beyond financial literacy. They make a conscious decision not to participate in systems that they perceive as harmful.

Again, these practices have been passed down to us generationally, thereby creating narratives that have been manifesting in our present lives for decades. These narratives lead to practices such as relying on informal means for financial security, including cash savings or even GoFundMe campaigns, when financial crises arise, such as covering funeral expenses.

As we saw in Stage 1 of the Model, historical and systemic factors play a significant role in shaping financial behaviors, and any approach to financial healing must acknowledge these realities. Many Black families have witnessed their elders invest in life insurance policies only to be denied payouts due to technicalities or institutional racism. These experiences create a sense of futility around financial planning, reinforcing the idea that these systems are not to be trusted.

Discriminatory practices were common in the life insurance industry in the 20th century. According to Mary Heen's comprehensive study published in the Northwestern Journal of Law & Social Policy, many insurance companies systematically used "race-based pricing," charging Black policyholders premiums up to 30% higher than their white counterparts for identical coverage. This research also documented how major insurance companies maintained dual-rate structures until the late 1970s, despite the practice being legally questionable after civil rights legislation in the 1960s. The discrimination extended beyond pricing. Black families were frequently limited to smaller "industrial" or "burial insurance" policies with benefit caps often not exceeding $1,000, while being denied access to more comprehensive whole-life policies commonly offered to white customers. Class-action lawsuits in the early 2000s acknowledged these historical disparities.[7]

Other scholars, apart from Mary Heen, also documented these racial disparities in life insurance access, creating a lingering impact on financial planning perspectives within Black communities. Books like *The Color of Money: Black Banks, the Racial Wealth Gap,* and Richard Rothstein's *The Color of Law: A Forgotten History of How Our Government Segregated America* explore how this systemic discrimination has affected the flow of wealth into Black communities, reinforcing mistrust in financial institutions.

This is why financial healing requires a community that understands not only the individual's personal financial history but also the broader socio-economic context. Healing doesn't only involve overcoming personal financial anxiety or trauma—it also requires challenging and changing the systems and beliefs that have shaped one's financial life. In many cases, this healing involves unlearning generational patterns of financial avoidance or mistrust.

As Brian Seymour powerfully points out, this mistrust isn't just rooted in historical injustices, such as the Freedman's Bank; it also extends to modern-day practices of major financial institutions. In Episode 24, Brian draws a compelling parallel between vaccine hesitancy in Black communities and the lasting impact of the Tuskegee experiments, noting how their shadow still influences medical trust today.[8]

To truly understand and address financial behavior in communities of color, we must acknowledge how these past and present experiences shape financial decision-making and trust-building. At the same time, seeking healing in a fractured community can be just as damaging as avoiding help altogether. If you're surrounded by people who share or reinforce negative Inherited Financial Narratives—whether it's a reluctance to save or invest, or an insistence on spending to maintain appearances—it becomes much harder to break free from those patterns. Instead of moving toward financial freedom, you may be stuck in the same cycles as you feel pressured to conform to the community's unhealthy financial habits.

The key is to find a community that supports financial growth and healing. That might involve connecting with people who are also on a journey of financial self-awareness or seeking financial professionals who understand the psychological and emotional aspects of money management. It also means being willing to admit when you're in over your head and seeking the right kind of help, even if it feels uncomfortable at first.

"Healing your relationship with money is not about budgeting harder; it's about confronting the pain you were never allowed to name."

True financial healing occurs when you can view your past without shame, understand its impact on your present, and make informed, empowered choices for your future. This journey extends beyond numbers and strategies; it cultivates a mindset that can withstand and transcend old patterns. The community you build (the people you choose to keep close to) becomes a vital influence on this path. They will either lift you or hold you back.

In many communities, there's an all-too-familiar phenomenon known as the "crabs in a barrel" effect, where those within the same environment may unintentionally hold one another back from success. This metaphor captures the struggle of rising against the odds, as some within our circles may pull us back into familiar but limiting beliefs and habits. Often, this resistance isn't rooted in malice; it stems from shared experiences, fears, and the comfort of the known. Yet, when we find ourselves surrounded by people who discourage growth or reinforce old, unproductive patterns, our journey toward financial healing can become stalled.

On the other hand, as Dr. Ruben highlights, surrounding oneself with positive, growth-focused, and supportive people can make all the difference. These are the individuals who encourage healing and help us to challenge outdated beliefs. They support our ambitions, gently nudging us forward, even when the path is uncertain. It's in the presence of these people—mentors, friends, and like-minded peers—that we can build the resilience needed to break free from generational cycles and truly heal financially.

Ultimately, financial healing is more than the strategies we employ or the assets we accumulate. It's also about the mindset and the power of intentional community. It's choosing people willing to help you rise out of that barrel and encourage you to reach heights you may not have dreamed possible. Financial healing doesn't happen in isolation but alongside those who see, support, and celebrate your journey to a better and brighter financial future.

The Universality of Financial Healing

However, earning more or being associated with the right company doesn't automatically solve the underlying issues. Financial behavior and beliefs also matter. A person can have a six-figure salary and still struggle with the same fears, anxieties, and destructive money habits as someone earning significantly less. They might feel more comfortable because their higher income provides them with temporary relief or access to more resources. But those deeper wounds—the financial scars from the past—still linger beneath the surface.

Financial healing is a universal process.

It's not how much money you make but how you interact with and understand it. It involves recognizing the patterns that have shaped your relationship with it, whether you grew up in a state of scarcity or had access to more than enough. As I mentioned earlier, the healing process begins with an honest examination of your financial history and an acknowledgment that past experiences continue to shape your present behaviors.

Many people equate seeking financial help with being bad at managing money or not earning enough. This misconception is a leading cause of why many internalize their struggles, thus becoming reluctant to seek guidance and help. It holds so many people back. Whether you're struggling to make ends meet or bringing in a high income, if you haven't dealt with the financial anxieties or traumas rooted in your past, those issues will continue to manifest in your present and future. Sure, a high income might allow for more flexibility and provide a buffer that low-income earners don't have, but it doesn't exempt anyone from financial stress or the need for healing. Some high earners find themselves living paycheck to paycheck, and they've amassed higher liabilities and or expenses than most. For that reason, those individuals may avoid confronting the deeper issues because, on the surface, it seems like they're managing well enough. However, beneath that surface, they may still feel the same fear of loss, insecurity, or guilt that stems from earlier financial experiences.

This cycle continues because of one central point: behavior matters more than income. It's easy to think that making more money will fix everything, but without addressing the beliefs and behaviors that drive your financial decisions, the same problems will persist. Financial healing is not just a case of learning to manage money better; it's a matter of rewriting the emotional and psychological code that influences how you think about and use money.

There is an argument that suggests that many people, regardless of income, experience similar struggles. The need for validation, security, or the desire to prove that they've "made it" often leads to financial decisions not grounded in long-term wealth-building. Whether overspending to maintain an image, avoiding discussions about financial planning, or simply staying silent about money matters, the underlying issue is the same.

There's an emotional resistance to facing the truth.

The truth is where the healing starts. It's in the realization that you're not alone in these struggles. Whether you're making $50,000 or $500,000 a year, the emotional toll of financial stress is universal. The focus is on unlearning the destructive patterns and rebuilding your financial mindset from a place of empowerment. This journey involves rewiring your beliefs about money, acknowledging the impact of past experiences, and allowing yourself the space to heal and grow into a more secure financial future.

Disrupting the Cycle of Generational Trauma

Although the journey toward financial healing is universally challenging, it is also deeply personal. When it comes to financial healing, one of the most important aspects that we often overlook is the impact of unresolved trauma and anxiety that plays out in relationships, especially the baggage we carry from our early life experiences.

This reality became clear during my recent youth mentorship workshops, where one young participant shared, "I can only speak personally on what I have seen in my family growing up—money was always argued about. When my grandmother died, she didn't write a will. They're still fighting about her house, and who it belongs to." Such experiences shape our earliest understanding of money and its role in family dynamics. It illustrates how financial trauma can persist across generations, creating patterns that affect entire families.

The absence of formal financial education often compounds these early wounds. "Money isn't something we touched base on at school, honestly," another mentee reflected. "If I am being completely honest, these financial workshops are the only events that have touched on that topic." This educational void leaves many young people handling complex financial decisions without proper guidance, often repeating the patterns they witnessed in those individuals who were responsible for their welfare.

It is especially significant when two people come together in any form of partnership, whether it's a business or a marriage. Each person enters the relationship with a Financial Genetic Code from Stage 1 and Stage 2 of the Model. Their backgrounds, attitudes, and experiences with money may be drastically different, which can create friction and cause stress because we often don't fully understand our own baggage, let alone that of our partner. Without financial healing, this friction continues to grow because we haven't taken the time to discuss or acknowledge our financial pasts openly. The depth of this friction often stems from their various childhood experiences. As one of my mentees poignantly expressed, "I grew up in poverty, so I think it influenced me not to expect to have any money saved or left to do nice things."

Another shared, "I learned to be cheap but also to spend when necessary... but I tend to overspend on dumb stuff because of how I was raised, like, just because something is on sale ..." These contradictory behaviors often stem from early experiences of scarcity or instability, and too often, create a perpetual cycle.

The path to financial healing becomes even more complex when we consider intersectional factors. "Being born below the poverty line, queer and trans, means that I constantly have to fight for my right to even take up space in public, let alone a livable wage," shared one mentee.

Another spoke about growing up. "I was born to a drug addict mother and an alcoholic father ... and I'm neurodivergent ... there's a lot of things that screw me over that I never asked for." This highlights how various forms of trauma interweave with financial challenges.

Growing up with such baggage, it becomes difficult for individuals to share their childhood traumatic experiences with their partners, so money remains one of those taboo topics we avoid in relationships. We might talk about everything else—hopes, dreams, even fears—but we tend to shy away from discussing finances. This avoidance keeps us from healing, as money remains an unspoken source of anxiety and stress. As one mentee articulated, "It's made me avoid talking about money, but constantly anxious that I'm gonna be broke and poor. I am always stretching myself thin to help those I choose to be my family, while also not asking for the same in return when I'm struggling." The impact of this silence is evident in the contradictory behaviors many develop.

Thankfully, more and more, people are realizing that financial trauma is real, and courses and resources dedicated to addressing it are beginning to emerge. This critical forward movement helps people understand the emotional and psychological barriers they face when trying to build wealth.

Consider those children who grow up in homes where financial insecurity is combined with instability due to parents battling issues like drug addiction or alcoholism. These children absorb the anxiety and chaos surrounding money from an early age. They might see bills going unpaid or experience the stress of not knowing where the next meal will come from. These experiences create deep-rooted anxiety, and as they grow into adults, they unconsciously carry these financial fears with them, even when their circumstances have changed. When entering a relationship, this trauma can manifest in several ways—fear of spending, an obsession with saving, or, on the flip side, reckless spending to cope with the deep-seated anxiety. Without open conversations and healing, these patterns disrupt the relationship's financial health.

As financial therapist Nate Astle emphasizes in Episode 23 of *The New Wealth Wave Podcast,* "Financial conflicts in relationships aren't about assigning blame—they're about acknowledging that both partners contribute to the dynamic."[9] He uses the powerful metaphor of partners fighting a shared enemy from different sides, where the real enemy isn't each other but their communication breakdowns and conflict cycles. Real progress becomes possible when couples can shift their perspective to see themselves as a team working together against these challenges.

Some couples take a more proactive approach from the start. Take Jasper Smith in Episode 6, who shared with us how he and his wife approached their finances differently from the beginning of their dating phase. Instead of letting financial discussions remain taboo, Jasper was completely transparent about his background, his family's approach to money, and his financial vision for the future.[10]

New Wealth Wave Podcast, EP 6: Jasper Smith

What made their relationship unique was his wife's willingness to engage in these conversations openly. They addressed financial challenges as they arose—whether it was deciding who would pay for dates or discussing future financial goals. They even established quarterly "money meetings" to check in on their financial health, a practice his wife eventually embraced so fully that she began scheduling these check-ins herself.

Their approach demonstrates how early, consistent financial communication can help couples avoid potential conflicts and build a stronger foundation.

I see this issue with many of the couples I consult. They're often stuck in Stage 3 of the Seven-Stage Generational Wealth Model©, trying to move past the trauma and anxiety of Stage 1 and Stage 2, but unable to do so because they haven't gone through the process of financial healing.

They're bringing unresolved financial trauma into their relationship, and it creates tension that holds them back from moving forward. This is the reason I emphasize that *Generational Wealth Begins with Generational Knowledge®*. You cannot build true wealth without fully understanding the emotional and psychological barriers surrounding money.

In a marriage or partnership, we must find alignment and work together to heal. For example, Dr. Ruben shared that shortly after she met her husband, and it was clear they would get married, they had open discussions about their views on finances. He'd grown up in a more financially stable environment, and as a result, he was more optimistic about money than she was. However, they agreed on key financial principles—like not spending more than they earned—and created a foundation of financial transparency and compatibility. This foundation helped them navigate their financial journey together and establish healthy financial habits.

"Many couples struggle to manage money together, even with shared goals, often because they were raised to treat finances as an individual responsibility. Without intentional alignment, partners may unknowingly work against each other, hindering financial well-being. Reaching Stage 5: Financial Well-being requires trust, transparency, and open communication. When couples align their strategies and communicate honestly, they build a stronger foundation for lasting financial health and generational wealth."

Unfortunately, many people wait far too long to have those critical conversations. They carry their financial wounds from childhood into adulthood and project them onto their partners and the next generation. One child recently told me, "My parents don't talk about money. But when they do, they argue about it and then use me as their therapist." The traumas in these adults continue to linger, influencing their financial decisions without their full awareness of the impact they're having.

When I work with couples now, I encourage them to explore their Financial Genetic Codes together, understanding that financial healing isn't just an individual journey; it can also be a partnership journey. It's not enough for one partner to heal while the other carries unresolved trauma. That is why generational wealth building is not just a money matter—it also involves healing generational patterns of financial trauma and creating new, healthier Encoded Financial Behaviors for yourselves and your partnerships.

A Holistic Approach to Your Financial Healing Process

Keep in mind that both your internal and external ecosystems profoundly influence your financial behavior. To achieve holistic well-being in financial healing, you must cultivate healing on both fronts: the internal and the external. Your outer world affects your inner world, and your inner world influences the external, creating a continuous cycle of impact. In financial terms, your mindset and emotional state are just as critical as your income, savings, and investments. This interconnection is well illustrated by Dr. Stephen Porges' Polyvagal Theory, which explains how our nervous system responds to perceived threats.[11]

When we face financial pressure, our body can interpret it as a danger signal, triggering a cascade of stress responses that make clear thinking nearly impossible. Understanding this biological reaction helps explain why financial stress can feel so overwhelming and why calming techniques are vital for making sound financial decisions.

David Rock, the founder of the NeuroLeadership Institute, presents an insightful concept in this regard.[12] His idea revolves around calming the brain and getting people to think clearly about their situations. In the context of financial healing, this becomes an essential practice. Often, the financial anxiety or trauma you experience clouds your ability to make sound decisions. When you can slow down, reflect, and properly understand your thoughts, you can identify where your thinking is clear and where it's stuck. This self-awareness, much like Rock's findings, enables individuals to devise their own solutions.

Rock's approach suggests that when you calm your mind, you uncover mental clarity, directly impacting your financial choices. If your mind is constantly overwhelmed by stress or negative financial experiences, it can be nearly impossible to think about solutions. You may find yourself caught in loops of doubt, fear, or mistrust—whether those entail avoiding financial professionals, feeling guilty about success, or struggling to set boundaries with loved ones who drain your finances.

However, once you manage to quiet those anxious thoughts, you can step back and assess your financial situation more rationally. Perhaps you'll realize that your spending habits are rooted in a desire to maintain appearances, or that your reluctance to save is tied to a fear of loss stemming from past financial failures. You might never gain these insights while stuck in a heightened emotional state, but they can surface when you give yourself space to think clearly and without judgment.

Thus, to break free from this mental imprisonment, the financial healing process must create room for these moments of introspection. It's essential not only to focus on the numbers but also on the mental and emotional clarity that allows for better financial decisions. Therefore, participating in "mental gymnastics" can position you to create and develop solutions that fit your specific needs, moving beyond generic advice and into personalized strategies that reflect your circumstances and goals.

A critical part of this healing process is recognizing where external factors, such as past financial traumas or negative community influences, impact your inner world. As discussed earlier, the community you belong to may not encourage the financial growth you need. In this case, healing means creating boundaries with that community or seeking out new networks of support that uplift your financial well-being.

The reverse is also true: the changes you make internally and the clarity you achieve in your mindset can begin to influence your outer world. When you start making decisions from a place of calm and understanding, you naturally begin to cultivate better relationships with money and with others who value financial growth. As you shift your thinking, you begin to attract and recognize opportunities and people who can support your healing journey, thereby strengthening your external environment. Take, for example, the experience of financial professionals.

If your first encounter with a financial professional left you feeling taken advantage of or unimportant, this experience can shape how you view any future financial advice. You might avoid getting the help you need because you're stuck in the trauma of that first negative experience. However, with mental clarity, you can begin to separate that single experience from the potential benefits of working with the right financial professional who genuinely cares about your success. This shift in thinking enables you to seek out professionals who align with your financial healing journey, opening up new growth opportunities.

Furthermore, understanding the psychology behind your financial behavior—your Inherited Financial Narratives, avoidance, or even vigilance—provides insight into how you can get unstuck (Chapter 2). These narratives, often passed down through family or community experiences, can be deeply ingrained and may not be immediately apparent until you take the time to reflect. Once you identify the underlying beliefs driving your financial habits, you can start to challenge them and create new narratives that support your financial health.

Neuroscience Tips for Reprogramming Your Financial Genetic Code

The neuroscience behind financial stress and decision-making provides valuable insights into our behavior. As we've seen, Dr. Stephen Porges' Polyvagal Theory helps explain why financial stress triggers such intense physiological responses. When we face financial pressure, our nervous system can interpret it as a threat, activating our fight-or-flight response and making it difficult to make rational decisions. That is why calming the mind before making financial decisions is so important; it helps us transition from a threat response to a state where we can access our prefrontal cortex for more informed decision-making.

The same principle of taking time to assess your thinking by calming your mind also applies to other aspects of financial healing. Often, we function on autopilot, much like driving to a familiar destination without remembering the route. Our brain quickly develops habits to conserve energy. While this efficiency can be helpful in daily tasks, it can also lead us to fall into the same unproductive financial patterns.

Our prefrontal cortex, the part of the brain responsible for decision-making, requires significant mental energy to engage deeply. When financial stress arises, it activates the amygdala, the brain's threat center, which triggers an immediate survival response, slowing down our ability to think logically and rationally. As explored in Chapter 2, this threat response is further complicated by the role of cortisol, the stress hormone that floods the brain in response to perceived danger. While the fight-or-flight response is beneficial in genuine emergencies, it becomes problematic when the perceived threat is a low bank balance or the fear of financial instability. Over time, chronic exposure to stress triggers from financial worry can have profound effects on mental and physical health, disrupting sleep, impairing decision-making, and reinforcing negative thought patterns.

Here, the work of financial healing becomes essential. Healing isn't just about accumulating wealth; it's also about calming that internal storm. Recognizing when your stress response is taking over—when your thoughts are driven by fear or scarcity—can help you re-engage the prefrontal cortex, shifting your decisions from survival-driven to strategy-driven.

However, this shift requires conscious effort and patience, especially if financial anxieties or traumas are deeply embedded in your hippocampus, the brain's memory center. As we saw earlier, the hippocampus is wired to retain negative memories more vividly than positive ones. This survival mechanism helps us avoid threats, but also means that financial traumas from the past can linger and influence our present behavior. When you understand this dynamic, you can begin to reframe your financial journey. Creating new habits requires breaking out of autopilot mode and interrupting the cycle of cortisol-induced decision-making.

For example, many people feel constant financial pressure because they lack an emergency fund or even a small financial cushion, which triggers the stress response whenever an unexpected expense arises. While the ideal recommendation may be to save six months' worth of expenses, many find this goal unattainable. Instead, aiming to save between $5,000 and $10,000 in liquid cash can significantly reduce financial stress, creating enough of a buffer to avoid falling into a state of survival mode when life's unexpected events occur.

While often viewed as a financial tool, this buffer also serves as a psychological safeguard, reinforcing a sense of security and control in one's financial ecosystem. Although this buffer may be considered a financial tool, I would argue that it can also be regarded as a psychological one. With a cushion in place, your amygdala is less likely to activate in times of financial uncertainty. Instead of reacting out of fear, you can approach financial decisions with a clearer and calmer mindset, which is vital for sustained financial growth. However, it's essential to reemphasize that financial healing isn't a linear process.

As the Seven-Stage Generational Wealth Model© suggests, people often cycle through different stages. You may find yourself at Stage 4, feeling secure, only to be pulled back to Stage 2 when an unexpected financial burden arises. The key is not to view this as a failure but as a natural part of the process. Healing requires revisiting old wounds and working through them with new insights. Even financial experts who have mastered the later stages of wealth-building, such as estate planners who deal with long-term financial strategies, didn't arrive at Stage 6 overnight. It took time, consistent effort, and, most importantly, a dedication to rewriting their Financial Genetic Codes.

Understanding the role of cortisol, along with the brain's memory storage in the hippocampus, is necessary in this process. Too much cortisol can keep you stuck in a cycle of fear and reaction, making it difficult to move forward. Learning to balance this with the release of positive neurochemicals like *dopamine* and *GABA*—the brain's natural calming agents—helps to break the chronic stress cycle. Whether through mindfulness practices, setting realistic financial goals, or shifting your self-talk, financial healing involves resetting your nervous system as much as balancing your budget, which is why mindfulness is essential in this process.

Yes, it is essential to maintain an engaging presence with a bank account, but also be mindful of how your body and mind respond to your financial situation. Are you stuck in a loop of stress and anxiety, with negative thoughts reinforcing your fear of financial instability? Or are you taking steps to calm your mind and body, allowing yourself to make decisions from a place of clarity rather than panic?

One practical strategy to combat this overwhelming sense of financial insecurity is gratitude. As simple as it sounds, taking a moment to reflect on what you're grateful for can profoundly impact your mental state. Neuroscience reveals that gratitude activates the brain's reward center, releasing GABA, a neurotransmitter linked to feelings of calmness and relaxation. This shift allows your body to move out of a stress response and into a state of balance. Even small acknowledgments like "I'm grateful I have enough money to put in the parking meter" or "I'm thankful for the bed I sleep in every night" can ground you in the present.

The focus isn't on dismissing your financial challenges but on recognizing the stability you already have, which provides a sense of safety and perspective. Dr. Ruben rightly pointed this out in Episode 5 of the podcast.[13]

She highlights that this kind of self-awareness can shift your focus, helping you manage financial anxiety.

New Wealth Wave Podcast, EP 5: Dr. Marcia Ruben

"It's really about self-care. When your self-talk becomes overwhelmingly negative, it's crucial to stop and ask yourself, 'What's real here?'"

Breathing exercises are another method to activate your parasympathetic nervous system, which serves as the body's calming agent. When we're stressed, whether about finances or other worries, our sympathetic nervous system goes into overdrive. It's as if our brain sympathizes with the stress, preparing our body for fight or flight. However, this heightened state isn't always helpful, especially when the perceived threat isn't physical. A simple act, such as pausing to take deep breaths, can shift your nervous system from fight-or-flight mode to a state of restoration, where the parasympathetic system takes over to soothe your mind and body. This shift helps open up your prefrontal cortex—the part of the brain responsible for reasoning and decision-making—allowing you to think more clearly and make better financial choices.

Connecting with others also helps manage financial stress. As social beings, we are wired for connection. Surrounding ourselves with people who are calm and grounded in their financial outlook can help us adopt a more measured perspective on our own financial situations. Studies like those by social psychologists James H. Fowler and Nicholas A. Christakis have shown that those around us can directly influence our emotions and stress levels through emotional contagion.[14] If you're surrounded by individuals who are equally stressed about money, that energy is contagious. On the other hand, connecting with people who are stable in their finances can reduce anxiety and provide a sense of support.

In the podcast session, Dr. Ruben further explained this through the lens of social baseline theory, referencing a study in which participants felt less pain when holding a loved one's hand while undergoing stressful situations such as receiving electric shocks. The brain's response to stress diminishes when we feel supported.

Another factor to consider is sleep. When we're sleep-deprived, our ability to make sound decisions is impaired. Financial anxiety tends to increase when we're not well-rested, and without enough sleep, we lose the mental capacity to handle complex financial situations. Prioritizing sleep, along with practicing gratitude and connecting with others, creates a foundation for emotional resilience, helping us approach financial healing with a clearer mind.

Mental Techniques for Financial Healing

When we discuss financial healing, a common thread suggests, "It's too late for me to change." This belief can feel almost woven into our thinking, especially if we've lived with certain financial habits or outlooks for a long time. However, the truth is that the brain itself, through a concept known as *neuroplasticity*, offers us the incredible capacity to reshape our thoughts about money and how we manage it. Neuroplasticity, discovered in the 1940s, tells us that our brains are not as fixed as once believed—they are "plastic," meaning they can reorganize and form new pathways in response to our experiences and intentional actions.[15] So, for anyone who feels indifferent or resigned to their financial circumstances, or even those frustrated by past attempts to improve their situation, neuroplasticity brings hope. Think of it this way: your brain is designed to adapt.

Say you've always taken a familiar freeway to work; it's automatic, and you hardly have to think about it. When you decide to change routes, you initially have to focus intently, making conscious decisions at each turn. Over time, though, this new route becomes second nature. Similarly, when it comes to your financial habits, changing your mental "route" may feel awkward and uncomfortable at first. Yet, with focused intention, these new pathways can become your new normal. In terms of financial healing, this means actively reshaping your approach to spending, saving, and wealth-building opportunities. You may have learned patterns from family and the external ecosystem that feel ingrained. However, the brain's remarkable ability to rewire itself means that you can shift these behaviors toward healthier financial habits with conscious effort.

This shift aligns with the principle of Hebbian learning, encapsulated in the phrase, "Neurons that fire together, wire together." Originally introduced by Canadian psychologist Donald Hebb in his 1949 book *The Organization of Behavior*, this theory explains that when neurons are activated simultaneously, their synaptic connections strengthen.[16] Over time, these strengthened connections form habitual pathways in the brain, shaping our responses and behaviors. Essentially, repeated actions and thoughts, when consciously directed, can forge new neural circuits, making them more likely to become automatic responses.

To apply this in a financial context, consider each moment as an opportunity to reinforce new financial habits. For example, if you notice yourself engaging in financial behavior that doesn't serve your long-term goals—like impulsive spending or mindless online shopping—you can pause, recognize the pattern, and consciously choose a different action, such as setting the money aside for an investment or saving goal. Each time you make this choice, you reinforce a healthier neural pathway. Gradually, as this new pathway becomes established, it gains strength, and the older, less beneficial circuits weaken. This rewiring process ultimately makes healthier financial decisions feel more natural and reduces the influence of ingrained, detrimental habits.

This practice of rewiring your brain is also helpful in cases where childhood environments were unstable, perhaps due to a parent's addiction, financial mismanagement, or lack of resources. Memories of financial insecurity often leave a deep imprint, creating a "snapshot" in the brain. This snapshot can lead to habits rooted in fear, such as over-saving or avoiding financial risks, which may hinder your ability to build wealth. Here is where neuroplasticity can be especially useful: by confronting and reframing these memories and taking new, proactive steps, you can reshape your financial outlook. For example, if growing up involved financial unpredictability, recognizing that those conditions no longer control your financial future can be the first step toward financial healing.

The key is approaching financial healing as a lifestyle change rather than a quick fix. Like adopting a new, healthier way of living, this approach allows time for growth, evolution, and proper alignment with your financial goals. Unlike a restrictive diet, which may yield short-term results but often ends once a target is reached, a lifestyle change is ongoing. What matters is fully embracing a new way of thinking and acting around money, one that becomes part of who you are. I often say, "If you are consistent consistently, your outcome will be consistently consistent. However, if you are inconsistently consistent, your outcome will be consistently inconsistent." This principle is at the heart of financial healing. At first, it requires mindful efforts to choose a new pathway, but with repetition, these connections become easier to access and eventually become the path of least resistance.

When financial healing becomes a lifestyle, you'll no longer battle with every decision. Instead, your actions will begin to align naturally with your goals, transforming your financial behavior from a struggle into a reflection of your true self. Through patience and consistency, this new foundation can help you thrive, not just in the short term but also in the long run, paving the way for a future of lasting financial well-being.

As you look ahead, recognize that in this healing process, setbacks aren't failures—they're simply part of the learning process. If you slip back into previous habits, use it as an opportunity to re-center and reaffirm your goals. Remember that healing is as much about self-compassion as it is about change.

Acknowledging each milestone, no matter how small, reinforces the neural pathways that support these positive habits, thereby strengthening them. Through consistency and a commitment to long-term vision, you're reshaping your financial future and setting a good example for generations to come. Stage 3 of the model is so transformative; it helps you redefine your relationship with money, choosing progress over perfection and growth over complacency. As you solidify your new Financial Genetic Codes, know that you're paving a path toward wealth and a legacy of financial well-being that reflects resilience, intention, and healing.

Financial Healing Journal: A Self-Reflection Guide

Introduction

This journal is designed to help you process and heal your relationship with money through intentional reflection and self-awareness. Take your time with each prompt, being honest and compassionate with yourself as you explore your financial past and present.

Part 1: Understanding Your Financial Flashpoints

Early Money Memories

- What is your earliest memory involving money? How did it make you feel?
- Describe a significant financial event from your childhood that still influences you today.
- What financial lessons did you learn from watching your parents/guardians handle money?
- Can you identify moments where money created tension in your family? How did these moments affect you?

Financial Trauma Reflection

- What financial experiences have left emotional scars?
- How do past financial hardships still affect your current decisions?
- When do you feel most anxious about money? Can you trace this anxiety to past experiences?
- What financial beliefs did you inherit that might not serve you well today?

Part 2: Examining Your Current Financial Relationship

Inherited Financial Narratives and Patterns

- What are your automatic thoughts when you think about money?
- How do you behave differently when you're financially stressed?
- What financial decisions do you tend to avoid or postpone? Why?
- What money habits do you have that mirror those of your family?

Community and Support

- Who influences your financial decisions today?
- How does your current community view money and success?
- What financial topics do you find difficult to discuss with others?
- Who are your financial role models, and what have you learned from them?

Part 3: Moving Toward Healing

Gratitude and Awareness

- List three things you're grateful for regarding your current financial situation.
- What financial skills have you developed that you're proud of?
- How have past financial challenges made you stronger or wiser?
- What positive changes have you already made in your relationship with money?

Future Vision and Boundaries

- What would a healthy relationship with money look like to you?
- What financial boundaries do you need to set with yourself or others?
- How can you better align your spending with your values?
- What new financial habits would you like to develop?

Part 4: Action Steps for Financial Wellness

Personal Growth Plan

- What is one financial belief you're ready to challenge?
- What small step can you take this week toward financial healing?
- How will you practice self-compassion when facing financial setbacks?
- What resources or support do you need to continue your healing journey?

Community and Legacy

- How can you contribute to breaking negative financial patterns in your family?
- What financial wisdom would you like to pass on to the next generation?
- How can you build or join a supportive financial community?
- What role do you want money to play in your life story moving forward?

Monthly Check-In Questions

Review these questions at the end of each month:

1. What financial triggers did I encounter this month?

2. How did I respond differently to financial stress?
3. What new insights have I gained about my relationship with money?
4. What progress have I made in my financial healing journey?
5. What support do I need moving forward?

Guidelines for Journaling

- Write without judgment.
- Be specific in your responses.
- Include both emotions and facts.
- Take breaks when needed.
- Return to earlier entries to track your growth.
- Celebrate small victories and insights.
- Use this journal as a tool for ongoing healing.

Remember: Financial healing is a journey, not a destination. Your experiences and feelings are all valid, and every step forward, no matter how small, is progress toward financial wellness.

Chapter 4:
Building Financial Intelligence

"An investment in knowledge pays the best interest."
—Benjamin Franklin

I f you've made it through the emotional work of financial healing in Stage 3, you've already done something remarkable. You've faced your financial wounds, acknowledged Inherited Financial Narratives, and begun recovering a healthier financial life. This process laid the groundwork; now, you're ready to construct a stable foundation rooted in knowledge, understanding, and proactive strategies. Building on this healing, you're prepared to transform that awareness into actionable knowledge through Stage 4 of the Seven-Stage Generational Wealth Model©. This stage focuses on building financial intelligence—or, as we term it, financial edification. Here, the goal is to strengthen literacy and inclusion, empowering you to make sound, strategic financial decisions that align with a broader vision for your life and legacy.

Financial edification is more than simply knowing how to manage money; it involves transforming your relationship with it. The focus is on making purposeful and informed financial choices that support your personal goals and a legacy that can resonate for generations.

The term "edification" itself carries a deeper meaning than mere education. It speaks to the complete intellectual and moral enrichment of an individual. The Seven-Stage Generational Wealth Model© integrates literacy with inclusion—two critical elements that work in unison to build a lasting foundation for wealth.

You might wonder why we don't dive directly into investment strategies or wealth-building tactics, especially after addressing past issues. The truth is that, much like building a house, a strong foundation is essential. The emotional part of financial healing in Stage 3 sets the stage, but now we're constructing a knowledge base to support your generational wealth-building journey. Remember, Generational Wealth Begins with Generational Knowledge®.

"Literacy gives you knowledge. Intelligence gives you power. But healing gives you the freedom to use both with purpose."

On this journey toward generational wealth, knowledge serves as the foundation that holds everything together. Just as you cannot build a secure home on unstable ground, you cannot establish enduring wealth on a shaky financial understanding. Each layer of knowledge reinforces the next, ensuring that your wealth is supported by a network of informed decisions, foresight, and resilience as you progress. This foundation of knowledge differentiates fleeting wealth from a legacy that can outlast you. Financial healing may have cleared away your past burdens, but financial edification—the advanced education and financial principles and practices extending beyond basic literacy—now becomes your present focus.

The relationship between financial healing and financial edification is deep. Healing addresses emotional scars from your Encoded Financial Behaviors, while edification empowers you to write the following chapters with clarity and confidence. Think of Stage 4 as the bridge between understanding your relationship with money and mastering its mechanics. This stage is crucial, but before you dig deeper into it, you should have completed your honest self-assessment: Where are you in your financial journey? What skills do you still need to acquire? Are you still building your financial knowledge base? Without knowing your starting point or your current situation, it becomes impossible to chart an effective course forward.

Stage 4: Financial Edification (Literacy and Inclusion) – Present

Now, reflect on how you first learned about money. Perhaps it was through observing your parents' behaviors, trial and error with your first paycheck, or learning from hard lessons after financial missteps. For many, formal financial education was notably absent. This knowledge gap is a systemic issue that has affected generations, especially in historically marginalized communities.

I recently spoke with a successful entrepreneur who had overcome significant financial trauma from his childhood. Despite healing these wounds, he felt overwhelmed by financial terminology and investment concepts. "I feel like everyone else received an instruction manual that I missed," he confided. This common sentiment speaks to the heart of why financial edification—both literacy and inclusion—is so necessary.

In Chapter 2, Brian Thomas rightly said, "Children are financial passengers in their parents' lives." What's fascinating is that we spend years teaching our kids how to walk, talk, and read. However, when it comes to money, we tend to leave them in the passenger seat. Imagine it's a typical evening at home. You've just told your child they can't have that new toy at the store. "We need to be responsible with money," you say. Then, what happens? The doorbell rings. Another stack of Amazon packages arrives with your name on them. See the contradiction? We're telling our kids one story while modeling another, inadvertently proving the adage, "Do as I say, not as I do." And here's the brutal truth: the more financially successful we become, the worse this gets.

Reflect on that for a moment. Passengers. They're just along for the ride, watching through the window as we navigate life's financial highways. Some people never leave the passenger seat. They hop from one car to another, never learning to drive on their own, and continue as passengers throughout their adult lives. The irony is this: when we think we're blessing our kids by giving them everything, we're handcuffing them. As parents, we often believe that by removing the financial barriers we faced growing up and fulfilling all our children's needs without hesitation, we're setting them up for success. In reality, we may be doing more harm than good. In some cases, we unconsciously adopt the role of Lawn Mower Parents, removing all barriers—both visible and hidden—smoothing every bump in their financial journey. While our intentions stem from a motive of love and protection, our actions can unintentionally prevent them from developing the critical thinking skills necessary to navigate today's economic landscape.

Without realizing it, we often trap our children in a financial maze where they struggle to find their way out on their own. This lifestyle we lovingly provide can become their financial prison. When they finally take the wheel of their financial vehicle by stepping out on their own, they find themselves unprepared and unable to drive. What happens then?

Credit cards.
Loans.
Debt.

They scramble to maintain a standard of living they never learned to build themselves. The skills required to sustain financial stability were never developed because they were never needed. Now, faced with reality, they are forced to play catch-up in an unforgiving financial climate.

The greater danger is that we risk raising individuals who may spend much of their adult lives battling financial anxiety and trauma. They could find themselves caught between managing these struggles and attempting to build their financial wealth in an increasingly challenging economic environment, or trying to preserve the inheritance passed down to them.

However, there's hope. The solution isn't complex, but it requires us to return to basics and adopt a more sustainable blueprint to guide the next generation of wealth builders effectively. It starts at home. Point blank, period. We must provide our kids with hands-on experience with money from the jump. I'm talking kindergarten, second, and third grade; giving them real responsibilities around the house with a small allowance. That's their first taste of providing value and getting paid for it. That needs to stay consistent through high school.

Here's what's real, though: the more money you make, the harder it gets to say, "No." I get it. We all want our kids to have more and better than we did. But listen carefully: giving them *knowledge* is way more valuable than giving them *things*. The more they learn, the more they can earn. That's not just a cute saying; it's a financial law. However, that learning must occur before the earning. Otherwise, we're just creating more passengers in a world that desperately needs drivers.

Every bit of knowledge your kids gain about money management, investing, and building wealth sets them up for better decisions tomorrow.

> "Most people believe that they'll learn to manage money when they get some more, but by that time, it's too late. The reason people have difficulty, primarily, is because they haven't practiced managing money before they start earning money. And so, how you manage a little bit of money is exactly how you're going to manage a lot of money."

Most people don't recognize that they don't know what they think they know. They think, "If I can just get a really good job, or if I can win the lottery, then I'm going to save some of that money, and I'm going to invest some. The reality is, if you're not doing that now with a small amount of money, you're probably not going to do it with a lot of money. This is why people tend to struggle with managing their finances and building generational wealth.

However, here's where I need to pivot and be candid, because if you're thinking, "My parents never taught me this," or "The system failed me," I need you to hear this: It's never too late for financial edification.

Never.

Your parents might have dropped the ball. However, we must show them grace, as their own internal and external ecosystems have shaped them. Therefore, we can't blame them for not passing down financial literacy and empowerment. We also acknowledge that our educational system has fallen short in teaching financial literacy to everyone. But you're here now, and that's what matters. Don't let anyone tell you you're too old to learn or change. The best time to learn about money was in your youth. The second-best time is right now.

Your financial education is now your responsibility. Not your parents'. Not the governments. Yours. And once you get this knowledge? Please share it. Build your community up. Because financial literacy is more than just building personal wealth, it's about empowering communities and creating opportunities to build generational wealth. That's how we turn passengers into drivers of their own financial futures.

So, what's your next move? Remember, financial literacy isn't just about knowing how to balance a checkbook anymore; it's about understanding the entire financial ecosystem we operate in. It involves learning how money moves, how wealth is built, and, most importantly, how to position yourself to win.

This form of literacy that generates and sustains wealth isn't standalone; it works hand-in-hand with financial inclusion. It's not so much having a bank account as having the proper knowledge to make that account work for you. The importance lies in understanding credit not just as a score, but as a tool. Also, recognizing that investments aren't just for "other people," they're for you. Financial edification extends far beyond basic literacy. While knowing how to budget or calculate compound interest is valuable, true financial intelligence involves a deeper understanding of the role of money in our lives and society. It consists of developing an intuitive grasp of financial concepts that guide informed decisions, ultimately enhancing your financial well-being, which is Stage 5 of the Model. Additionally, it includes recognizing and identifying our "Walls in" and "Walls out," which is Stage 1 (internal and external ecosystem).

In this context, the process of educating and enlightening oneself financially becomes necessary. Understanding the "why" and "how" behind each financial decision matters. This means moving beyond simple financial terms and engaging with the psychological and societal influences that shape our financial behaviors.

A truly educated financial mind doesn't operate in a vacuum; it understands risk, values patience, and appreciates the need for adaptability in the face of life's inevitable changes. This deeper level of knowledge aligns seamlessly with the previous stages, enabling us to recognize and combat our *cognitive biases*, manage anxiety, and foster a healthy financial mindset.

Research in cognitive psychology and behavioral finance reveals that financial decision-making involves both analytical and emotional brain processes. Dr. Richard Peterson's research on the neuroscience of financial decisions shows that even seasoned investors can make irrational choices when emotions override analytical reasoning. This underscores the importance of developing emotional resilience and intellectual capacity to manage finances effectively.

Effective Approach to Financial Edification

Resting on the understanding that financial edification must evolve beyond basic literacy to incorporate complex frameworks and practical applications, theories from behavioral economics, such as Richard Thaler's Nudge Theory, demonstrate how subtle shifts in framing and structure can lead individuals to make better financial decisions without feeling pressured or overwhelmed (Stage 2).[2] Thaler's work further showed that financial habits are not solely a result of logical thinking but are influenced by how options are presented, which can support more responsible decision-making in areas like saving and investing.

Stage 4 of the Seven-Stage Generational Wealth Model© emphasizes this development of financial edification. It's where theory meets practice, transforming abstract concepts into practical tools for wealth creation. This stage addresses the "financial knowledge gap"—the distance between what we think we know about money and what we need to know to build lasting wealth.

Financial edification also brings about a shift in mindset, moving beyond seeing financial goals as isolated tasks to understanding them as part of a broader vision for life and legacy. What matters is cultivating a financial philosophy that extends into every decision, from day-to-day expenses to long-term investments. Empathy and real-life experience become important resources. As you advance in financial edification, you develop a stronger sense of purpose in your financial decisions, making choices that align with your personal values and overarching goals.

Transitioning from Stage 3 to Stage 4 isn't always smooth. Many individuals may find themselves in what behavioral economists refer to as the "competence-confidence gap."[3] In this gap, an individual's *objective* financial competence (knowledge and skills) does not always align with their *subjective* clarity and control, or the self-assurance required to apply that knowledge effectively in real-world scenarios. This discrepancy can lead to hesitation, underinvestment in opportunities, or, conversely, to overly cautious behavior that limits potential growth. You may have healed from financial trauma, but still lack the confidence to apply your knowledge to building sustainable wealth. That's why Stage 4 emphasizes not just acquiring knowledge, but also putting it into practice in real-world scenarios.

It is important to note that when discussing financial inclusion, we also address systemic barriers that have historically limited marginalized communities' access to financial knowledge and opportunities. When paired with a more intentional and trauma-informed financial literacy curriculum, these elements form the backbone of proper financial edification where knowledge is not just taught, but internalized, healed, and passed forward. Your journey through Stage 4 recognizes that financial education isn't one-size-fits-all. Your path to financial security will be unique and influenced by your cultural background, life experiences, and personal goals.

This stage is not so much about conforming to traditional financial wisdom, but about developing the knowledge and confidence to make informed decisions that align with your values and vision for generational wealth. One effective way to approach financial edification is to engage in it alongside Stage 3, which is dedicated to financial healing from trauma and anxiety. In essence, by focusing on reprogramming your Financial Genetic Code (Stage 2). By intertwining financial education with healing, we create a comprehensive approach that helps replace outdated money management and growth beliefs and reprogram the mind with actionable and profitable knowledge to build and sustain wealth.

During Episode 23 of *The New Wealth Wave Podcast*, Nate Astle, a marriage and family therapist and certified financial therapist, highlighted the benefits of alternating between these two processes. He recommended dedicating one week to financial healing and the next to edification.[4] This allows the mind to process and integrate new beliefs while releasing outdated ones. This approach aligns with findings in neuroscience suggesting that actively replacing ingrained patterns requires a deliberate infusion of new information essential for meaningful change.[5] In the context of financial edification, this emphasizes the importance of active learning. The brain learns most effectively through stimulation, interaction, and surprise, rather than passively receiving information. After all, the brain doesn't operate well in a vacuum. As we dismantle old, unproductive beliefs, filling this space with a sound understanding of financial principles becomes essential.

Studies in behavioral finance reinforce this strategy, as they indicate that actively engaging in financial edification improves financial habits and rewires our emotional associations with money.[6] When financial healing and edification are combined, the mind becomes better equipped to embrace constructive financial narratives—those that support wealth creation and financial resilience. This dual approach can ultimately build a robust mental framework that rejects harmful myths about money while actively promoting informed and positive financial behaviors that align with your goals. As you progress, you may notice the anxiety surrounding financial decisions gradually fading and being replaced by quiet confidence. This shift doesn't mean the financial world has become less complex; you've developed the tools to navigate it effectively.

If you're still caught up in thought patterns that undermine your best intentions or lead you to make choices against your own interests, please revisit Stage 3 and address these early on. Moving into edification without dealing with these barriers only weakens the foundation you're building. Often, these deeply rooted mental habits, such as self-doubt or limiting beliefs about money, can pull people back into cycles they thought they had left behind. Therefore, before approaching edification, you need to shed light on these tendencies and confront them directly, setting the stage for a more informed and well-rounded understanding of financial literacy.

Unpacking unhealthy habits and understanding how they formed can accelerate financial growth. Learning to break down these patterns not only strengthens personal financial health but also builds empathy for others facing similar challenges. This is especially powerful for financial professionals and educators who have personally navigated the struggles their clients experience. There is a unique credibility that comes from having lived it, creating a relatability that turns complex financial concepts into meaningful, practical guidance. Speaking from personal experience enables you to move beyond theory and share real-life lessons that transform knowledge into actionable insights.

Bridging the Gap Beyond Financial Literacy: Building Inclusive for Sustainable Wealth

One of the biggest gaps in financial education and one of the reasons Stage 4 is so necessary is that traditional education rarely prepares us for real-life financial management. Whether in high school, college, or even at the graduate level, finance remains a blind spot in our education system. Many reach adulthood, even with advanced degrees, without a genuine understanding of financial principles beyond basic spending and saving. Many must navigate complex financial decisions, often for the first time, with little guidance. They're left vulnerable to costly mistakes or, worse, feeling inadequate when confronted with financial issues that seem far more manageable with even a baseline of knowledge. This reality creates a disconnect. People with advanced education and credentials, such as MDs, JDs, MBAs, PhDs, and others, may be experts in their professions but often lack a basic financial foundation for managing their finances.

This isn't just a personal issue; it's also an educational shortfall that affects society as a whole. Colleges drill us in product strategies, pricing tactics, and market trends, but they overlook personal finance essentials. Most classrooms barely scratch the surface when it comes to tax credits, personal investments, and budgeting. These essential life skills are paramount and often treated as afterthoughts, leaving many of us to stumble through financial adulthood without guidance. At the same time, those with access continue to excel while holding the keys. Therefore, the question begs: What messages are we sending when the foundations of financial freedom are left off the syllabus entirely? We're prepared for the corporate world but not necessarily equipped to build a financially stable life for ourselves after receiving our "Cap and Gown."

After graduation, the gap in this kind of knowledge becomes real. Many people find that the only way to learn these financial essentials is by seeking out mentors or networking with those who already understand these intricacies. Connecting with people who can share insights on managing money, investing wisely, and making strategic financial choices often takes effort and initiative. If you're lucky, you might have family members or friends who can offer guidance. But for many, the journey to financial literacy starts from scratch, often through self-teaching, trial and error, and asking questions. This situation reveals a deeper issue: financial literacy is not so much knowing the right strategies as it is having access to the right conversations and people who can help you grow.

The absence of this knowledge isn't accidental; it's the result of longstanding systems never designed to educate, empower, and equip everyone equally. Too often, key financial principles remain out of reach or hidden in conversations that never reach the communities that need them most. This problem is even more complex in communities that haven't traditionally been included in the financial system. For a long time, the financial industry hasn't felt welcoming to everyone. In marginalized communities, for example, there's a history of financial exclusion that has led to mistrust. It's understandable. Without a feeling of safety and support, many people hesitate to engage fully with banks, investments, or other financial institutions.

Financial edification confronts this by bridging that divide, empowering you to grow your wealth, and even bringing others along on that journey. The key here isn't only getting financial knowledge into people's hands; it's making that knowledge accessible and inclusive, so everyone has a real chance to build a stable future. Financial literacy isn't just about understanding; it's about creating an environment where financial systems are accessible to everyone, empowering more people to break free from living paycheck to paycheck.

Reflect on this idea for a moment: If you've learned to understand money, you've gained a rare and highly valuable skill. Why not share it? Financial edification shifts you from a *"me"* mindset to a *"we"* mindset, where wealth is seen not as an isolated achievement but as something that grows best when nurtured collectively. As Jasper Smith, the visionary behind the #BuildWealth Movement®, shared in Episode 6 of *The New Wealth Wave Podcast*, "If I can do this and learn, why can't I tell a family member or a friend and watch all of us grow together?"[7]

This mentality drives home the point that edification isn't just an individual journey. Historically, money matters have been shrouded in mystery, creating barriers that prevent open discussion. However, when financial literacy is woven into everyday conversations, we begin to break down the cultural taboos that can keep us, our families, and friends silent about finances. This shift empowers us and begins to normalize the idea that financial literacy is a critical, everyday skill. This action will transform our personal finances and create a ripple effect, uplifting entire networks and communities by sharing knowledge that is typically exclusive or out of reach.

Research shows that communities where financial education is shared and accessible experience stronger economic resilience. For instance, a study by the National Endowment for Financial Education found that adults who were taught financial concepts early in their lives exhibited higher levels of financial well-being, specifically at Stage 5.[8] This belief aligns with what psychologists term *collective efficacy*, an idea championed by social psychologist Albert Bandura. Collective efficacy refers to the shared belief in a group's ability to achieve its goals, suggesting that as more people become financially literate, the community's overall financial health improves.[9]

As someone once wisely observed, "*When good men do nothing, evil prevails.*" Similarly, when financially knowledgeable individuals withhold their knowledge, the cycle of financial inequality continues. When you share financial knowledge within your circle, you plant seeds of empowerment that ripple outward, overcoming the restraints of financial ignorance and supporting a more informed, resilient society. Therefore, this isn't simply a case of individual empowerment; it's a collective and inclusive responsibility with the potential to bring about long-term generational change in yourself and those around you.

Think about it—what ideas about money do you carry? Do you see wealth-building as accessible to you, or does it feel like something only "other people" achieve? To build wealth, you now know that understanding your financial past and your attitudes toward money is essential. You can now help others see that financial literacy isn't just external; it takes examining and sometimes challenging the ideas we've internalized over the years. At other times, we also need to explore and challenge external influences.

For generations, the financial landscape marked by limited options, systemic bias, and at times outright exploitation has left many African Americans struggling with basic concepts such as credit, savings, and investment that are critical for financial stability and wealth building. It goes beyond simply a failure of individual planning or personal effort; it results from a historical structure that has withheld resources and opportunities from specific communities, creating a ripple effect that is felt through generations. One of the key contributors to financial vulnerability in African American communities stems from the generational impact of redlining. This discriminatory practice restricted homeownership opportunities and access to favorable credit.

Recent studies show that even today, African Americans are denied mortgages at higher rates than their White counterparts with similar financial profiles. Data from 2022 reveals that Navy Federal Credit Union approved 77.1% of conventional home purchase loans for White applicants, but only 48.5% for Black applicants.[10] Even after controlling for variables such as income, debt-to-income ratio, property value, down payment percentage, and neighborhood characteristics, Black applicants were more than twice as likely to be denied a loan compared to White applicants—a reminder that past barriers continue to impact financial opportunities in the present.[11]

You've seen how this generation of economic exclusion has resulted in generations of injustice and a unique "financial inheritance" in African

American communities, one rooted in survival strategies that, while functional in the short term, do not support long-term wealth-building.[12] Many of us inherited silent money rules shaped not by wealth, but by survival, passed down through financial trauma rather than financial literacy. These subconscious money schemes, rooted in scarcity, self-sabotage, learned helplessness, and loss aversion, are behavioral responses to generational exclusions from wealth-building systems such as homeownership, personal investing, and fair lending. Thus, loss aversion becomes a significant collaborator and partner in our decision-making process as it places an enormous amount of energy and passion, emphasizing the possibility of loss versus the opportunity to grow or gain, which shows up in how we avoid risk, hoard cash, or delay opportunities, often mistaken for protection progress. These patterns didn't emerge by accident; they're psychological defenses born from systemic injustice, reinforced by silence, shame, and cultural normalization of financial avoidance.

Behavioral economists suggest that this "financial inheritance" reinforces beliefs that money is scarce, not meant to be accumulated, or inherently unstable.[13] Academic studies on behavioral economics have also found that individuals who grow up in environments of financial scarcity are more likely to make immediate financial decisions out of necessity, often at the expense of future financial growth.[14] In African American communities, this inherited scarcity mindset has hindered many from taking calculated financial risks, such as investing in the stock market or starting businesses that could help create generational wealth.

Many predatory financial practices continue to compound these challenges. In areas with limited access to traditional banking services, payday lenders and title loan companies frequently target Black neighborhoods. Research by the Center for Responsible Lending reveals that Black Americans are disproportionately affected by these high-interest loans, with nearly half of all payday loan storefronts located in predominantly Black and Latinx neighborhoods.[15] These practices exploit financial vulnerabilities and perpetuate cycles of debt, leaving individuals and households even more financially constrained. Many predatory lenders capitalize on this lack of financial education and banking resources, creating a landscape in which entire communities are left to navigate financial decisions in high-risk, and often high-cost, environments.

These longstanding financial disparities in African American communities have broader societal impacts, affecting educational access, healthcare affordability, and even life expectancy. Studies from the National Bureau of Economic Research indicate that children who grow up in financially disadvantaged homes often face reduced educational opportunities, which impacts their earning potential in adulthood.[16] Additionally, the stress of financial insecurity has been linked to a variety of health issues, with African Americans experiencing higher rates of hypertension and related health conditions, partly due to financial stress. Financial insecurity isn't merely an individual burden; it's a societal concern that reverberates across generations and can be broken through effective engagement practices.

A renewed focus on financial literacy and inclusion that brings deep, applicable financial knowledge to individuals who have long been excluded offers a path toward changing this narrative. When we begin to demystify complex financial concepts and make them accessible, we can then reclaim these tools for financial advancement. We achieve this by first engaging in a well-rounded financial literacy development program.

Strategies for Developing Financial Literacy

Let me break down what fundamental financial literacy looks like, because reading a few books or watching some YouTube videos is not enough and won't provide much help. When you wanted to master anything else in your life, what did you do? You immersed yourself in it. Whether it was sports, music, or your career, you didn't just dip your toe in; you dove deep. Financial edification demands the same level of commitment. However, let me keep it real with you: I know not everybody has thousands of dollars to spend on seminars or countless hours attending retreats. That's the beauty of where we are right now. Knowledge isn't locked behind golden doors anymore. You have access to resources that previous generations couldn't even imagine.

You see, every wealthy individual you admire had to learn about money at some point. Some were fortunate enough to learn at home, while others learned through mentors, and many learned through their own dedicated study and practice. The path to financial literacy isn't so much about where you start as it is your commitment to the journey of learning and application.

This journey begins with understanding the fundamentals of money movement. That means studying not just basic financial concepts but also the psychology of money, the principles of wealth building, and the strategies for maintaining and expanding financial success. Don't forget also to learn the strategy for passing on and leaving a legacy for the next generation. It starts with gaining knowledge about various income streams, personal investment options, and methods for preserving wealth.

However, knowledge alone isn't enough. Proper financial edification requires implementation. It means taking those concepts off the page and putting them into practice in our daily lives. It means starting where we are; whether that's opening our first personal investment account with a small sum, establishing credit, or repairing damaged credit while gaining knowledge in areas such as reading, but most importantly, understanding financial statements. Each step, no matter how small, builds upon the last.

Anmol Singh, a trader, investor, author of *Prepping for Success,* and a successful financial educator, shared in Episode 25 of *The New Wealth Wave Podcast*[17] how he started an intentional engagement in financial literacy.

New Wealth Wave Podcast, EP 25: Anmol Singh

"Many of us carry invisible barriers around money that limit our financial potential. These barriers, though real, are not permanent. Through dedicated financial edification, we can recognize and dismantle them, one by one."

Knowing this, he spent years and significant resources accumulating financial wisdom. While not everyone has access to high-level coaching or expensive seminars, we *can* all commit to consistent and focused learning. It might mean dedicating time each week to studying financial concepts, joining investment clubs, or seeking out mentors in our communities who have achieved the financial success we aspire to.

The beauty of financial edification is that it compounds, just like interest. Each piece of knowledge we gain opens doors to deeper understanding. Every principle we master gives us the ability to grasp more complex concepts. As we learn, we become better equipped to teach others, creating a ripple effect of financial literacy that can transform entire communities. Therefore, financial edification is not a case of personal enrichment. It's a matter of breaking cycles of financial ignorance that have held back generations. When we commit to our financial edification, we're changing our futures and at the same time creating new possibilities for those who come after us. We're establishing new narratives about what's possible and giving direction for others to follow.

This journey requires patience, persistence, and dedication. We must be willing to face our financial fears and misconceptions. We must accept that we'll make mistakes along the way, but understand that these missteps are part of the learning process. Most importantly, we should maintain a child's mindset, one that is always ready to learn, adapt, and grow.

As we engage in financial literacy, we must remember that this isn't a race to some fictional finish line. It's a continuous process of growth and development. The financial world is constantly evolving, presenting new opportunities and challenges. Our commitment to learning must be equally dynamic, adapting to new realities while staying grounded in timeless principles of wealth building.

Dr. Trina Shanks, a social work professor who studies asset-building strategies in low-income communities, emphasizes that financial edification tailored to culturally specific needs can be transformative.[18] Programs that teach wealth-building in a relatable way, addressing past experiences and validating the financial anxieties that exist from Stage 2, allow individuals to start reprogramming their Financial Genetic Code. This type of targeted financial edification provides practical knowledge and encourages a mindset shift: money becomes something that can be managed, grown, and ultimately used to secure a better future.

Addressing these gaps is more than a matter of information; it's a matter of financial equity. National Endowment for Financial Education studies highlight that individuals who engage in consistent financial edification report greater peace of mind, reduced anxiety, and an increased likelihood of achieving financial goals.[19] For African Americans, cultivating this knowledge is especially powerful because it acts as a protective layer against the "Walls Out" that often contribute to wealth disparities.

The impact of this approach is profound. With greater financial literacy, you begin to see money not just as a means of transaction but also as a strategic tool for empowerment.

Understanding wealth accumulation and distribution enables you to make informed decisions that support personal financial growth, community reinvestment, and a generational legacy. It encourages a culture of inclusive and transformative wealth-building, emphasizing collective progress alongside individual success.

Reprogramming your financial beliefs with edifying knowledge also builds a supportive environment that allows you to thrive financially and be free from the weight of culturally imposed limitations and resistance. Financial educator and author Tiffany Aliche, known as "The Budgetnista," emphasizes that for Black Americans, breaking free from cycles of financial misinformation involves creating a healthy community ecosystem.[20] In her view, "When we build our knowledge, we build our community. We don't just lift ourselves up; we're lifting one another." This shift is both personal and communal, creating an environment where accurate financial information can flow freely and empower others.

Discernment: A Necessary Skill for Financial Edification

However, before you begin bridging the knowledge gap in your own community, it's essential to first ensure that you have the right knowledge actively working and applied in your life. Financial literacy is more than amassing information; it's about discernment and understanding which knowledge truly empowers and aligns with sustainable wealth-building practices, and which to discard.

A study conducted by the National Bureau of Economic Research (NBER) reveals that individuals with basic financial literacy are significantly more likely to make informed financial decisions, particularly in areas such as debt management, retirement savings, and investment.[21]

However, acquiring that literacy requires more than cursory knowledge— it demands a commitment to understanding principles that are both effective and ethical. It becomes particularly crucial in communities where financial literacy has historically been limited, leading to a cycle where misconceptions are perpetuated, often with serious financial consequences.

How do we discern the right knowledge in a world where financial advice is readily available but often unvetted?

This question becomes even more pressing for African Americans and other marginalized groups who have long been underrepresented in financial education and services. According to a survey by the TIAA Institute, only 37% of Black Americans demonstrate high levels of financial literacy. This gap has been linked to structural inequities and a lack of targeted financial resources.[22] This deficit in knowledge doesn't just impact individual financial health; it has broader ramifications for economic stability and generational wealth in these communities.

Financial edification requires an understanding of an increasingly complex financial landscape, given that traditional concepts now intersect with emerging technologies, alternative investments, and global economic forces. This begs for an adaptive and discerning mindset that can filter through the overwhelming influx of financial information and focus on long-term stable growth rather than short-term trends and high-risk moves.

A key aspect of this adaptive mindset is the ability to assess the credibility of financial information critically. With the rise of digital finance platforms, social trading networks, and cryptocurrencies, access to financial opportunities has never been easier; yet, this access comes with unique challenges. Take, for example, the phenomenon of cryptocurrency. While it offers new opportunities for wealth-building, its volatility and speculative nature require a sophisticated level of financial intelligence to navigate profitably.

Historically, Bitcoin's daily volatility average rate has been approximately 3%, making it significantly more unpredictable than traditional assets.

For comparison, traditional assets like gold have an average daily volatility of around 1.2%, while major fiat currencies typically range between 0.5% and 1.0%.[23] Evaluating whether assets like these align with your financial goals requires a sophisticated understanding of potential returns and the broader implications of high-risk assets on your present portfolio and long-term financial health. This skill enables you to focus on your financial decisions rather than getting sidetracked by trends or impulsive moves.

One of the clearest illustrations of the risks of chasing quick profits over sound financial strategy is the story recorded by *Forbes* of Alex Kearns, a 20-year-old college student who turned to the Robinhood trading platform in 2020.[24] Eager to take advantage of the apparent ease and excitement of options trading, Alex invested in high-risk trades without a full understanding of the complex and fast-paced world of options. Unfortunately, he lost everything, with devastating consequences.

In the world of high-risk investing, particularly in options trading and cryptocurrency, misunderstood financial data can have devastating consequences. There have been cases where trading platforms displayed large negative balances due to unsettled transactions, which were temporary figures that did not represent actual debt. Yet without clear communication, proper education, or adequate support, some users have interpreted these figures as irreversible financial ruin. These incidents reveal how critical financial edification is when navigating volatile markets. When investors lack a solid foundation in risk management, even enthusiasm and ambition can be overtaken by fear, confusion, and impulsive decisions. The allure of high returns can mask the emotional and financial volatility involved, making it essential to equip wealth builders with the knowledge, tools, and mindset to navigate uncertainty without being derailed by it.

When you bypass careful edification and jump into high-risk investments hoping to replicate quick success stories, you may end up facing financial distress and return to Stage 2. However, by prioritizing edification and cultivating a disciplined approach to investing, you can avoid the lure of shortcuts and build a portfolio that aligns with your unique financial goals. Whether it's learning about the nature of the risk involved or understanding the mechanics behind the investment, financial knowledge enables you to focus on sustainable growth. This approach seeks to preserve your assets while growing your wealth over time, even in unpredictable situations. The same goes for social trading platforms. While they enable amateur investors to follow and emulate experienced traders, they also risk perpetuating the "*herd mentality,*" where investors blindly follow trends without fully understanding the underlying factors.

The GameStop trading frenzy in early 2021 is a stark reminder of this phenomenon.[25] During that time, many inexperienced investors joined the buying spree without a clear exit strategy, resulting in substantial losses for those who acted without a sound understanding of the market. Financial edification involves learning when and how to evaluate trends critically and weighing personal values and goals against popular sentiment.

Understanding the Distinction between Trading and Investing

The financial markets often feel like an emotional rollercoaster, especially for those taking their first steps into investing. Many of us carry deep-seated financial trauma and anxiety about the markets, whether from personal experiences, cultural narratives surrounding losses, or the confusing cacophony of so-called experts throwing around predictions and warnings. This emotional burden can paralyze and keep us from building wealth.

However, one important distinction people must make early on is the difference between trading and investing. While they are both involved in the same market, the skills, mindset, and time horizon required for each are worlds apart. Trading, in essence, is an intense, skill-based discipline—it's like a professional sport. Just as you wouldn't expect to perform at a PGA level without a history of practice and skill development, you can't expect to succeed in trading without a grounded understanding of the market, comprehensive strategies, and rigorous testing. Jumping into trading without a clear strategy isn't bold—it's reckless. It mirrors the idea of showing up to the NASCAR circuit expecting to race, without understanding the system, the rules, or even having a car assigned to your name.

In wealth-building, like in racing, there are critical steps most people never learn because they were never taught. Securing the 'sponsorship'—the financial education, mentorship, and emotional readiness required to navigate risk—isn't just a professional formality. It's the difference between building a portfolio and burning one. For that reason, when individuals are lured into high-risk financial arenas without a solid foundation in financial education, they're not being empowered—they're being exposed. It isn't about limiting ambition; it's about protecting legacy.

Furthermore, trading requires technical knowledge, a plan, and, most importantly, patience in honing one's craft, which can take at least a year to grasp fully. For those who may be following the latest tip from a relative or a sensational headline, this kind of trading can easily backfire. Trading can lead to more harm than good when the source is unreliable or the information is delayed. Success in this field comes with dedicated learning, deliberate practice, and resilience to manage the ups and downs inherent in trading. On the other hand, investing has a different rhythm and goal. It's a slow, methodical process that prioritizes stability and long-term growth over short-term gains.

Traditional financial theory provides a clear framework; concepts such as diversification, Modern Portfolio Theory (MPT), and the Efficient Market Hypothesis (EMH) are often considered the cornerstones of sustainable wealth building. While that structure has value, these models rarely acknowledge the emotional weight, cultural barriers, and generational realities that many of us bring to the table.

Wealth isn't created in a vacuum.

These strategies can only take root when they're introduced into soil that's been nurtured, where trauma has been addressed, knowledge has been passed down, and the mindset has been prepared to receive and apply the information with intention. Combining these time-tested approaches acknowledges that markets are generally efficient, information is quickly reflected in prices, and spreading investments across various asset classes may help manage risk. Yet, our emotions are often aligned and intertwined in our decisions. Unlike the adrenaline-fueled world of day trading, this methodical approach optimizes your risk-return profile through carefully constructed portfolios that align with your long-term financial objectives.

The focus here isn't on timing the market but *on the time you're in the market.* Investing wisely means contributing a consistent percentage of your monthly income, setting it aside in the market without looking back. Whether 5%, 10%, or more, the objective is to make investing a habit. Market fluctuations, such as elections, wars, and recessions, often create anxiety. Over time, the market will experience dips and crashes. However, historical data shows that, over the long term, these ups and downs are cyclical. This assumes a positive rate of return. Those who understand this principle know they don't need to check their investments daily because their focus is set on a horizon of ten, twenty, or even thirty years.

This concept blew my mind when I first learned it!

When I share this information during a consultation or review of a client's portfolio, I must continually remind them of the emotional aspect of decisions we typically yield to. The Standard & Poor's 500 Index is a capitalization-weighted index of 500 stocks designed to measure the performance of the broad domestic economy through changes in the aggregate market value of 500 stocks representing all major industries. Yet, the S&P 500 has never lost money over any 20-year period when accounting for dividend reinvestment. For instance, the average annual return of the S&P 500 over the last 20 years, as of the end of February 2025, is 10.392% when including dividends. Adjusted for inflation, this figure stands at 7.618%. Between 1980 and 2019, reinvested dividends accounted for approximately 75% of the S&P 500's total returns.[26] Not during wars, not during depressions, not during anything. That's the power of long-term investing. Of course, historical performance is not a guarantee of future wealth.

It's important to understand this key difference: *trading* involves understanding price movement, while *investing* is about understanding value growth. Trading is when you couldn't care less about a company's long-term prospects. You're looking at supply and demand, price patterns, and market sentiment. However, when investing, you consider demographic trends, technological shifts, and economic cycles.

The beautiful thing is, you don't have to choose one or the other. Many successful people I know do both. They have their long-term investment portfolio, which they rarely touch, and their trading account, where they apply more active strategies. It's like having a savings account and a business. They serve different purposes but can coexist beautifully.

It's tempting, though, for many to let fear drive their decisions. A prime example is the 2008 financial crisis, which left countless people wary of investing again. Movements like "Occupy Wall Street" fueled a sense of distrust, leading people to miss out on the remarkable market recovery that followed. Research indicates that exposure to anti-market rhetoric associated with the movement led to a decrease in investment activity. Specifically, individuals exposed to such rhetoric invested between 15% and 30% less than those who were not, with the effect more pronounced among women, older investors, and the college-educated.[27]

Those who stayed out of the market due to fear missed a significant opportunity to grow their wealth, while others who invested consistently saw their portfolios flourish. The emotional component of investing—particularly the fear of losing money—holds many back, causing them to make decisions that feel safe in the short term but ultimately erode their wealth in the long run.

For instance, many turn to high-yield savings accounts or conservative bonds, feeling assured in the stability they offer. In reality, these "safe" accounts often don't outpace inflation. When inflation averages around 6–7% and savings accounts provide returns closer to 4%, this creates a scenario in which the purchasing power of one's money is actually eroding, even in savings accounts meant to preserve it. Investing for the long term is one way to counteract this erosion and strive to beat inflation. When you systematically put funds into the market over the long term, without letting daily fluctuations or news cycles affect your decisions, it's possible to avoid the gradual loss of value and instead steadily build a solid foundation.

Still, the generational divide in financial knowledge and perspectives on wealth remains a significant barrier that prevents many from embracing investing. Many people, especially in marginalized communities, grew up with practical aspirations—careers in medicine, engineering, or law were considered reliable paths to a stable life. Discussions around wealth-building, compounding interest, and financial strategy often weren't part of the picture.

Generational trauma surrounding money is common in these communities and is characterized by a deep-seated hesitation around investing and a lingering sense of risk aversion. This hesitancy is often reinforced by well-meaning but cautious advice passed down from family members. Many base their guidance on past experiences, usually shaped by financial struggles or limited access to modern investment tools. For example, investing in the stock market is sometimes viewed as too risky or akin to gambling, reflecting a fear of losing what little has been built over time. These beliefs, while protective, can inadvertently hold people back from exploring opportunities to grow wealth.

A patient, long-term approach is vital. Wealth isn't something that appears overnight; it's built incrementally. Riches can be transactional and momentary, tied to individual paychecks or a windfall, but wealth is different—it's not sexy; it's gradual and sustained over time. An approach that involves regularly investing a set portion of income month after month may not yield flashy immediate results, but it can lead to substantial growth through compounding. Over the course of 20 or 30 years, these investments can grow exponentially.

For those carrying emotional baggage related to money, it is essential first to recognize how these feelings influence their financial behaviors. Financial trauma, as we saw in Stage 2, isn't always obvious—it might manifest as anxiety around making financial decisions, fear of losing money, or the tendency to follow advice from sources that aren't well-informed.

Breaking away from this cycle involves actively choosing trusted, research-backed investment approaches. As I always emphasize to clients, understanding the root of one's financial anxieties is key. For that reason, the Seven Stage Generational Wealth Model© emphasizes Stage 1, which intentionally focuses on our internal and external ecosystem, identifying and addressing the underlying emotional triggers that can obstruct financial progress.

Many people are *"going broke safely"* by sticking with conservative choices out of fear. In these cases, understanding the actual risk of missed opportunities becomes essential, as it relates to Loss Aversion. Yes, investing requires patience, discipline, and tolerance for temporary dips, but the cost of not investing is a silent, gradual erosion of financial potential. Holding money in accounts that barely keep pace with inflation is like running in place; adopting a strategic, consistent approach to investing is essential to move forward.

A practical and emotionally balanced approach to investing can lay a solid foundation for financial security for those just starting. The key is to move past fear and start creating a disciplined and sustainable habit that leverages time, compounding, and the market's inherent resilience.

Your Investment and Risk Tolerance

What this means in the real world is that it's not the complex strategies or technical terms that hold people back. It's the emotional and mental barriers we create. Listen, you don't need to dump your life savings into the market on Day One. That's like trying to run a marathon without achieving your first mile (timed or not). Instead, think about starting with just $100 a month. You could start with an index fund that tracks the S&P 500. It's like owning a small but significant piece of 500 of America's biggest companies. In this way, you're not relying on a single opportunity but positioning yourself to benefit from the broader financial ecosystem.

The wonder occurs when you examine compound interest. Einstein supposedly called it the eighth wonder of the world, and man, he wasn't kidding. Let me break this down with a simple example. Say you invest $200 monthly; that's like skipping a few fancy dinners out. If you earn the historical market average of about 6% annually (though keep in mind, returns vary year to year), after 30 years, you would have approximately $200,000. So remember, that $200 per month totals $72,000. $378,000 is compound interest. Now that is growth! The hypothetical rates of return used do not reflect the deduction of fees inherent to investing, but still show how compound interest works in your favor. Research shows that the biggest obstacle isn't a lack of money, but rather a lack of consistency.[28] I've seen people with excellent salaries who never build wealth because they keep jumping in and out of the market based on headlines or emotions. Meanwhile, someone making a modest income who consistently invests a small amount each month often ends up way ahead.

Think about it like growing a garden. You don't plant seeds and then dig them up every week to check if they're growing, right? Same with investing. Once you've set up your automatic investments, your job is to let them grow. As explained earlier, the market will have its ups and downs. That's just like having some rainy days and some sunny days in your garden. However, with proper care and patience, things tend to grow over time.

Start small. Even if you can only invest a modest amount each month, the act of investing consistently is what matters. It helps you develop the habit of building wealth, explains how markets work, and demonstrates that investing isn't as intimidating as it may seem.

The research backs this up, too. Studies from Vanguard show that investors who use dollar-cost averaging—a fancy way of saying investing a fixed amount regularly—tend to do better over time than those who try to time the market.[29] That's because they take emotion out of the equation. They're not trying to guess if the market is too high or too low; they're just steadily building wealth over time. However, before investing, you must consider what level of risk you can tolerate. Risk tolerance is not only about stocks or bonds–that's just scratching the surface. Every single way of making money has its risk profile. Even keeping cash under your mattress is risky because inflation is eroding its value every single day.

According to the U.S. Bureau of Labor Statistics Consumer Price Index (CPI), if you had $100,000 in cash in December 2000, by December 2020 that same amount would have the buying power of just about $66,465, meaning it would take approximately $149,697.70 to purchase what $100,000 could two decades earlier. This reflects a cumulative price increase of approximately 49.7% over the 20-year period, meaning the dollar's purchasing power decreased to roughly 66.8% of its 2000 value by the end of 2020.[30] This substantial erosion due to inflation is what we refer to as the "silent wealth killer."

Real estate is fascinating because it presents multiple layers of risk. You've got your standard residential real estate—your primary home or rental properties. According to the S&P CoreLogic Case-Shiller U.S. National Home Price Index, the average annual nominal home price appreciation from 2001 to 2024 was approximately 5.2%. However, when adjusted for inflation, the real annual appreciation rate is closer to 0.7%.[31] This indicates that, over the long term, residential real estate tends to appreciate at a rate slightly above inflation. Then you've got commercial real estate, real estate investment trusts (REITs), and real estate development projects, each with its own risk-reward profile.

Here's something most people don't think about: your career itself is an investment with its risk profile. I know doctors who think they're risk-averse, but they spent 12 years and hundreds of thousands of dollars on medical training. That's a massive risk! What if healthcare regulations change? What if AI transforms their specialty? The Bureau of Labor Statistics shows that the average person changes jobs several times in their lifetime.[32]

Let me give you a classic example. Let's consider someone who was super conservative with their stock investments and wouldn't touch anything but bonds. However, it was later discovered that 90% of their net worth was tied up in a business. That's like saying you're afraid of swimming while you're skydiving! *Furthermore, let me clarify that diversification does not guarantee protection against potential losses.* One must consider both systemic and non-systemic factors when constructing a portfolio. For that reason, consultation with a trusted financial planner is encouraged and recommended. Therefore, different wealth-building vehicles have different risk levels. Take traditional employment, for example. Traditional employment is what most people consider "safe," but after what we saw during the COVID-19 pandemic, it's clear that this is not entirely true. Its stability depends heavily on your industry, skills, and ability to adapt. However, it does provide something valuable: it can serve as your "risk foundation," allowing you to take calculated risks in other areas, such as business ownership.

Business ownership is quite fascinating because it allows you to control your risk level. You could start a low-risk service business with minimal overhead or invest heavily in a manufacturing business with substantial capital requirements. The risk level here is often more about execution than the type of business itself. While success rates can vary widely, research from the U.S. Small Business Administration underscores that proper planning and access to sufficient capital are among the most critical factors influencing whether a business thrives or fails.[33] Thoughtful preparation and sound financial footing don't eliminate risk, but they significantly improve your chances of building something sustainable.

Then, we can explore alternative investments, including private equity, venture capital, cryptocurrency, art, collectibles, and other options. Each has its own unique risk profile. Private market investments, for instance, can offer higher returns but have less liquidity. You might not be able to access your money for 5-10 years. If that matches your time horizon and risk tolerance, it could make perfect sense.

"This is where understanding your personal risk tolerance becomes important. It's not just about whether you can stomach market volatility; it's about understanding your entire wealth picture. What's your time horizon? What are your income needs? How stable are your other income sources?"

Most millionaires don't rely on just one source of income, which is why it's important to understand the various options available. Studies, such as Tom Corley's "Rich Habits," reveal that many self-made millionaires typically maintain three to five income streams.[34] These may include earned income, dividends, rental income, business profits, royalties, and so on. Each stream might have a different risk level, but together they create a relatively stable wealth-building system.

Keep in mind that risk tolerance isn't static. It evolves with your age, wealth level, and life circumstances. What's risky for someone else might be conservative for you, and what's aggressive today might be conservative for you in five years. The key is to regularly reassess and rebalance not just your investment portfolio, but your entire wealth-building strategy.

Insurance: Your Financial Safety Net

Building on the evolving nature of risk tolerance leads us to something many people overlook: protecting what you've built. Insurance is an integral part of your wealth-building foundation. Often, we see individuals taking the correct approach, doing everything exceptionally well, investing regularly, and building businesses, but one health emergency comes their way, and they are derailed. This eventually wipes out their savings because, due to their age at the time, they thought, "Oh!

I'm too young" for comprehensive health insurance. The reality is that wealth protection is just as important as wealth creation.

Think of insurance as a safety net for a trapeze artist. Sure, they might never fall, but having that net allows them to perform confidently. Research from the Life Insurance Marketing and Research Association (LIMRA) reveals that approximately 42% of American households would face financial hardship within six months if the primary wage earner were to die, and a quarter would struggle within just one month.[35] Yet many people delay purchasing life insurance because they prefer not to confront worst-case scenarios. However, having insurance doesn't mean you're dwelling on negative possibilities; it means you're prepared so you can focus on positive opportunities.

Different life phases require different types of protection. When you're young and single, your insurance needs might be fundamental. However, adding a spouse, kids, a mortgage, or a business requires your insurance strategy to evolve accordingly. It's like building a house; as you add rooms, you need more comprehensive protection. Most successful wealth builders adjust their insurance coverage periodically as their needs change.

There are various types of insurance designed to cover specific needs. Take disability insurance, for example. The Social Security Administration reports that one in four 20-year-olds will become disabled before reaching retirement age.[36] That's a sobering statistic. It's not so much the probability as the impact. Your income is your most significant asset when building wealth. Protecting it isn't just smart; it's essential. Think about it. All those careful investment plans we discussed earlier depend on your ability to earn and invest consistently.

Property and casualty insurance is another key component, covering risks associated with your home, car, or other assets. While many focus solely on premiums, it's essential to have adequate coverage. Take homeowner's insurance, for example. According to the Insurance Information Institute, the average claim is around $15,000.[37] However, that number can skyrocket if you live in an area prone to natural disasters or have valuable assets. You need to find the sweet spot between adequate coverage and affordable premiums.

Insurance is even more of an issue for business owners. From professional liability to key person insurance, coverage can mean the difference between recovery and closure during a crisis. According to the Federal Emergency Management Agency (FEMA), nearly 40% of small businesses never reopen after a disaster.[38] Not because they couldn't rebuild, but because they didn't have the right insurance coverage to help them through the crisis. It's like having a spare tire; you hope you never need it, but you'd never drive without one.

As you plan for risk, it is also important to consider long-term care insurance, which many people feel uncomfortable discussing. The Department of Health and Human Services reports that someone turning 65 today has a 70% chance of needing long-term care services in their lifetime.[39] Long-term care insurance protects both your comfort and your family's financial stability.

While discussing insurance as a financial safety net, it's worth highlighting annuities as another strategic financial tool. Annuities can be a valuable supplement to traditional investment vehicles, Social Security, and pension plans when properly structured and managed. According to the LIMRA Secure Retirement Institute, annuities can provide a guaranteed income stream that helps mitigate the risk of outliving one's retirement savings.[40] The American Association of Retired Persons (AARP) notes that fixed-indexed annuities (FIAs), in particular, can offer retirees a way to generate reliable income while potentially participating in market gains without direct market risk.[41] While insurance can be a valuable part of a broader financial well-being strategy, as discussed in Stage 5 of the Model, it's important to understand the purpose and limitations of the products being considered.

Fixed annuities, including Fixed Indexed Annuities (FIAs), are long-term insurance products commonly used in retirement planning. They offer features such as principal protection, tax-deferred growth, and the potential for lifetime income. However, FIAs can have complex structures that require a thorough understanding before purchase. While earnings grow tax-deferred, withdrawals are taxed as ordinary income, and distributions made before age 59½ may incur a 10% IRS early withdrawal penalty. Additionally, surrender charges may apply based on the specific terms of the contract. It's essential to remember that all guarantees depend on the claims-paying ability of the issuing insurance company; therefore, due diligence is crucial before investing in these products.

Because individual goals, time horizons, and risk tolerance vary, *it is strongly recommended that you consult with a licensed financial professional to determine if a fixed indexed annuity aligns with your unique financial objective*s. This book presents financial tools as part of a broader behavioral and strategic framework, rather than as one-size-fits-all solutions. Proper education, suitability review, and timing are critical when considering any long-term financial product.

Permanent life insurance policies, such as Whole Life, Universal Life, Index Universal Life, and Variable Universal Life Insurance, combine protection with investment components. Many of these policies also offer various Long-Term Care and Critical Illness riders, which can be advantageous to include. While these policies should not be your primary investment vehicle, they can provide tax advantages and estate planning benefits that complement your overall financial strategy. Riders are additional guarantee options available to an annuity or life insurance contract holder. While some riders are part of an existing contract, many others may incur additional fees, charges, and restrictions; therefore, the policyholder should review their contract carefully before purchasing. Guarantees are based on the claims-paying ability of the insurance company that issues them.

The most successful wealth builders I have worked with view insurance as an integral part of their overall risk management strategy. They understand it's not so much having policies alone as having the right coverage at the right time. They regularly review and adjust their coverage as their wealth grows and their circumstances change. It's a little like updating your smartphone's security features as new threats emerge.

Insurance not only protects you against loss. It also creates a sense of security that allows you to take calculated risks in other areas of your financial life, while avoiding a return to Stage 2. When you know you're properly protected, you can focus on growth opportunities without constantly worrying about what might go wrong.

Planning for Retirement

This naturally brings us to retirement planning, as all these customized strategies ultimately contribute to your long-term financial security. Retirement planning isn't just about reaching a certain age with sufficient funds; it's about creating sustainable income streams that will last throughout your retirement. The Employee Benefit Research Institute found that only 50% of Americans have tried to calculate how much they'll need for retirement.[42] That's like starting a road trip without knowing your destination or checking your fuel gauge!

Modern retirement planning has evolved far beyond the traditional "save 10% of your income" rule. Today's retirees are living longer, facing different challenges, and often pursuing more active lifestyles than previous generations. The Centers for Disease Control report that life expectancy continues to increase, meaning your retirement savings might need to last 30 years or more.[43]

From the perspective of someone who has lived the journey, let's be honest about what this "third phase" truly signifies. It's intriguing. I see many people treat retirement as a finish line when, in reality, it's more like the beginning of a whole new race. At 58, I'm at a crucial point that most people in their 20s and 30s can't even picture, and that viewpoint is invaluable. Consider this: while younger individuals sprint through the accumulation phase from 28 to 45, aiming to grow their savings and then carefully protect them during the preservation phase from 45 to 60, you're now facing something more sophisticated. The retirement phase isn't just about sitting back and watching your savings weaken over time; it's about strategically applying everything you've learned and accumulated.

The Federal Reserve's Survey of Consumer Finances shows something interesting: retirees who actively manage multiple income streams in retirement typically have more stable and satisfying retirements than those who rely solely on traditional retirement accounts.[44] But here's what's powerful: When you combine that financial knowledge with the wisdom of experience, you've got something priceless to share.

Let's be clear, retirement planning isn't just about the numbers. Sure, we can analyze data about safe withdrawal rates and portfolio allocations all day, but what about the human element? Your current situation, which allows you to assist others through wealth education, is a perfect example of what modern retirement can look like. The focus is on creating value, staying engaged, and, yes, possibly generating additional income streams while doing something meaningful.

If many retirees knew then what you know now, things might be different. That's exactly the kind of insight that makes your perspective so valuable. For instance, data from the Employee Benefit Research

Institute shows that only about 28% of retirees feel very confident about having enough money to live comfortably throughout their retirement.[45] You're in a position to help change that statistic for the next generation!

Consider how retirement has evolved. Back in the day, it was simple. Work for 30 years, receive a pension, travel, spend time with grandkids, take on a new hobby, and play golf. Today, we're exploring dynamic retirements that may include consulting work, teaching, podcasting, or building online communities. The Bureau of Labor Statistics reports that the fastest-growing segment of entrepreneurs is people over 50.[46] They're leveraging their experience, just like I am doing with my podcast and educational outreach.

However, there's something more important about this third phase than just making money. You're able to share knowledge, experience, and wisdom. My podcast, for example, isn't just about content creation; it's about building a legacy. I draw on decades of financial lessons, including both successes and failures, to create a knowledge base that might influence future generations. That's a kind of compound interest that traditional retirement calculators can't measure!

That said, let's get practical about this phase, too. When you're helping others understand financial planning, you're also staying sharp about your strategy. Teaching financial concepts is like teaching math—you can't just skim the surface. You have to deeply understand the material yourself if you're going to break it down in a way that makes sense, especially for those who've never seen it taught with care or context.

This engagement keeps you connected to market trends, emerging opportunities, and potential pitfalls that could affect your own retirement plans. The beauty of my current position is that I can speak to all three phases from personal experience. I've navigated the accumulation sprint, tackled the preservation of capital challenge, and am now pioneering what modern retirement looks like. That's incredibly valuable in a world where, according to the U.S. Census Bureau, approximately 10,000 Baby Boomers turn 65 each day, a trend that began in 2011 and is expected to continue through 2029. This demographic shift, often referred to as the "silver tsunami," has significant implications for retirement systems and the economy, as many Baby Boomers are ill-prepared for the new challenges of a longer life and a more dynamic retirement.[47]

Research from the National Institute on Retirement Security (NIRS) indicates that nearly half of working-age households have no retirement savings, and many of those nearing retirement age are facing an uphill battle to achieve the financial security they had anticipated.[48] This trend is evident in the 2020 Retirement Confidence Survey conducted by the Employee Benefit Research Institute (EBRI) and Greenwald & Associates, which confirms that retirees often struggle with maintaining a steady income in retirement.[49] For many, the transition from the accumulation phase to the preservation phase is difficult due to insufficient knowledge of how to manage multiple income streams or protect their wealth from inflation.

Remember that your retirement phase isn't only about how much you've saved; it's also about what knowledge and wisdom you've accumulated that you can share. For example, every podcast episode and every piece of financial education I provide is also part of my retirement strategy. It creates impact, generates income, and most importantly, gives purpose to this phase of life. Traditional financial planning textbooks focus on the numbers, withdrawal rates, asset allocation, and tax strategies. However, real retirement planning, especially in this third phase, involves leveraging your position to create ongoing growth, both financially and personally. Instead of contraction, the emphasis is on expanding and giving back while moving forward.

Strategies to Filter Sound Financial Edification from Noise

As we look at Stage 4 of the Seven-Stage Generational Wealth Model©, it becomes increasingly clear that financial success isn't a case of overnight gains; it's a matter of understanding and committing to strategies that align with your risk tolerance and long-term goals. A disciplined approach guards against losses and fosters a mindset that prioritizes consistency over fleeting victories. It's a mindset that's especially critical today, as the financial landscape is flooded with a mix of genuine advice, misleading claims, and dangerous promises from self-styled "financial preachers."

As Brian Seymour eloquently pointed out in Episode 24 of *The New Wealth Wave Podcast*[50]:

New Wealth Wave Podcast, EP 24: Brian Seymour

"When it comes to investing, many young Black investors are now actively participating in the market. However, they are also more inclined to seek advice and guidance from social media. This creates a distinct difference between certified professionals, who have a fiduciary duty to act in their clients' best interests, and influencers, or 'fin-fluencers,' who may prioritize product promotions or receive kickbacks for each signup rather than truly prioritizing their audience's financial well-being."

While scrolling through social media, you've likely seen influencers claiming they can turn $10 into $10,000 in just a few days. These bold promises often come from so-called "financial experts" who rely more on hype than genuine knowledge or experience. The ease of creating and sharing content online has fueled numerous accounts that present financial strategies as magical formulas, with little attention to the real risks or realities involved. They promote methods to "build generational wealth" or "double your investments" without credible proof or measurable success to support their claims. Many of these approaches resemble guesses, designed more for likes and views than for meaningful financial progress.

The allure of these promises is understandable. Everyone wants to maximize their wealth with minimal effort, and in a world where attention equals revenue, it's not surprising that influencers gravitate towards sensational claims. How can you tell which voices to trust and which to avoid? Filtering this influx of information starts with a few core strategies.

One essential first step is knowing how to verify credibility. With the fiduciary rules governing financial advisors, professionals are legally obligated to act in their clients' best interests related to their advisory accounts. For instance, accounts follow the suitability standard. This standard doesn't apply to influencers, whose recommendations may be influenced by commissions or kickbacks. If someone is promoting a financial product on social media, you should look up their credentials through a service like FINRA's (Financial Industry Regulatory Authority) BrokerCheck. You can access this by visiting https://brokercheck.finra.org. It's not just a tool—it's a layer of protection.

BrokerCheck enables you to verify whether an advisor is licensed, view their professional history, and discover any past disclosures that may indicate bias, misconduct, or a potential conflict of interest. In a financial world where trust must be earned, this level of transparency is essential for those seeking to build and protect generational wealth. If you can't find their name, consider it a red flag. This extra step may feel tedious, but it can reveal whether the person giving you advice has genuine expertise or is simply promoting products they are paid to endorse.

The increased visibility of certain financial products on social media—such as Indexed Universal Life (IUL) insurance policies—highlights the importance of informed decision-making. IULs are often presented as flexible tools that combine life insurance protection with the potential for cash value accumulation linked to the performance of a market index. Indexed Universal Life (IUL) insurance offers permanent death benefit protection, accompanied by the potential for cash value accumulation that tracks the performance of a market index, subject to caps, participation rates, and other product-specific features. It's essential to note that these policies can be marketed and sold by individuals who hold a state life insurance license, without requiring a securities or investment advisory license. As such, clients are encouraged to evaluate whether the professional offering the product has the appropriate background to help them assess how an IUL fits into their overall financial strategy. Careful consideration of policy costs, features, and long-term suitability is essential.

While IULs can be a part of a comprehensive financial strategy for some individuals, they are not one-size-fits-all solutions. The structure, fees, caps, participation rates, and long-term policy performance should be carefully reviewed and fully understood. As with any insurance product, policy guarantees are subject to the claims-paying ability of the issuing insurance company.

Before purchasing an IUL—or any financial product—consumers should consult with a licensed and qualified financial professional to evaluate whether the product aligns with their financial goals, risk tolerance, and long-term planning needs. In a financial landscape increasingly shaped by digital marketing and influencer content, education and due diligence remain essential. Yet, in many consultations with potential and incumbent clients, I've sat across the table from families who were sold products they didn't understand—policies that sounded promising but lacked the strategy and intention required to build generational wealth truly. One common thread I often observe is a person selling a product but lacking the necessary training to provide comprehensive financial guidance in the first place.

Let's break this down.

When you work with a financial professional offering investment products like mutual funds, variable annuities, or managed accounts, they must pass a series of exams, like the Series 6, 63, 65, 66 or even the Series 7, depending on what products are offered. These licenses aren't just red tape. They represent a baseline understanding of financial markets and regulatory compliance. To be clear, although someone may have successfully passed the requirements to sell a financial product(s), it doesn't necessarily mean they're acting in your best interest. Licensing indicates that they've met the minimum requirements to offer certain products legally—it doesn't guarantee expertise or alignment with your goals.

That's why it's important to ask questions, understand how professionals are compensated, and know whether they're offering advice or simply selling a product. The more informed you are, the better positioned you'll be to make decisions that reflect your values and long-term financial well-being.

When evaluating any financial product, especially one positioned as an "investment alternative" or "retirement strategy," it's wise to ask detailed questions, request illustrations, and ensure you fully understand the risks, fees, and long-term implications. The responsibility to make informed decisions is shared, and your clarity begins with asking the right questions.

This is why financial education must come before financial products.

Don't let someone's title—or a shiny brochure—fool you. Ask the hard questions. Who are they licensed with? Are they registered with

FINRA? Can they explain the product beyond the buzzwords? If they hesitate or deflect, that's a bad sign.

Because the truth is, your legacy deserves more than a sales pitch—it deserves a strategy rooted in knowledge, trust, and intention.

Let me be crystal clear: Products like Whole Life, Universal Life, Indexed Universal Life, and Variable Universal Life can be excellent components of an overall financial portfolio—but only when they genuinely align with the client's specific financial goals and circumstances. Recommending any financial product—whether it's an insurance policy, annuity, or investment—without fully understanding a client's financial goals, risk tolerance, and long-term needs can lead to outcomes that fall short of expectations. While licensed professionals are authorized to offer specific solutions, the effectiveness of those solutions often depends on how well they're aligned with the individual's broader financial picture.

Some financial professionals earn commissions from selling products, while others charge ongoing advisory fees based on assets under management. Both compensation models are standard and regulated in the financial industry, but they come with different incentives that can influence recommendations. As a consumer, it's essential to inquire about how your advisor or agent is compensated and whether their advice is part of a comprehensive strategy tailored to your specific goals. Understanding these dynamics doesn't mean being skeptical—it means staying informed and taking an active role in your financial journey. Transparency around fees and services helps ensure that the advice you receive supports your long-term interests, not just a transaction.

This same awareness applies when you receive financial advice from social media, online platforms, or peers. Ask yourself whether the person offering guidance is licensed, affiliated with a specific company, or being compensated to promote a particular product. Their incentives don't automatically render the advice incorrect, but understanding the context helps you assess how well it aligns with your needs. No single credential guarantees good advice; what matters most is that you feel confident asking questions and comparing options. Staying informed empowers you to make decisions that truly align with your values, goals, and financial well-being.

When seeking trustworthy financial guidance, some critical factors separate the experts from the opportunists:

First, look for professionals who provide evidence-based strategies and maintain transparent discussions about potential risks. Genuine financial advisors prioritize education—teaching durable principles you can apply over time, rather than dangling tantalizing shortcuts or promising miracle financial solutions. They understand that sustainable wealth-building is a marathon, not a sprint.

Second, evaluate the consistency of their messaging. Trusted financial professionals demonstrate a clear and coherent approach to wealth management that remains adaptable without becoming contradictory. If tactics constantly shift or the latest trend is promoted without providing fundamental insights into why it works, that's a red flag. Real expertise is grounded in time-tested principles, not in jumping from one trend to another to stay relevant.

Third, take the time to investigate the real-world outcomes of any given strategy. A reliable financial professional is often transparent about their own journey, sharing both successes and setbacks. This honesty is frequently lacking in online spaces, where the focus is primarily on curated success stories and filtered images of "wealth." Genuine educators will be transparent about the practical steps and timeframes required to achieve meaningful financial growth.

Finally, focus on financial advice that encourages education rather than dependence. People who are genuinely invested in your financial growth will aim to empower you, teaching principles you can apply independently, rather than simply offering "hot tips."

If the advice encourages you to explore further, read more, learn, and expand your knowledge, it's probably more trustworthy. This mindset helps you think critically about each financial choice, cutting through the noise and concentrating on what genuinely benefits your long-term financial health.

Working with a Financial Educator

Many people think they need to wait until they're close to retirement or have significant assets before seeking a financial advisor. Part of this is the industry's messaging, which focuses on reaching milestones such as $250,000, $500,000, or even $1 million in assets. But how many people in their twenties or thirties have that kind of wealth? Financial planning is valuable from the start, and our greatest resource is time, especially for young people.

When we consider the financial industry, it's clear that we have work to do. Not everyone seeking advice looks the same, has the same background, or even speaks the same language. Yet, those providing unsubstantiated advice tend to come from a narrow demographic, limiting access and perpetuating exclusion cycles. This is why it is essential to engage with young people and demonstrate the diverse range of career paths in finance, beyond the stereotypical Wall Street roles. If we bring more perspectives into the industry, we can better serve a wider, more representative population.

Understanding that not everyone has the same financial needs is vital in this process. Within the financial industry, there are multiple roles, each serving a unique purpose. These professionals include financial therapists, financial educators, financial counselors, financial advisors, and financial planners. However, not everyone is ready to meet with an advisor. Many individuals, particularly those from marginalized communities, might benefit from foundational financial education first.

For instance, someone might believe they need a comprehensive financial planner when they're at Stage 1 of the Seven-Stage Generational Wealth Model©. A financial educator, counselor, or financial therapist could provide more immediate and impactful guidance. The key is recognizing and addressing individual needs rather than applying a generic one-size-fits-all approach. The industry often groups everyone, which can be a significant disservice to individuals. Accurate financial guidance means meeting people precisely where they are and understanding their authentic requirements.

While professional credentials are valuable, they do not guarantee success. You must thoroughly vet potential financial professionals, seek robust referrals, and conduct comprehensive interviews with potential partners. Remember, a genuine financial partnership requires your active participation. You cannot be a passive recipient of advice; you must be willing to engage, learn, and implement strategies. Therefore, do not become a prisoner of your current moment. Thoroughly assess your present location, understanding what's genuinely required for your unique success trajectory. Keep in mind that we are all different and exist at distinct stages of our financial journeys.

Ultimately, financial edification is not a matter of finding one guru or one perfect strategy. It's a matter of cultivating a knowledge base that allows you to discern and apply sound principles in ways that align with your values and goals. When you equip yourself with the proper knowledge, you can cut through the noise and build a financial future founded on understanding, patience, and genuine growth.

Building wealth isn't a straight path; it requires remaining steadfast during economic downturns, investment losses, and personal setbacks. This resilience is not just emotional but also intellectual, rooted in a deep understanding of your strategy and confidence in your knowledge base. As part of the edification process, remember that setbacks are not the end of your financial journey but a natural part of it.

Let this knowledge guide you in setting boundaries with money, both in your personal and professional life. It might mean learning to say *no* to high-risk opportunities that don't align with long-term goals. It can also mean establishing boundaries with loved ones, perhaps learning how to lend support without compromising your financial stability. With a well-developed financial GPS, you can navigate these financial situations with clarity and a sense of responsibility to both yourself and your legacy.

As we've seen, financial edification involves creating a set of guiding principles. These might include sticking to a diversified investment strategy, maintaining an emergency fund, or consistently prioritizing long-term goals over short-term gains. Your principles may also involve regular check-ins with financial mentors or advisors, which can help keep you grounded and focused. Such practices lay the groundwork for wise, informed financial decisions and become an integral part of how you approach wealth-building.

Yet, as important as individual knowledge and discipline are, financial edification also requires consideration of inclusion and accessibility. In many communities, financial resources and opportunities have historically been concentrated among a select few, with access limited by systemic barriers like income inequality, educational disparities, and racial discrimination. Building generational wealth meaningfully requires consideration of these structural inequities, which is why inclusivity is a foundational pillar in this stage of development.

Inclusivity doesn't only mean advocating for more equitable access to financial services. It also involves building awareness of cognitive biases that can affect decision-making. We've seen how studies show that individuals from marginalized backgrounds may, for example, exhibit heightened financial caution or distrust of financial institutions due to generational experiences with economic instability or discrimination. Understanding and overcoming such biases is crucial for anyone seeking to build generational wealth with a clear and unbiased perspective on risk and opportunity.

In addition to dismantling biases, financial edification involves expanding your literacy around retirement planning, insurance, and estate management—often overlooked areas in traditional financial education. For instance, comprehending the complexities of retirement funds, such as those offered through your employer, and understanding the difference between term and permanent insurance are foundational skills that many individuals lack. Yet, these are instrumental in securing long-term financial stability. Equally, understanding estate management can empower you to plan for wealth transfer effectively, ensuring that the financial legacy you've worked hard to build is passed down according to your wishes.

For many, financial edification also means engaging in continuous education, especially as technology and economic forces evolve. It's a commitment to lifelong learning in the area of finance. This could mean staying informed about economic trends, tax law changes, new investment opportunities, or even participating in financial literacy workshops or mentorship programs. As you deepen your understanding of finances, you're also equipping yourself to teach and empower future generations, bridging the financial knowledge gap that may exist within your family or community.

As you move forward in Stage 4 and build upon the foundations established in Stage 3, remember that financial edification is an ongoing process. It involves becoming adaptable, well-informed, resilient, and committed to inclusivity. Each choice, lesson, and challenge in this stage builds a legacy that goes beyond mere wealth. It is a GPS of knowledge and wisdom that can guide your journey and the paths of those who follow in your footsteps.

Through this journey, financial edification becomes your most potent tool for empowerment. With a firm grasp of financial principles and an inclusive perspective, you are no longer just managing money—you are mastering it and using it as a tool to support your purpose, values, and legacy.

Financial Edification: Self-Reflection Worksheet

Introduction:

Financial edification involves building a strong foundation in financial knowledge, learning to make informed decisions, and gaining confidence in managing money. This worksheet will guide you through a series of reflections and exercises designed to deepen your understanding of financial literacy and its role in your life. Take your time with each question, allowing yourself to reflect honestly and openly.

Section 1: Examining Your Financial Beliefs

1. Childhood Influences

- What messages about money did you hear growing up? Who taught you about money, if anyone?
- How have those early experiences shaped your current views on saving, spending, and investing?

2. Core Beliefs

- Describe three beliefs you hold about money. Are these beliefs generally positive, neutral, or negative?
- Which of these beliefs support your financial goals, and which ones may be holding you back?

3. Attitudes Toward Financial Institutions

- How comfortable are you with using banks, investment firms, or other financial institutions?
- Do you feel these institutions have your best interests in mind? Why or why not?

Section 2: Building Financial Knowledge

4. Financial Education Background

- On a scale of 1 to 10, how would you rate your financial knowledge in these areas:
    - [ ] Budgeting as a lifestyle choice
    - [ ] Credit management and building generational credit
    - [ ] Investing for long-term wealth creation
    - [ ] Retirement planning across generations
    - [ ] Insurance as a wealth protection tool
    - [ ] Tax strategies for wealth preservation
    - [ ] Estate planning and wealth transfer
    - [ ] Real estate as a generational wealth builder
    - [ ] Entrepreneurship and creating family business legacies
    - [ ] Financial inclusion and navigating systemic barriers

- Which area do you feel most comfortable with, and which do you feel needs the most attention?

5. Setting Learning Goals

- List three topics within financial literacy that you would like to learn more about (e.g., compound interest, stock market basics, retirement accounts).
- What resources (books, podcasts, courses, mentors) could help you grow in these areas?

6. Self-Education Habit Check

- How much time do you currently dedicate to learning about finances each month?
- What small changes can you make to incorporate financial education into your routine (e.g., reading a finance book each month or following a financial news site)?

- Create a learning schedule
- Set specific, measurable learning objectives
- Establish accountability mechanisms

Section 3: Financial Inclusion and Equity

7. Financial Inclusion Awareness

- Reflect on whether you've had equal access to financial services and knowledge compared to others in your community.
- What barriers (if any) have you faced in gaining access to financial resources or services?

8. Goals for Inclusivity

- How would increasing financial literacy and access to resources impact your community?
- Are there actions you can take to support financial inclusion in your circles (e.g., sharing what you learn, mentoring others)?

Section 4: Financial Habits and Mindset Shift

9. Current Financial Habits

- Describe your current financial habits regarding budgeting, saving, and spending. Which habits are beneficial, and which might be worth adjusting?
- What small change could you make today that would improve your financial health in the long term?

10. Long-Term Vision

- What does financial freedom look like to you? How do you define it beyond simply having "more money"?

- Write down three specific financial goals that align with your vision of financial freedom (e.g., debt reduction, investing for retirement, supporting a family member's education).

11. Mindset Shift Exercise

- Think of a financial decision you've been avoiding or are unsure about. What fears or limiting beliefs might be holding you back?
- Visualize yourself making this decision with confidence. Describe how achieving this goal would positively impact your future.

Section 5: Reflection and Action Plan

Key Takeaways

- After completing this worksheet, what are three key insights or "Aha!" moments you've had regarding your relationship with money?

Commitment to Growth

- Write down one action you will take to improve your financial literacy or work toward financial inclusion within the next month.
- How will you hold yourself accountable to this commitment?

Financial edification is a journey. With each step, remember that building a solid foundation of financial knowledge empowers you to make informed and confident decisions. Small, consistent actions today can lead to a more secure and financially independent tomorrow.

PART III:

PLANNING FOR YOUR FINANCIAL FUTURE

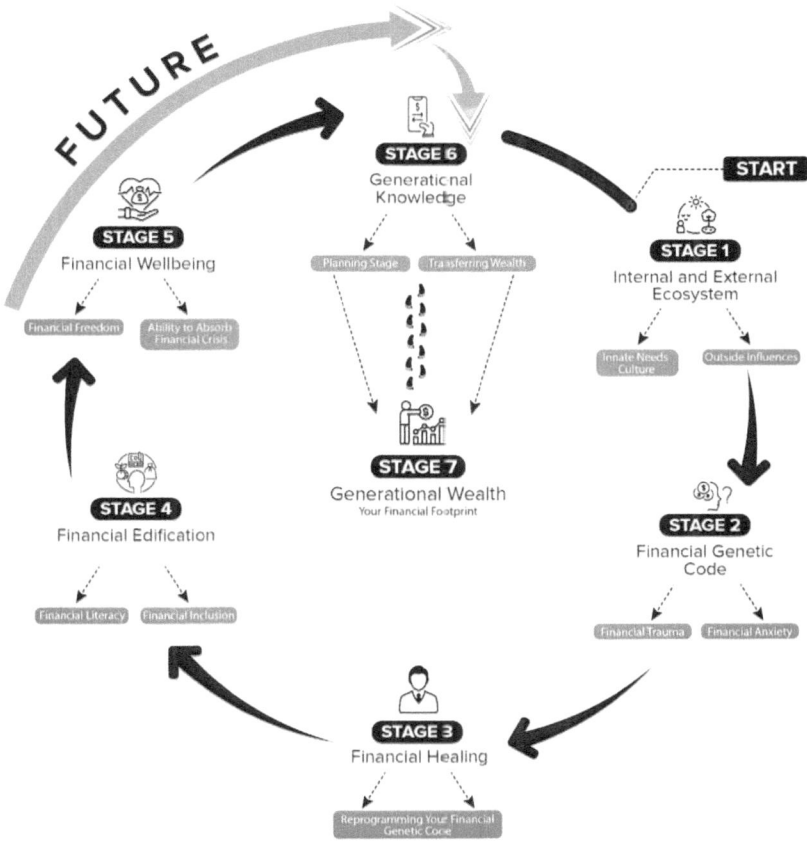

GENERATIONAL WEALTH BEGINS WITH GENERATIONAL KNOWLEDGE®
REG. COPYRIGHT © 2023 DR. JOAQUIN WALLACE.

Chapter 5:
Your Soft Landing

"It is not the man who has too little, but the man who craves more, who is poor." —Seneca

Imagine you've spent time studying, learning, and gathering knowledge about money. You've read countless books, attended seminars, and followed every financial influencer on social media that has piqued your interest. You've also watched YouTube videos and absorbed every piece of financial wisdom you could find. If you're not actively implementing what you've learned, you might as well be reading fiction. Knowledge alone won't build your wealth. Without action, it is just idle information. It's like having a sleek, polished car with no engine—impressive to look at, but useless.

This issue mirrors the findings of the *Harvard Business Review*, which states that while knowledge acquisition is essential, the "knowing-doing gap" remains one of the largest barriers to progress in both personal and organizational growth.[1] Similarly, according to the TIAA Institute-GFLEC Personal Finance Index, the average financial literacy rate among U.S. adults is relatively low, with a 49% correct response rate on financial literacy assessments, and many failing to act on their financial knowledge to improve outcomes.[2]

Consider the analogy of medical doctors who struggle with their health. They counsel patients on eating right, exercising, getting enough sleep, and managing stress, yet they often fail to practice these habits themselves. A study reported that about 53% of physicians were either overweight or obese, mirroring their patients, despite their extensive knowledge about health and wellness.[3] Therefore, knowledge without action is insufficient; the implementation makes the difference.

More importantly, we face two key outcomes if we ignore our financial health even after investing time and effort into financial literacy. First, we risk struggling to attain personal financial well-being and stability. Like an untreated medical condition, poor financial habits such as debt, stress, and a lack of savings can continue to worsen regardless of how much we know about budgets or investments. Second, we limit our ability to build meaningful financial footprints that could strengthen our path toward lasting generational wealth.

Stage 5: Financial Well-Being (Future)

As we've seen, knowing is essential, as it serves as a starting point for creating generational wealth and achieving financial freedom. Yet, knowledge alone isn't enough to propel you forward. This is where many individuals often find themselves, needing guidance and support to take actionable steps. The financial journey that we have been exploring isn't a one-time destination but a dynamic, ever-evolving ecosystem. It's a living, breathing system that demands consistent care, attention, and intentionality. Therefore, consider your financial journey a perpetual work in progress that will require your intentional commitment to revisit and consistently adjust, much like a procedure.

Think of it like cultivating a garden; it starts with acquiring the valuable seeds of knowledge. These seeds have great potential, but their promise stays dormant without regular care and attention. The true blessing comes from daily rituals: watering, weeding, and nurturing the garden. It's through these steady, deliberate actions that the seeds grow into thriving plants. Similarly, financial literacy is just the beginning. The knowledge you gain can only produce results when it's turned into a tangible wealth-building lifestyle, maintained and passed down to the next generation.

The key phrase here is "sustainability." It requires a long-term perspective that acknowledges that wealth isn't built in a moment, but through a series of critical steps taken in the present. These deliberate actions lay the groundwork for financial independence and resilience—the kind of legacy we long to leave behind. Just as a gardener must adapt to changing seasons and ensure the soil remains fertile, this sustainability requires foresight, discipline, and a willingness to adjust, providing the seeds of knowledge take root and continue to grow for generations.

This transformation process is at the heart of Stage 5 in the Seven-Stage Generational Wealth Model©. It shifts the focus from what you've learned in Stage 4 or the insights gained from your financial past to what you actively put into action. This is the stage where knowledge becomes practice and practice develops into habit. At this point, the seeds of financial literacy are no longer dormant ideas but a living, growing system of wealth stewardship. Sustainability is not simply about reaching a destination; it requires embedding practices that keep the journey alive across generations.

Stress-Free Money: The Key to Financial Confidence

I've seen it too many times—people grinding themselves down, believing that working harder and longer is the path to success. However, that's misinformation we've been sold. As I said earlier, true financial well-being is not a matter of how much you earn but of how strategically you manage what you have. I have also had several clients explain to me that being rich was their goal. However, as Seneca rightly said, "It is not the man who has too little, but the man who craves more, who is poor."[4]

Many feel an urgency to "get rich quick," spurred by observing past generations who worked tirelessly yet struggled to achieve financial stability. The result is a paradox: we crave financial freedom but often pursue it through strategies prioritizing speed over sustainability. This approach neglects the true essence of financial well-being, which lies not in accumulating wealth quickly but in building a stable foundation that endures.

As we revisit Abraham Maslow's hierarchy of needs, it is essential to remember that at its base lie our most fundamental human requirements—those physiological needs that drive survival and shape every other aspect of our engagement with the world, including our relationship with money. However, beyond these, we seek safety, social belonging, self-esteem, and self-actualization. These fundamental and higher needs inform our financial aspirations. For some, the desire for wealth is rooted in a need to escape the insecurity that previous generations experienced. The financial behaviors we inherit often stem from generational experiences, such as the Depression-era mindset, where extreme frugality was a survival mechanism for many families. This mindset, passed down from parents to children, cultivates habits of relentless saving and a reluctance to spend, fostering money vigilance. While such habits may secure financial stability, they can limit joy, flexibility, and the ability to invest in meaningful experiences.

I often advise my clients to enjoy life while also emphasizing the importance of planning for the future. It's crucial to find a balance between living in the moment and maintaining the discipline and focus necessary to secure tomorrow. Yet some individuals, shaped by past financial instability, lean toward the opposite extreme. Behavioral economics reveals that many individuals prioritize immediate gratification, often engaging in impulsive spending or taking on risky investments at the expense of future rewards. This pattern leads to decisions that overvalue the present, often conflicting with long-term goals. Emotions frequently drive these choices, fueled by a desire to avoid the delays and sacrifices experienced earlier in life.

However, neither hoarding wealth nor seeking quick gains leads to true financial well-being. The key is intentionality—being purposeful with resources, aligning decisions with long-term goals, and planning for a sustainable future. Achieving this balance promotes financial security and creates a life rich in meaning, experiences, and joy.

Financial freedom, however, is a deeply personal concept. For some, it might be as modest as winning a small lottery prize—enough to clear debts, invest in a dream, and enjoy small indulgences. Freedom, for them, is the absence of financial burdens and the ability to live without constant worry. For others, financial freedom may mean building substantial wealth, pursuing ambitious goals, and living a life of luxury. Both perspectives are valid, as financial well-being is not so much about achieving a universal benchmark as it is about aligning resources with personal values and aspirations.

For me, this understanding crystallized while working on this project and transitioning into the *Preservation of Capital Phase* within the Financial Planning Model. It was during this phase that I gained clarity on what financial well-being truly meant for me. I identified and embraced this vision, then crafted a personal roadmap that focused on what truly mattered, not a false sense of what was important.

I vividly recall a defining moment while waiting in line at the bank to make a deposit. Ahead of me was a gentleman in a wheelchair, accompanied by his caregiver. With an oxygen tank by his side, he turned to me and said something that has since shaped my personal credo: "I would give up a large portion of my money if I could have my faculties." He elaborated, speaking about the simple yet profound abilities to walk, breathe, and care for oneself, daily routines that are often taken for granted.

Then, he uttered a phrase that has guided my perspective ever since: "Health is Wealth."

At the time, I was 35 and didn't fully grasp the depth of his words. However, as I transitioned into my role as a financial planner and witnessed clients coping with long-term care challenges, assisted living expenses, and the delicate balance between financial and physical well-being, the phrase took on a profound meaning. It forced me to take inventory of my own life and reimagine financial planning, not merely as a pathway to wealth but as a holistic approach to address three critical phases we may all face:

Living Too Long: Planning for the financial demands of longevity, such as retirement and healthcare, to ensure you do not outlive your income.

Dying Too Soon: Protecting loved ones through insurance, estate planning, and legacy building.

Becoming Disabled: Preparing for the unexpected is a key part of financial well-being. This includes building savings, securing long-term care or disability insurance, and creating a strong support system. Most importantly, proper estate planning involves establishing a Power of Attorney (POA) and considering the use of revocable or irrevocable trusts to protect your wishes and assets. This information is not intended to replace legal advice. I firmly recommend discussing your specific situation with a qualified legal advisor.

These reflections became the foundation of my personal mission: to help myself and others navigate these three phases with clarity and purpose. While not everyone will experience all three phases, I always recommend planning for each one. By preparing for these key areas, you'll be better equipped to navigate whichever life stages you may encounter. This approach aligns with Stage 6 of the Seven-Stage Generational Wealth Model©: Generational Knowledge, where financial planning is not only a case of wealth accumulation; it's a matter of addressing life's vulnerabilities with wisdom and compassion. As we delve into Stage 6 in the upcoming chapter, we will explore how health, wealth, and legacy intertwine to create a truly sustainable financial future.

For now, remember that financial well-being and freedom are often misunderstood as reaching specific financial milestones or accumulating certain amounts in a bank account. While these numbers are useful as progress signs, they don't capture the full meaning of being truly financially free. Real financial freedom goes beyond just money; it's about creating a life where your time, talents, and resources are fully yours to manage. It's the freedom to choose how and where you spend your days, unbound by debt, societal pressures, or financial limits.

"Financial peace isn't just the absence of debt. It's the presence of direction, discipline, and dignity in every dollar you spend."

In their study on subjective financial well-being, Brüggen et al. (2017) define it as "the perception of being able to sustain current and anticipated desired living standards and financial freedom."[5] This perspective underscores that financial freedom is not solely a matter of wealth; it is also a matter of achieving alignment between financial resources and personal values. Financial well-being encompasses both *objective* measures, such as income and savings, and *subjective* elements, including the sense of security, autonomy, and the ability to pursue meaningful goals. For instance, a person earning a modest income but managing their resources intentionally, aligned with their goals and values, may experience greater financial freedom than someone with substantial wealth burdened by excessive obligations or financial insecurity. This holistic approach challenges the narrow, materialistic view of wealth, encouraging individuals to focus on *financial edification*, mindful resource allocation, and long-term planning.

Autonomy, in the context of financial well-being, refers to the ability to make financial decisions independently, without undue stress or external influence. This sense of financial self-determination is vital, as it fosters a sense of empowerment and confidence, enabling you to take charge of your financial journey and align your choices with your values and long-term goals. To get this right, you must master your cash flow— understanding where your money comes from and where it goes. By maintaining a clear picture of income and expenses, it's quite possible that you can avoid the cycle of living paycheck to paycheck and instead create room for purposeful financial planning. For example, individuals who allocate resources effectively toward their needs, wants, and other financial goals minimize their financial stress and build a foundation for achieving larger financial goals.

As Dasarte Yarnway insightfully noted[6]:

 New Wealth Wave Podcast, EP 15: Dasarte Yarnway

"Communication is the gateway to vulnerability, and vulnerability is the only way you can align with your mission." He shared how he and his wife hold weekly family meetings to discuss upcoming events, share partner feedback, and align on their goals.

Yarnway emphasized that open dialogue is essential in personal relationships and professional and business partnerships. Through consistent communication, individuals and teams can create alignment and joint planning, ultimately laying the groundwork for achieving financial well-being and generational wealth.

This strategic allocation of resources goes beyond managing day-to-day expenses to include investment in opportunities that align with one's ambitions and values. For example, pursuing higher education, launching a business, or transitioning into a fulfilling career are pathways that require thoughtful financial planning. Each of these endeavors represents a step toward not only personal growth but also financial security and independence.

The beauty of financial autonomy lies in its ability to unlock opportunities that might otherwise seem inaccessible. When you are free from the constraints of financial stress and external pressures, you can focus on what truly matters to you—whether that's achieving professional milestones, nurturing personal relationships, or contributing to causes you care deeply about. Financial autonomy is, therefore, not just a state of being but also the dynamic process of growth and empowerment. However, achieving this freedom requires a paradigm shift in mindset. Many people work tirelessly without considering why they work or what their finish line looks like. They fall into the trap of believing life is only about work and earning, all while postponing the essence of living. However, the essence of your life isn't solely in earning—it lies in how you spend that essence.

The capitalist structure perpetuates a narrative that convinces people to work endlessly, contributing to an economy that rarely supports them in achieving their dreams. Many people do not realize they've already achieved financial freedom because they remain conditioned to pursue more, believing they must always work and save more, never entirely stopping to reflect on their progress or enjoy their achievements. Unfortunately, this makes many people live like elephants in captivity, tethered to their financial past or societal expectations. Just as a chained baby elephant grows into a powerful adult but remains bound by the illusion of its chains, individuals condition themselves to limitations that no longer hold them. True financial freedom begins when we break free from our Inherited Financial Narratives and understand that wealth, at its core, is a means, not an end. It's not the destination; it's the vehicle for choice, impact, and generational transformation.

Align Your Finances with Your Life's Mission

Purpose is the cornerstone of meaningful financial planning, bridging the gap between numbers and the life we aspire to live. Purpose ensures financial decisions are not just a case of accumulating wealth but a matter of creating a life aligned with what matters most—family, community, personal growth, or philanthropy. Research by the Consumer Financial Protection Bureau underscores that individuals who connect their financial goals to meaningful aspirations are more likely to achieve lasting financial satisfaction.[7]

Traditionally, the financial industry has focused heavily on a single, monumental goal: retirement. While retirement planning is crucial—it represents freedom from the daily grind and the security of a stable financial future—this singular focus often overlooks the richness of life's journey. Along the way, numerous milestones and aspirations deserve attention, each representing an opportunity to shape a fulfilling life. Life's financial mission is far more nuanced than a singular endpoint. There's a reason we work, plan vacations, dream of starting a family, or aspire to own a vehicle or a home. Each desire reflects an underlying mission: providing for loved ones, pursuing personal growth, or contributing to a greater cause. However, articulating that mission is often challenging. It requires introspection and vulnerability, which can feel daunting, especially when opening up to a financial advisor or counselor.

When clients are asked, "What is your mission?" Many default to answers like "retirement," not because that's their sole goal but because they haven't fully explored their deeper motivations. Identifying this mission involves uncovering the values and dreams that drive them, transforming financial planning from a transactional process into a deeply personal journey. A skilled financial advisor or planner can facilitate these conversations. For example, during onboarding meetings, asking open-ended questions like "What is your mission?" encourages clients to reflect on what truly matters to them. This process often reveals more than initial responses, such as "retirement." A family might share their dreams of traveling as an adventure, funding their children's education, or starting a charitable foundation. These aspirations become central to their financial plan, meaningfully shaping decisions and resource allocation.

If Stage 4 is about empowering the mind with financial knowledge, Stage 5 is about empowering your financial health. It involves ensuring that what you've learned becomes a part of who you are and, more importantly, a part of your everyday financial habits. As I said earlier, you can't create a legacy of generational wealth by simply knowing—no, it's the sustained action, the intentional living, and the discipline that ensures your money works for you over time.

As we discussed in Stage 3, neuroscientific research shows that habit formation is a neurological process where neural pathways become more efficient with repetition. In financial terms, this means your money management skills become more instinctive and automatic with consistent practice. Every mindful financial decision, whether tracking expenses, making strategic investments, or resisting impulsive purchases, strengthens neural connections that make sound financial choices feel more natural.

To move forward in building your financial freedom, you need to understand the psychological frameworks that govern your money management. One such framework is Charles Duhigg's concept of the habit loop, which consists of a three-part process: cue, routine, and reward.[8] This loop plays a significant role in how we form habits, whether they relate to spending, saving, or investing.

The first element, the cue, is the trigger that sets the cycle into motion. In financial behavior, a cue could be as simple as seeing a sale advertisement or feeling stressed about money. These triggers lead us to the next phase—the routine. If the cue is an advertisement, the routine might involve impulsively buying something we don't need. The final phase is the reward, which may be the short-term satisfaction of a purchase but often leaves us feeling more anxious or regretful in the long run, known as buyer's remorse.

The habit loop is compelling because it's often unconscious, operating in the background of our daily lives. We might not even realize how we repeat certain behaviors over time. For instance, compulsive spending can become ingrained when small rewards, such as temporary relief from stress or feelings of excitement, continually reinforce it. Similarly, consistent contributions to savings or investments may begin as a conscious effort but become automatic once the habit has been established. Understanding this is key to creating lasting financial habits. To change your financial future, you must first identify the cues that trigger unhealthy financial behaviors. Do you tend to make impulsive purchases when you're bored or stressed? Once you recognize these cues, you can replace old routines with healthier ones.

For example, instead of immediately adding items to your cart and proceeding to the checkout on your Amazon Prime app or computer, take a moment to reflect on whether the purchase aligns with your financial goals. In this case, the reward could be the sense of accomplishment and empowerment you feel by sticking to your budget or increasing your savings.

The insight from Duhigg's habit loop suggests that it's not enough to simply try to change our behavior; we need to reinforce the new habits with a meaningful reward. The more satisfying and consistent the reward, the more likely the new behavior will become a lasting habit. In terms of financial well-being, rewards may come in the form of reaching a savings milestone, feeling less stressed about money, or watching your investments grow.

When you understand how your brain forms habits, you can utilize this knowledge to develop more effective financial habits. This allows you to be intentional about changing your behavior and creating lasting change that will enhance your overall financial well-being. Over time, these financial habits become ingrained, and your financial well-being improves.

You can think of financial well-being as the soft landing you anticipate when your airplane pilot instructs you to return to your seat and fasten your seatbelt in preparation for landing. The pilot has done their due diligence, working with air traffic controllers to provide a weather outlook, identify nearby airplanes, and plan the safest route for your descent. Now, consider the air traffic controller your financial professional, guiding you toward your financial goals. Together, you've done all the preparation: reviewed your investments, assessed discretionary income, analyzed the numbers, and gathered the necessary tools and guidance. However, just like in aviation, even with all the preparation, the landing itself is critical. Turbulence could turn a well-planned journey into a challenging experience. You can plan the perfect flight, but it's the execution of the landing that ultimately determines whether you reach your destination safely. Similarly, just as a smooth landing brings relief and satisfaction while a rough landing creates stress and instability, your financial success depends not just on your planning but also on your execution—the daily management of your money and adherence to your strategy.

This stage, Stage 5, is your "financial soft landing." It involves ensuring you have the right mindset and strategy to protect the wealth you've built and to grow it further. This is where the real work begins, where you put the financial knowledge you've accumulated into practice to create a flourishing financial life. Without careful planning and execution, financial landings can be turbulent or even missed altogether. In our flying analogy, this equates to a missed approach, where the plane is forced to return to the skies abruptly, and gravity pulls you back into your seat unexpectedly. Individuals who fail to execute their financial plans often revisit earlier stages of the Seven-Stage Generational Wealth Model©, trapped in cycles of instability and missed opportunities.

Financial well-being is a state where your income, investments, and savings enable you to navigate life smoothly. What matters isn't quitting work entirely but rather gaining the freedom to choose what job you do, when you do it, and how it aligns with your values and goals. Financial autonomy gives you the liberty to live life on your terms, focusing on purpose and fulfillment instead of just survival. To maintain this balance, it's essential to reassess your financial priorities. Are you working toward goals that provide lasting satisfaction? Have you thought about the number that represents your financial independence? This intentionality helps prevent resource misuse and keeps your journey toward financial well-being beneficial for you and future generations.

The Path to Financial Well-Being

Often, it's tempting to keep chasing more knowledge. There's always a new book, podcast, or workshop promising to reveal the secret to wealth. Financial well-being isn't something you achieve in a classroom or just by reading about it; it's built through actions, decisions, and long-term habits.

This is where you need to pause and be mindful of continuous academic consumption of knowledge, which could create an illusion of progress and a comfortable intellectual space where you feel productive without actually producing tangible financial results. It's like running on a treadmill: there's plenty of motion, but you're not moving forward.

While financial edification is the foundation, the actions toward financial well-being are the structure that turns that foundation into a secure and livable home. At some point, you have to step off the treadmill of constant learning and start walking the path of implementation.

Think of it this way: knowing how to cook doesn't make you a chef, just as knowing about money doesn't make you wealthy. You can read a hundred recipes and watch countless cooking tutorials, but until you light the stove, mix the ingredients, and plate the dish, you haven't created anything. Similarly, the path to financial well-being demands that you take what you've learned and put it into practice, no matter how imperfectly you start.

"Mistakes are simply tuition fees for the school of life, and the sooner you make peace with that, the sooner you can start creating meaningful change."

This is often where fear creeps in for many. Fear of making a mistake, fear of the unknown, or fear of failing. Thus, we carry decades and generations of behavioral biases that have impeded our ability to change this debilitating narrative. It's easier to sit with the safety of knowledge than to face the vulnerability of action. Let's be honest: You will make mistakes. Everyone does. The most successful people in finance, business, or life didn't get there by avoiding errors—they got there by learning from them.

The path to financial well-being requires turning the abstract principles you've learned from financial education into concrete practices. For example, you may know that diversification is a sound strategy, but have you established a diversified portfolio? You may have learned the importance of saving for retirement, but do you have a dedicated retirement account and a plan to contribute consistently? Knowledge without application is like owning a power tool but leaving it in the box; it holds potential, but it's not doing any work for you.

Stability: The Foundation of Financial Well-Being

Financial wisdom implores you to see financial well-being as more than the absence of financial struggle. It is a state of security, empowerment, and control, enabling you to cope with uncertainties while maintaining reduced financial stress. At its core, this well-being hinges on financial stability—the ability to consistently meet our basic needs without the chronic stress of financial insecurity. Understanding this will provide a support framework for higher levels of financial planning and freedom.

Imagine trying to build a house on shifting sands. Without a firm foundation, every storm threatens to undo your progress. Similarly, financial stability provides the foundation for your broader financial goals. This begins with practices such as proper budgeting and creating an emergency fund, which we will explore in more detail later in this chapter. Neglecting this safety net can be likened to running a race with weights tied to your feet. The progress will be painfully slow, and setbacks will be almost guaranteed. Credit card debt, for instance, can become a significant obstacle, trapping individuals in a cycle of high-interest payments and limited financial flexibility. However, planning early and extending your preparedness to areas like insurance is wise. Many people mistakenly forgo this area, viewing it as an unnecessary expense. However, it's a critical component of risk management. Whether it's health, disability, life, or property insurance, having these protections doesn't mean you're fearfully expecting disaster; instead, the emphasis is on ensuring you can recover if it occurs. Just as schools conduct fire drills to prepare for emergencies, you must stress-test your financial plans to anticipate potential crises.

Similarly, in the journey to creating generational wealth, preparation differentiates those who thrive from those who struggle. While no one desires misfortune, life's uncertainties—job loss, illness, or market downturns—are inevitable. Planning for such events doesn't mitigate their impact. It ensures you remain on track toward your financial goals and keep yourself financially fit as you continue your journey toward creating generational wealth.

As I mentioned earlier, I often advise my clients on three key areas to prepare for: living too long (making sure your savings and investments last through retirement), dying too soon (protecting your loved ones with life insurance and estate planning), and becoming disabled (covering your income and lifestyle with disability insurance, long-term care, and emergency funds).

Each pillar requires foresight and intentional planning, rooted not in fear but in knowledge and financial literacy, Stage 4 of the model. By progressing through the earlier stages—reprogramming your Financial Genetic Code through healing from financial trauma (Stage 3) and financial edification (Stage 4)—you can approach these challenges with clarity and confidence rather than anxiety.

The Basics of Your Financial Health

Starting with the basics of financial health is non-negotiable for building lasting financial well-being. Much like maintaining physical health through regular exercise, nutritious eating, and routine check-ups, financial health requires intentional care and consistent effort. It involves ensuring your income, spending, and savings are in harmony, creating a sense of stability and control over your financial life.

This foundation of financial health begins with understanding your current position. Too often, we try to make vague guesses about our current financial situation. However, there's no need to guess or hope for the best, even though in today's salary and gig economy, our income isn't always a straightforward paycheck. You might have to consider your primary job earnings, side hustle revenues, passive income streams, potential freelance opportunities, and even investment returns. Here, you have to take stock of all your income: How much do you bring in monthly, weekly, or daily?

Apart from your income, you must also analyze your expenses: Where is your money going, and are there areas where you could adjust? According to the Federal Reserve, 37% of Americans are unable to cover an unexpected $400 expense, highlighting the critical need for financial stability.[9] These expenses can be classified under three main categories: essential expenses, discretionary expenses, and savings and investments. Understanding these classifications will help you to budget effectively and identify your spending patterns. These classifications shape how you allocate your income and reveal the broader financial realities in marginalized communities.

The *essential expenses* category, for example, forms the foundation of everyday living, encompassing housing, food, healthcare, education, and transportation. These are the unavoidable costs that sustain a household's basic needs. For many, the largest share of their income is dedicated to housing, including rent or mortgage payments, as well as utilities. This is particularly true for African American families, where systemic barriers such as redlining and discriminatory lending practices have historically limited access to affordable housing and homeownership. Transportation, another essential expense, often consumes a significant portion of income, especially for those living in areas with limited access to public transportation. Coupled with rising healthcare costs and educational expenses, the burden of meeting these essential needs often leaves little room for financial flexibility.

Beyond these necessities, *discretionary expenses* represent the choices individuals make to enhance their quality of life. These include entertainment, dining out, vacations, and luxury purchases. For African

American households, discretionary spending often reflects cultural priorities. For example, contributions to church and community events are more than financial transactions—they are an expression of identity and support for communal ties.

Similarly, spending on personal appearance, such as fashion or grooming, can reflect a deeper narrative of navigating societal perceptions and affirming individuality in environments where image matters. While these expenses are non-essential, they hold significant social and emotional value.

As we've seen, the final category—*savings and investments*—is a cornerstone of financial stability and wealth building. It includes setting aside emergency funds, contributing to retirement accounts, purchasing life insurance, and exploring opportunities in stocks, real estate, or other investments.

When planning for your emergency savings, ask yourself: "Could I handle an unexpected expense without resorting to debt?" Financial health is not just about thriving, but also about being prepared for the unexpected. It is highly recommended that you aim to set aside three to six months' worth of living expenses in an easily accessible account. This safety net will protect you from spiraling into debt when life throws a curveball, whether it's a medical emergency, job loss, or even something that may look as small as an urgent car repair.

Let's talk about debt. If there are any, you must face your debts honestly: What do you owe, and what's your plan to pay it off? If you don't have the answers to these questions, it shows you're flying blind—and that's a quick way to hit turbulence in your financial journey. Now, not all debt is created equal. Debt itself isn't inherently bad—credit can be a helpful tool when used wisely—but it becomes a problem when it limits your options or drains your income through high-interest payments. You must distinguish between *high-interest debt* (such as credit cards) that erodes your financial health, *strategic debt* (like mortgages and student loans) that can be part of long-term wealth building, and *productive debt* that potentially generates more value than its cost.

If you have significant debt, tackle it systematically. Both the snowball method, where you pay off smaller debts first for quick wins, and the avalanche method, which focuses on high-interest debts, are effective strategies. You must choose the approach that aligns with your psychology and financial situation.

Once you've pinpointed your current financial situation, the next step is to take control. Financial well-being is not only a case of how much money you make; it's a matter of how you manage, grow, and protect what you have. It's about the sense of control you feel over your finances and the confidence to meet future goals while living a fulfilling life today. This often begins with creating a budget.

Let's clear up a misconception: a budget isn't a punishment or a tool to restrict your lifestyle. It's a strategic plan. Think of budgeting not as a restriction but as guidance that directs your money to work in line with your values. A well-designed budget allocates funds for essentials like housing, food, and utilities, while helping you identify what can be reduced or redirected. More importantly, it creates space for saving, investing, and building a legacy. This is where financial clarity begins, not with perfection but with purpose.

On this journey toward creating generational wealth, one of the most pervasive barriers to financial well-being is financial stress. This stress often stems from uncertainty, lack of control, or unforeseen challenges. However, proper budgeting has proven to be a practical remedy. For instance, a survey by the Certified Financial Planner Board of Standards (CFP Board) found that 62% of consumers who maintain a budget feel more in control of their finances, while 55% report increased financial confidence and 52% experience greater financial security.[10] Why does this work? Because knowledge is power, and clarity is calming. When you understand your financial story and craft a purposeful plan, taking charge of your narrative becomes easier, reducing anxiety and stress, and promoting emotional relief.

Implementing a structured budget can alleviate stress by providing clarity and a sense of control over your finances. According to the NFCC, only about 2 in 5 Americans (42%) have a budget and keep track of their spending, indicating a substantial opportunity for improvement in financial management.[11] Furthermore, the NFCC's "Sharpen Your Financial Focus" program has demonstrated that clients who receive financial counseling experience increased peace of mind, confidence and improved money management skills. Specifically, 70% of participants reported an enhanced sense of peace of mind, 73% indicated that they now pay their debts more consistently, and 67% reported improved money management following the program.[12]

This improvement in financial management skills directly correlates with reduced stress levels and increased financial stability. A follow-up study by The Ohio State University found that participants in the NFCC's program reduced their revolving debt by an average of $6,000 within 18 months of counseling. This was a statistically significant reduction of $3,600 compared to a matched comparison group that did not receive counseling.[13] These findings underscore the potential of budgeting and financial education as tools for managing finances and enhancing overall well-being.

Budgeting, however, must extend beyond rigid spreadsheets or overly ambitious frameworks that fail to reflect real-life circumstances. Instead, it should be approached as a dynamic resource—think of it as a GPS guiding you toward your financial goals. An adequate budget prioritizes clarity and intention, breaking down income into categories such as essentials, discretionary spending, and savings. For instance, the 50/30/20 rule, a widely recognized framework introduced by Senator Elizabeth Warren and Amelia Warren Tyagi in *All Your Worth: The Ultimate Lifetime Money Plan* (2005), offers a balanced approach: 50% of income is allocated to necessities, 30% to discretionary expenses, and 20% to savings and investments.[14] This method promotes equilibrium, ensuring financial well-being is maintained while pursuing long-term objectives.

Yet, it's important to recognize that the traditional 50/30/20 rule isn't a one-size-fits-all solution. Regional differences, individual circumstances, and cultural nuances can significantly influence how budgets are structured. This framework may require adjustments for individuals in high-cost-of-living areas or those facing unique financial challenges. What truly matters is creating a budget—or rather, a lifestyle plan—that evolves with your needs and remains adaptable. By framing budgeting as a lifestyle shift, you can "trick" your amygdala, the part of the brain that reacts to stress, into perceiving this change as a positive, sustainable choice rather than an inflexible obligation. This approach mitigates the frustration and discouragement often arising from unrealistic or overly strict budgets. Davis discussed this concept in Episode 12 of *The New Wealth Wave Podcast*[15], emphasizing that:

New Wealth Wave Podcast, EP 12: Saundra Davis

"Instead, consider budgeting as a flexible, ongoing process. Begin by using your budget to address immediate concerns, such as repaying high-interest debt or building an emergency fund. Over time, as your financial literacy deepens, you'll be better equipped to refine your financial plan. With this knowledge, you can make informed decisions tailored to your specific circumstances, ensuring your budget supports both your current needs and future aspirations."

However, budgeting alone isn't enough; financial health demands a vision. You need goals that inspire and motivate you. What does financial success look like for you? Is it the security of owning a home, the freedom to start your dream business, or the peace of retiring early? Defining these goals gives your budgeting a purpose. From here, you can break the goals into actionable steps. During this stage, it's important to set realistic goals. These goals must be specific, measurable, and achievable within a given timeframe. For instance, a person might aim to save for a down payment on a home, pay off high-interest debt, or establish an emergency fund. Such clear objectives provide direction and ensure that financial decisions are made intentionally rather than impulsively.

If homeownership is the dream, start by setting a savings target for a down payment and researching mortgage options. If retirement is your primary focus, consider exploring investment accounts and committing to regular contributions. This realistic and attainable goal-setting fosters discipline and patience, two vital traits for managing the inevitable ups and downs of financial life. As you work toward these goals, you are building your financial habits along the way. So, how do you make the habits you're building stick, and how can small, consistent actions snowball into a legacy of financial well-being?

Moving into Financial Freedom: Start Small, Stay Consistent

One way to overcome the inertia of doing little to nothing is to create a plan prioritizing small, actionable steps. Building financial habits doesn't mean overhauling your life overnight. Trying to do too much at once often leads to burnout and a sense of giving up. Instead of tackling everything at once, focus on one area of your finances. Perhaps that involves building an emergency fund, paying down high-interest debt, or setting up automatic contributions to an investment account.

You can choose one of your goals at a time and commit to it, breaking it down into bite-sized tasks so it feels less overwhelming and more achievable. Progress, no matter how small, has the potential to build momentum. Your aim here is to ensure that each small, manageable change becomes a part of your daily routine. Think of it like brushing your teeth; you do it automatically without much thought. For example, if you're prone to impulsive purchases, decide on a small amount you're "allowed" to spend each day on non-essential items. This habit builds mindfulness and encourages you to prioritize your needs over wants. Also, if you are someone who waits until the end of the month to save, chances are that there'll be nothing left to put away. Automating a portion of your income directly into a savings or investment account ensures that saving will happen without effort.

Another small task you can do is to track your expenses. There are several apps out there that you can use for this process as well. Find one you are comfortable implementing and, most importantly, can be committed to. To create this habit, you can commit to spending five minutes each day logging your transactions—it's a small habit with a big payoff in financial awareness. This critical component of financial well-being builds consistency. You're aiming to take small, steady steps over time. Wealth isn't built in a day; it's built daily. The habit of setting aside a portion of your income, regularly reviewing your financial goals, and sticking to your budget is what creates a strong financial foundation. When compounded over the years, these habits produce almost magical results. However, they're not magic; they're discipline in action.

Remember that what was effective for you when you first started may no longer be as helpful as your income increases or your financial goals change. Therefore, it is crucial to regularly review and update your financial strategies. Think of it like tuning a car engine. Routine maintenance keeps the vehicle performing at its best, and sometimes, you need to replace parts to meet new challenges or seize new opportunities. Financial well-being is an ongoing process, not a single achievement.

This journey to financial well-being doesn't just involve the practical side. It's also deeply tied to mindset. Many people carry limiting beliefs about money, such as "I'll never earn enough" or "I'm just not good with numbers." These beliefs can return from the previous stage and then hold you back, even if you have all the tools and knowledge at your disposal. Part of building financial well-being is challenging these narratives and constantly replacing them with empowering ones, like "I'm capable of learning and improving" or "I have the discipline to manage my money wisely."

It's also worth mentioning that financial well-being isn't about perfection. You don't need to have everything figured out or hit every target exactly as planned. Life is unpredictable, and financial plans must often adapt to unexpected circumstances. What matters most is your ability to stay resilient and keep moving forward, even when the path gets rocky. A missed goal or financial setback isn't the end; it's a chance to recalibrate and continue the journey.

Financial well-being is also more than just avoiding debt. It's not even about accumulating wealth or showcasing your investments. It involves creating a lifestyle that prioritizes long-term well-being and wealth-building strategies while still allowing you to enjoy the present. This is the sweet spot we aim for: balancing responsibility with pleasure while being mindful of how we spend and invest and staying disciplined enough to stay on track.

What else? Being financially healthy means having the resources and strategies to live comfortably, handle life's unexpected bumps, and, most importantly, not run out of money when you need it most. You want to reach a level in your financial journey where your money is working for you, not stressing you out, and thus pulling you back to Stage 2 (financial anxiety and trauma).

Financial health isn't a luxury. It's a necessity for anyone serious about creating generational wealth. The foundation of financial well-being lies in your ability to handle money wisely, make it work for you, and ensure that your financial decisions align with the life you want to lead. It involves transformation: moving from merely *understanding* financial principles to *applying* them in daily life. You can create a sustainable financial ecosystem that supports your dreams, protects your family, and builds a legacy that extends beyond your lifetime. It is important to note that financial well-being is not a destination but a continuous journey of mindful choices, strategic planning, and intentional living.

The Real Threat: Outliving Your Income

One of the most common financial fears is running out of money, especially after your working years are over. It's not just about covering the essentials; it's about living confidently, knowing you won't have to sacrifice your quality of life to survive. That fear is real and justified. However, it doesn't have to control your future. With the right planning and a commitment to your financial health, you can build a future that feels secure rather than uncertain.

The key to avoiding this fate lies in thinking beyond the present and embracing a long-term vision. Saving enough for retirement is essential, but it's only part of the equation. Inflation, rising healthcare costs, and unexpected lifestyle changes can quickly eat into savings if not accounted for. As we saw in the previous chapter, a dollar today won't have the same value in ten or twenty years. Medical expenses, too, can skyrocket as we age; without a plan, these can become a heavy burden. Preparing for these realities now, when you have the time and resources to act, can make all the difference.

Part of making sure you don't outlive your income is understanding the power of diversification. A single income source is no longer sufficient in today's unpredictable economy. This is where diversification becomes your most powerful ally. Your financial health is like a table: one leg represents your job, another your investments, and a third your side hustle. The more legs you add to that table, the sturdier it becomes.

Having multiple income streams provides stability and resilience. For example, investing in real estate or the stock market can provide the returns you need to continue building wealth. However, you must also consider having passive income streams, like rental properties or stock dividends, that generate money even when you're not actively working.

Online platforms also enable freelance work, digital products, affiliate marketing, and numerous other income streams that were previously unimaginable just a decade ago. Remember, the goal isn't to become extraordinarily wealthy overnight. It's to create a sustainable, flexible financial framework that provides security, allows for unexpected opportunities, and allows you to make choices aligned with your values and aspirations. This will equip you to avoid relying solely on what's coming in from your 9-to-5 job or a single source of income. Remember that active income, like a salary, is limited by how many hours you can work, while passive income doesn't have that restriction. By building a mix of active and passive income sources, you create a financial ecosystem that can support you at all stages of life.

Always remember that achieving financial well-being is not a linear process. It is a dynamic, multifaceted concept, deeply rooted in the experiences and perspectives we carry from our earliest financial memories. It comes with setbacks, learning curves, and the need to redefine priorities. But through intentional decisions, resilience, and an unwavering sense of purpose, you can create a legacy that empowers you and those who follow. Understanding the need for stability, autonomy, and purpose in your finances provides a framework to confidently navigate life's uncertainties, ensuring that your financial healing (Stage 3) endures throughout your financial journey.

This perspective enables you to refine your Encoded Financial Behaviors even further, shifting from chasing wealth to embracing well-being. Ultimately, financial freedom is not merely the accumulation of money—it's the realization that going through Stages 3 and 4 of this model, you already have the tools to live a life aligned with your values and free from the invisible chains of limiting societal expectations. You'll be in control of your money, making choices that align with your long-term goals and ensuring that your wealth grows in a way that supports your present and your future. You'll be able to live with greater assurance, knowing that you have the resources to handle life's ups and downs and that your financial health will support you throughout your life.

As we move into Stage 6, we'll dive deeper into creating your financial legacy—how to ensure that your wealth not only serves you but also benefits future generations. For now, take a moment to reflect on your financial well-being. Remember, it's not about perfection but about progress. With the right tools and mindset, you're already on the path to building the life you've always wanted and living it on *your* terms with confidence in the future and financial freedom.

Your Financial Well-being Vision Board Worksheet

Personal Reflection Areas

1. Current Financial Landscape

- Where am I financially right now?
- What are my immediate financial challenges?

Notes:

_____

_____

_____

_____

_____

_____

2. Financial Security

Short-Term Goals (Next 1-2 Years)

Emergency Fund Target: $_____
Debt Reduction Goal: $_____
Monthly Savings Target: $_____

Long-Term Goals (3-5 Years)

Retirement Savings Target: $_____
Major Investment Goals: $_____
Passive Income Stream Target: $_____

3. Lifestyle Vision

What does financial freedom look like to you? Describe in detail:

My ideal financial freedom looks like:

_____

_____

_____

_____

_____

_____

4. Wealth Generation Strategy

Potential Income Streams

    Current Job/Primary Income
    Side Hustle/Additional Income
    Investment Returns
    Passive Income Sources

Skills to Develop

    Financial Education
    Investment Knowledge
    Entrepreneurial Skills
    Other: _____

5. Personal Growth Financial Mapping

Financial Mindset Transformation

Current Limiting Beliefs:

1. _____

2. _____

3. _____

Empowering Beliefs I'm Cultivating:

1. _____

2. _____

3. _____

6. Giving and Impact

Financial Contribution Goals

- Personal Charitable Giving Target: $_____
- Family Support Plan:

_____

_____

Community Impact Vision:

_____

_____

7. Quarterly Review Tracker

Quarter	Financial Milestone	Status	Date Achieved
Q1			
Q2			
Q3			
Q4			

Quarterly Reflection Questions

1. What financial victories did I achieve this quarter?
2. What challenges did I encounter?
3. How am I closer to my financial vision?
4. What adjustments do I need to make?

Reflections:

_____

_____

_____

Chapter 6:
Building Your Legacy Through Thoughtful Planning

*"The art of becoming wise is the art of knowing what
to overlook and what to plan for."*
—Ralph Waldo Emerson

The journey to financial well-being isn't complete without considering what lies beyond our own horizon. It extends into the lives of those who follow us, ensuring that the wisdom gained along the way continues to ripple through time. Imagine standing at the edge of a tranquil lake and tossing a small pebble into the water. The ripple that follows starts small but grows outward, continuing until it reaches the surface far beyond its original point of origin. This is the essence of creating generational wealth through thoughtful planning.

As we master the art of wealth creation and understand the language of money, it prompts a fundamental question: "How do we turn our financial success into a lasting legacy?" This question takes us to the core of generational knowledge, the bridge that links wealth creation with the lasting impact of wealth transfer. Wealth, when lacking wisdom, is a fleeting gift; but when paired with knowledge, it becomes a foundation for future generations.

Take the often-heard saying, "Knowledge is power." In wealth creation, this power is more than just an advantage; it becomes the bedrock for creating our financial footprint. Passing down wealth isn't simply a case of transferring assets like property or investment accounts; it's a matter of embedding the emotional and intellectual frameworks that give money meaning. These include values and lessons from financial successes and failures, as well as the deeper purpose that money serves in living a fulfilling life.

Let's examine the story of the Rockefeller family, one of the most enduring examples of intergenerational wealth in the United States.[1] Their approach to building and preserving wealth is a masterclass in strategic financial planning and legacy management. John D. Rockefeller, the family patriarch and founder of Standard Oil, didn't just amass one of the greatest fortunes in history; he also instilled values of stewardship, philanthropy, and discipline in his descendants through long-term planning.

These principles became the foundation of a structured system in which they established trusts that allowed for the growth of wealth while safeguarding it from mismanagement and unnecessary taxation. These trusts ensured that each generation received resources for education, business ventures, and philanthropy, but not without accountability. The family governance structure includes regular meetings and the Rockefeller Family Office, which play a central role in educating younger family members about the responsibilities and opportunities that come with wealth. This framework, combined with a culture of philanthropy, has preserved their financial legacy and reinforced a shared purpose among family members, allowing the Rockefeller name to remain synonymous with wealth and influence for over a century.

In families like these, wealth is not just a case of big numbers on a balance sheet—it's an integrated way of life. Budgeting becomes a collaborative act among family members. Investments are seen as seeds for future harvests, and financial discipline is celebrated as an empowering practice rather than a restrictive one. In such families, wealth is not only preserved but also deeply understood. Even if external challenges arise, the roots of their financial wisdom ensure resilience, enabling the family to rebuild and thrive.

It doesn't happen by accident. Making wealth transfer a process rather than a singular event requires deliberate and strategic effort. Too often, wealth is lost because the inheritors are unprepared for the responsibilities that come with it. Studies have consistently shown that the second generation loses 70% of wealth and 90% by the third.[2] The issue isn't just financial mismanagement; it's also the absence of generational knowledge about the mindset and principles that created the wealth in the first place. The most successful families understand that wealth preservation begins with equipping the next generation to be stewards of their inheritance. This involves nurturing financial acumen, instilling shared family values, and ensuring that everyone understands the responsibilities tied to wealth. Such preparation demands conversations about money that are as intentional as the efforts to create it. The importance lies in transforming wealth into a tool for growth, unity, and purpose rather than letting it become a source of division or loss.

"A legacy without a plan is a liability. True legacy is love made permanent through preparation."

The goal isn't just to accumulate wealth, but also to educate those who will inherit it, ensuring they can nurture the legacy for years to come. This is the heart of the sixth stage of creating generational wealth, where we transition from individual achievement to legacy building through the transfer of generational knowledge. It's a call to become not just custodians of wealth but also mentors for the future. By distilling personal experiences into lessons, we bridge the gap between possessing wealth and understanding it. This process transforms personal success into something far greater: a legacy that empowers and inspires generations.

When money is understood as a universal language, it becomes a resource for creating a lasting impact. However, without proper guidance, its lessons are reduced to fleeting transactions. Teaching financial edification, sharing stories of resilience, and passing on principles of purpose and stewardship are the acts that breathe life into a legacy. They ensure that the ripple started by one generation continues to expand and touch the lives of those who come afterward. It is the ultimate fulfillment of generational wealth: not merely passing down resources but equipping those who follow with the wisdom to use them well.

Stage 6: Generational Knowledge (Legacy)

Interestingly, in my years of working with various clients, I've noticed something striking. While many individuals are diligent about the basics of financial planning—they have their emergency funds sorted, actively save and invest, and even have their insurance needs covered—there's often one glaring blind spot: planning for what happens next.

One way to plan is through estate planning. To look deeper into its critical role in building generational wealth, I spoke with Martin C. Johnson, Esquire, an experienced estate planning attorney, in Episode 4 of *The New Wealth Wave Podcast*. With decades of experience helping individuals and families navigate the complexities of estate planning, Martin shared invaluable insights about how proper planning connects to generational wealth transfer.[3] He explained:

 New Wealth Wave Podcast, EP 4: Martin C. Johnson

"There is a misconception that estate planning is just a set of documents. And I hope, as you can tell from this discussion, a lot of the consulting and advice that goes into the planning is what you're paying for."

Martin also discussed the challenges that prevent many people from engaging in estate planning, particularly in underserved communities. For a lot of individuals, thinking about their eventual death or possible incapacity makes them feel very uncomfortable, which often leads to avoiding the topic. In the African American community, this reluctance is made worse by cultural discomfort and fear linked to discussions about death and disability. Martin pointed out that these attitudes come from deep-rooted historical and social causes, including trauma, mistrust of institutions, and limited knowledge passed down through generations.

This reluctance has profound consequences. Many individuals focus narrowly on wealth accumulation while delaying or avoiding the vital step of securing their legacy through estate planning. As Martin observed, this oversight not only affects the individual—it creates a ripple effect that leaves loved ones unprepared and, in some cases, jeopardizes the stability of the wealth that has been painstakingly built.

Even for those who recognize the importance of estate planning, misconceptions often hinder progress. Martin pointed out that clients frequently assume estate planning is reserved for the wealthy or the elderly. "During my client consultations, when I ask, 'Do you have an estate plan?' The answer is almost always a resounding no. Not surprising considering that estate planning is rarely discussed openly in many communities," he explained.

You Need an Estate Plan

According to a study by Caring.com, statistics reveal the challenges many communities face in achieving this ideal, particularly people of color. More than 50% of Americans do not have an estate plan in place, and the percentage is even higher among African American and Hispanic communities. Only 31% of African American adults have estate planning documents, such as a will or living trust, compared to 34% of White adults.[4]

This disparity often stems from systemic issues, including a lack of access to financial education and professional guidance, with significant implications. Families without proper planning frequently face prolonged legal battles, increased financial strain, and the emotional toll of navigating these challenges during already difficult times. Without a clear plan, assets can become tied up in the probate process. Probate is the legal process by which a deceased person's assets are distributed and debts settled, often requiring court involvement. Probate can be a costly process. In many cases, the cost of probate includes attorney fees, executor fees, and court costs, which collectively can erode the value of the estate being passed down.[5] Additionally, the time it takes to settle an estate through probate can be extensive, leaving families in limbo for months or even years while assets are tied up in the legal system.

Avoiding probate should be a top priority for families attempting to build and transfer generational wealth. Probate delays the transfer of assets and makes the process public, exposing sensitive financial details to anyone who might be interested. In contrast, properly executed estate plans—especially those that include living trusts, whether revocable or irrevocable—facilitate a smoother, private transition of assets, ensuring that families can preserve as much wealth as possible for future generations.

Take the example of Aretha Franklin, the Queen of Soul. Despite her immense wealth and fame, she passed away in 2018 without a formal will. Her estate, valued at over $80 million, became embroiled in a lengthy legal dispute among her heirs.[6] While most people may not have estates of this magnitude, the underlying lesson is universal: Failing to plan invites confusion, contention, and costly delays. The same lesson applies when we look at other high-profile figures like Chadwick Boseman and Prince, whose untimely deaths also exposed the vulnerability of unplanned estates. While these names may resonate on a global scale, the reality is that the same risks exist for everyday people. Your neighbor, your relative, or even you may face similar challenges if proper planning isn't prioritized. Estate planning isn't reserved for the wealthy; it's an essential tool for anyone seeking to secure their family's future.

Now, there's a lot of buzz about generational wealth on social media, with influencers emphasizing the importance of building assets like homes or businesses. However, they often forget to mention this: without generational knowledge, there is no true wealth passed down. Simply buying a home doesn't automatically create a legacy. Without proper planning, that property could be lost when you pass away or even if you become incapacitated.

Imagine working your entire life to build something meaningful, only to have almost half of it disappear because of avoidable legal fees and delays. For instance, in California, a $1 million estate, a figure that could easily represent the value of a modest home in many areas, would incur a minimum of $46,000 in probate fees if it went through probate. That's money taken directly from your family's inheritance—money that could have funded a grandchild's education, started a family business, or provided for your loved ones' needs! And here's the kicker: probate fees are based on the gross value of the estate, not your equity. Even if you still owe $800,000 on a $1 million house, the fee is calculated on the full $1 million.

It gets even more complicated. While the estate is tied up in probate for between 9 and 24 months, who's paying the mortgage on that house? Without a plan, your children or heirs might struggle to keep up with payments, risking foreclosure. All of this could be avoided with proper estate planning, which typically costs around $4,000—a fraction of the potential loss.

Estate planning involves much more than just financial issues. It's about making sure your loved ones are taken care of, your wishes are respected, and your legacy remains intact. Without it, families risk losing wealth and missing out on opportunities that wealth offers, such as better education, healthcare, and housing. Good planning requires a conscious effort to ensure that all aspects of your life, both big and small, align with your vision when you are no longer there to oversee them. This process demonstrates care, leaving a significant financial legacy that embodies the values, stories, and struggles that shaped your life. For some, it's about giving their children opportunities they never had. For others, it involves creating a charitable legacy or supporting causes they care about.

Consider this: everything built over a lifetime, whether it is a modest savings account, a cherished family home, or a watch passed down through generations, holds far more than material worth. Each item carries the weight of struggle, triumph, family history, and years of hard work. Yet without a clear plan, these meaningful symbols can become sources of confusion, conflict, or even fractured relationships among those left behind. This reality is both sobering and empowering. It offers an opportunity to take deliberate action now and shape a legacy that extends beyond material possessions into lasting clarity, peace, and security for future generations.

Components of an Estate Plan

Of course, estate planning can feel like a labyrinth. Terms like "living trust" or "probate" sound abstract and distant until they directly affect you. Imagine losing someone close and being left to sort through their affairs. Without a clear plan, families too often face the grueling probate process. This strain, layered on top of the grief, can fracture even the closest relationships. Yet, it's a reality many families face simply because estate planning is often viewed as something to address "someday."

However, you don't need to be a Rockefeller to need an estate plan. If you have a checking account, a car, or even just a collection of family recipes, you've got an estate. And if you've got people you love, you need a plan for it. Why wait? Planning isn't a case of anticipating the worst; it's a matter of preserving the best of what you've got. This is where something as straightforward as a "trust" comes in.

In Episode 14 of *The New Wealth Wave Podcast*, Martin explained that a trust is like a box where you place your wishes, not your belongings, and it's part of an estate plan.[7] Unlike a will, which is a set of instructions that must go through probate court and tells where your things go after you pass, a trust allows you to transfer ownership of your assets while you're still alive, keeping control over them. When you pass away, the trust ensures that your assets are transferred smoothly to your beneficiaries, without the delays or costs associated with probate.

Some people hear the word "trust" and immediately think it is for the ultra-wealthy. That's a misconception. A trust is for anyone who wants their affairs handled with care and precision, whether you're leaving behind a portfolio of investments or a small collection of mementos. Trusts aren't one-size-fits-all; they adapt to your needs and those of your heirs. A *revocable trust*, for instance, offers flexibility. It can be altered during the grantor's lifetime, allowing changes to beneficiaries, trustees, or even the terms of the trust. This adaptability makes it a popular choice for individuals who anticipate life changes or prefer to have ongoing control over their assets.

On the other hand, an *irrevocable trust* is established once and remains fixed, with no modifications permitted. While this lack of flexibility may seem restrictive, it offers significant tax benefits. The assets placed in an irrevocable trust are removed from the grantor's estate, thereby reducing estate tax liabilities and shielding assets from creditors. Complementing the trust is the pour-over will, which acts as a safety net, ensuring that any assets inadvertently left outside the trust are "poured over" into it upon your death.

Wealthy families often favor irrevocable trusts to minimize the financial burden of estate taxes on heirs. However, it's important to recognize that a living trust—revocable or irrevocable—is just one component of a comprehensive estate plan. A well-rounded estate plan encompasses a range of documents and strategies tailored to an individual's specific needs. A durable power of attorney and a healthcare directive are critical yet frequently overlooked elements. These documents ensure trusted individuals can manage your finances or make essential medical decisions if you become incapacitated.

When incorporating life insurance into an estate plan, many wonder whether naming a trust as the beneficiary is beneficial. In such cases, the trust can act as the beneficiary of the policy, providing greater control over how funds are disbursed. This strategy enables the distribution of assets according to a structured timeline, preventing young beneficiaries from prematurely squandering large sums.

Consider this example: Suppose a life insurance policy leaves a $1 million inheritance to an 18-year-old beneficiary. While the intention is generous, the reality is that such a large lump sum may overwhelm a young adult who lacks the financial maturity to manage it responsibly. Without guidance, they could make impulsive or unwise financial decisions, derailing their long-term financial stability. However, a well-structured trust can mitigate this risk. By designating a trustee to manage the funds, the inheritance can be distributed in stages—for example, a portion at age 21, another at age 25, and the remainder at age 30—while providing financial education and oversight along the way. This approach safeguards the assets and helps the beneficiary develop the skills and discipline needed to manage wealth responsibly. Of course, your situation will differ. I recommend consulting with a financial professional who can help you determine the products and services that will meet your personal needs.

Strategic trust-based planning highlights the importance of building generational wealth through careful asset allocation, establishing systems that promote responsible financial habits and long-term stability. Therefore, the core of estate planning truly resides in our choices about the individuals entrusted to carry out our wishes or step in if we cannot. Choosing a trustee or fiduciary involves more than just paperwork—it requires genuine trust. Although some families naturally choose a relative, believing it's the easiest option, this choice can sometimes create complications. For example, appointing a sibling to manage a trust might unintentionally cause conflicts among beneficiaries.

Similarly, when one or more children are named as trustees, it can lead to conflicts, particularly when financial decisions are involved. Imagine a parent designating two daughters as co-trustees while excluding a third due to financial irresponsibility. While the intention might be to protect the estate, such a decision could create resentment and escalate tensions, especially when large sums of money or high-value assets are at stake.

In such situations, appointing an impartial professional can often be the wisest choice. The goal is not to distance yourself from loved ones but to protect those relationships from unnecessary strain. A neutral party can remove emotional biases from the equation, ensuring that decisions are made objectively and aligned with the trust's terms. I have heard countless stories of families embroiled in disputes for years over estates, with money tied up in the probate process. These battles not only delay the distribution of assets but also risk permanently damaging relationships. Hiring a fiduciary can eliminate much of this drama. Fiduciaries are licensed professionals with extensive training in asset management, trust administration, and estate law.

Furthermore, they are legally bound to act in the best interests of the beneficiaries and are held to high ethical standards. While hiring a fiduciary may involve a cost, the benefits far outweigh the expense. Their expertise and neutrality can save families from lengthy legal disputes and ensure the estate plan is carried out as intended. For that reason, my wife and I hired a fiduciary to manage our estate plan. It provided our family with legacy confidence, knowing that the process would remain impartial and efficient, safeguarding our assets and relationships.

Here's something important to consider about timing when selecting trusts or fiduciaries: you must do this while fully aware and present. I can't tell you the number of times I have received calls from family members, including children, stating that their "mom needs a living trust." After conducting fact-finding, we often discover that Mom is 90 years old and the other siblings are unaware of this conversation. That's a recipe for disaster. Estate planning is not a one-size-fits-all blueprint—it's a personal roadmap shaped by your unique life, your loved ones, and your long-term vision. Suppose you're a homeowner with children, for example. In that case, your plan may center on a *revocable living trust*, which allows you to retain control of your assets while providing flexibility to adapt as life evolves—whether that means welcoming a new child, transferring property, or responding to changing family dynamics.

But no two families look exactly alike, and no two legacies should either. The right estate plan considers more than just assets—it reflects your values, your responsibilities, and the legacy you intend to leave behind. Whether you're just getting started or fine-tuning what you've already built, your estate plan should serve as a living document that grows with you and protects what matters most.

For those without children or significant assets, the focus may shift to making sure healthcare decisions and personal wishes are documented. No matter the details, the main goal is to protect your assets, lower tax liabilities, and ensure clarity and control for your loved ones and other stakeholders.

Estate planning in a broader sense extends beyond asset distribution. Critical documents, such as a certificate of trust, an advance healthcare directive, and a living will, address specific scenarios that might arise during your lifetime. The certificate of trust, for instance, serves as proof of the trust's existence and authority without revealing the entire trust document. This certificate can be presented to banks, financial institutions, or other parties as needed. The advance healthcare directive is a document specifying your medical wishes should you become incapacitated. It includes a living will that details the kind of care you desire, as well as HIPAA authorization, which allows designated individuals access to your medical information.

The importance of HIPAA authorization cannot be overstated. Under privacy laws enacted in the late 1990s and early 2000s, healthcare providers are prohibited from sharing medical information without explicit patient permission. Imagine the distress of being unable to access your spouse's or child's medical information in an emergency because the necessary authorization wasn't in place. This issue is especially prevalent for parents with children over 18. Without HIPAA authorization, parents may be left in the dark about their adult child's condition, even in critical situations. Such scenarios underscore the importance of having comprehensive estate documents that address both financial matters and medical contingencies.

Another essential component I stated earlier is the durable power of attorney. This grants a trusted individual the authority to manage your finances and business matters in the event of your incapacity. Whether paying bills, managing investments, or ensuring a business continues to run smoothly, this document can prevent significant disruptions. It's essential, however, to establish this authority while you are still of sound mind, as it cannot be granted retroactively. For example, if an accident occurs and a power of attorney hasn't been established, it's often too late to execute one effectively. The durable power of attorney typically requires a doctor's confirmation of incapacity to activate, which safeguards against misuse.

Estate planning involves additional complexities for business owners. Without proper arrangements, businesses may face probate, leading to delays and disruptions. Structuring ownership, such as transferring LLC or S Corp shares into a living trust, helps ensure business continuity and avoids probate complications.

A comprehensive estate plan should also include an assignment of personal property, memorial instructions, and a personal property memorandum. These components address the distribution of specific items, such as family heirlooms or sentimental belongings, ensuring they are allocated according to your wishes.

Significance of Life Insurance in Your Estate Plan

Equally important in estate planning is the strategic use of life insurance, which provides benefits that complement other planning tools. Its most notable advantage is that life insurance proceeds bypass probate completely, allowing immediate access to funds when they're most needed. This is especially crucial for covering immediate expenses and maintaining property after a death, ensuring that real estate assets aren't affected while the estate is being settled.

The structure of your life insurance coverage should align with your specific estate planning needs and obligations. For instance, homeowners should consider matching their term life insurance policy with their mortgage duration: a 30-year mortgage paired with a 30-year term policy of equivalent value. This strategic alignment ensures that your family can maintain the property and preserve your real estate legacy even if you're no longer there to make the payments.

Beyond traditional term insurance, there are permanent life insurance policies that offer lifetime coverage and may include a cash value component. These include Whole Life, Universal Life, Indexed Universal Life (IUL), and Variable Universal Life Insurance (VUL). Although each type operates differently, they are designed to provide death benefit protection along with the ability to accumulate cash value over time, which can be accessed under specific conditions.

- **Whole Life** offers fixed premiums and guaranteed cash value growth.
- **Universal Life** provides flexibility in premium payments and death benefits, with interest credited to the cash value.
- **Indexed Universal Life (IUL)** credits interest based on the performance of a market index (like the S&P 500), subject to caps and participation rates.
- **Variable Universal Life (VUL)** allows policyholders to invest cash value in sub-accounts similar to mutual funds, which involves market risk.

Many newer policies also include optional riders, such as long-term care or chronic illness benefits, which allow policyholders to access a portion of the death benefit while living if certain conditions are met.

These products are not one-size-fits-all, and their structure, costs, and long-term implications should be carefully reviewed. Consulting with a licensed financial professional is essential to determine whether a permanent policy aligns with your estate planning goals and financial situation. When properly structured, these policies build cash value over time, offering living benefits while maintaining death benefit protection. Many modern policies now include long-term care or chronic illness riders, effectively addressing multiple estate planning concerns through a single financial instrument.

Working with an experienced insurance professional becomes essential in structuring these policies to complement your estate plan. They can help align your coverage with both immediate needs and long-term legacy goals. In some cases, permanent life insurance can serve as a diversification tool within a broader strategy, offering potential tax advantages, liquidity options, and market-linked features, depending on the policy type and structure. However, it's essential to note that there's no guarantee that a diversified portfolio will consistently enhance overall returns or outperform a non-diversified portfolio. Diversification does not protect against market risk. That's why any insurance-based planning should be realistic, individualized, and aligned with your specific financial objectives.

Going Forward with Your Estate Plans

When considering how to proceed with estate planning, there are three main pathways: do-it-yourself (DIY) planning, document preparation services, or hiring a professional estate planning attorney. Each option has its merits and limitations, but the right choice often depends on the complexity of your situation and the long-term goals you envision for your legacy.

DIY planning, often facilitated by online tools, may seem cost-effective and straightforward. However, these tools rarely account for the nuanced legal requirements or unique circumstances that can arise. While they might suffice for individuals with fundamental needs, they often leave significant gaps that could result in costly oversights. As Martin aptly put it, "This is not something you should be dabbling in. The DIY approach might look appealing, but you have to pay the cost to be the boss."

Document preparation services, which offer customizable templates and a more structured approach, present a middle ground. These services typically cost between $2,000 and $2,500. While they provide more support than DIY options, they often lack the comprehensive customization required for complex estates or families with growing assets. As Martin pointed out, "You may be able to get this done for less than $2,500, and it could be a solid plan for you. But fast forward 10 years—if you've grown your assets, landed a better job, or have five kids, how does this fit into it? Now is probably the time to invest in a professionally curated estate plan."

The most reliable and robust option is to work with an experienced *estate planning attorney*. These professionals provide tailored guidance, ensuring your plan is enforceable and comprehensive. Estate planning attorneys can address specific needs, adapt to evolving family circumstances, and navigate the intricate legal landscape that varies from state to state. Depending on your estate's complexity, hiring a licensed attorney can cost anywhere from $3,500 to $30,000 or more, particularly for families with property in states like California, where probate laws and fees are notoriously burdensome.

The variation in cost reflects the depth of planning and expertise provided. A professionally curated plan does more than transfer assets— it also protects against potential disputes, ensures legal compliance, and offers strategic protection. As Martin emphasized, "The cost will vary depending on the complexity of your situation, but it's an investment in the security of your family and your legacy."

This investment becomes especially valuable when coordinating different parts of your estate plan. For example, your estate planning attorney should work closely with your insurance professional to ensure your life insurance portfolio aligns with your overall estate planning goals. A well-designed insurance strategy can provide the liquidity needed to cover estate taxes, balance inheritances among heirs, or ensure business continuity—all while avoiding delays and costs associated with probate. But it's not just about the expense; the quality of the plan and how well its parts work together are equally important. Many attorneys rely on templates, which can sometimes lead to mistakes. This underscores the importance of working with a professional who is familiar with state-specific probate and trust laws. For example, California's probate laws differ greatly from those of North Carolina. While the Full Faith and Credit Clause keeps your plan valid if you move to a different state, consulting an attorney in your new state can reveal opportunities to improve your plan by incorporating local benefits.

As we plan for the future holistically, we recognize that preparation is about adaptability. It's essential to keep your estate plan up to date. As a general rule, revisiting your estate plan every two to three years is critical to ensure it accurately reflects your current wishes and circumstances. Life changes, such as the birth of a grandchild, purchasing new property, relocating to a different state, or experiencing family transitions like divorce or remarriage, may require adjustments to your plan. To add a new property to a living trust, you can do this through a title company or escrow service without altering the trust's core terms.

The complexities grow when blended families are involved. These situations require careful deliberation, as partners may have differing priorities regarding the distribution of assets. For instance, one partner might wish to leave their investments solely to their biological children, while the other envisions a more inclusive approach, considering stepchildren as well. In such cases, separate trusts can provide clarity and avoid potential conflicts. However, if a joint trust is preferred, it requires both parties to align their visions, a process that can take weeks of introspection and dialogue.

As we navigate these decisions—trusts, wills, directives—it's easy to see that estate planning isn't just about finances. It's also deeply personal. It's a case of asking questions like, "What do I want my legacy to reflect?" and "How can I ease burdens for those I care about most?"

The answers aren't found in legal jargon but in the values you hold dear: fairness, protection, and love.

Many clients I've worked with, even those well-versed in other aspects of finance, struggle to differentiate these tools. I, too, was once in the financial advising business without fully appreciating the importance of an estate plan. I thought estate planning was reserved for the rich, those with sprawling estates and high net worth. It wasn't until I delved deeper into the subject that I realized anyone, regardless of their financial level, can and should have an estate plan.

The misconceptions about estate planning that stem from a lack of generational knowledge can be addressed through proper wealth transfer, as cycles of financial disorganization make it more challenging to build generational wealth. Therefore, estate planning can be summarized as the deliberate act of making provisions for transferring wealth, whether to heirs, charities, or other entities. It is more than just drafting a will; it encompasses a variety of tools and strategies to ensure your financial legacy aligns with your values and goals. When you begin to see estate planning as part of a larger financial wellness journey, you'll be able to effectively engage the process of framing it accordingly. Many believe estate planning can wait until later in life. However, life's uncertainties make early planning essential. In Episode 4 of the podcast, Martin brilliantly summarized this[8]:

New Wealth Wave Podcast, EP 4: Martin C. Johnson

"Beyond death, consider the 20% chance of becoming incapacitated and unable to make decisions effectively. These realities underscore the importance of preparing not just for death but also for life's unpredictable turns that could render you unable to continue creating, managing, and accumulating wealth."

Now, if you've looked at this as part of your financial well-being journey, you'll see that this is not just a case of having a will or an estate plan; it's a matter of laying a foundation of knowledge, so your family understands not just what you've left behind but why. Let me be frank: most people I meet in my practice haven't put a proper plan in place for their future care and asset transfer, not because they don't care, but because they don't fully understand the implications. Often left untouched, this critical piece is a vital element that can either preserve or devastate the legacy they are working so hard to build. The reality is stark. When I say "plan," I'm not just talking about having insurance. I'm talking about having meaningful conversations with your family, financial advisor, and planner about what happens when you are gone or if you need care. Many avoid these necessary conversations out of fear or discomfort, which leaves their loved ones vulnerable to emotional and financial strain after they are gone or in need of long-term care. This silence can become costly as it tends to hurt the entire family's well-being.

Managing Your Physical Health for the Long Term

A study by the Center for a Secure Retirement found that fewer than 1 in 3 individuals have planned for their long-term care needs and costs with their families.[9] This lack of preparation can undermine even the most carefully constructed financial legacy. With costs potentially exceeding $7,000 per month, long-term care can quickly drain family resources, creating a financial and emotional burden that ripples across generations. I've witnessed families struggle under the weight of these challenges, not just financially, but also in ways that profoundly affect their quality of life. The stress of caring for aging parents often extends far beyond monetary costs. It impacts relationships, with siblings and spouses grappling over who will shoulder the responsibility. These tensions can strain marriages and family dynamics, leaving caregivers emotionally and physically exhausted. This isn't mere conjecture; the statistics are clear. When examining demographics, the demand for long-term care is surging as the Baby Boomer generation ages. Even more concerning, Generation X is on track to surpass Baby Boomers in terms of care needs, creating an even larger wave of people who should be planning for this now, not later.[10]

Failing to address this critical aspect of aging can jeopardize financial stability and place an enormous strain on families. The true essence of generational knowledge thus lies in understanding that wealth preservation is as important as wealth creation. By proactively planning for long-term care, you can preserve your family's financial legacy, safeguard relationships, and reduce the stress and uncertainty that often accompany caregiving.

Therefore, the transfer of generational wealth must include the transfer of generational knowledge, encompassing the understanding of the difference between having assets and protecting those assets. This means having difficult conversations with family members about topics many prefer to avoid, such as aging, care preferences, role responsibilities, and financial preparations. It also means asking questions like, "Who will coordinate care if needed? How will we modify our living spaces? Which assets are designated for care costs?" These teachable moments demonstrate to the next generation how to think holistically about wealth preservation. They involve preserving dignity, maintaining family harmony, and ensuring the wealth you've built serves its intended purpose across generations.

Let's break this down clearly. When most people hear "long-term care," their minds immediately jump to nursing homes. That's a misconception we must address because it holds people back from proper long-term care planning, which is the kind of practical wisdom that must be passed down alongside our financial assets. Most extended care happens in people's own homes, and it's primarily non-medical. We're talking about help with daily activities that most of us take for granted. Think about your morning routine: getting out of bed, dressing, showering, and eating breakfast. These are among the activities of daily living (ADLs): transferring, toileting, bathing, dressing, eating, and managing continence. You need extended care when you require assistance with two or more of these activities or if you develop cognitive impairment like Alzheimer's, dementia, or Parkinson's, which require supervision. Unlike recovering from surgery or a temporary illness, we're talking about ongoing support and care that extends beyond 90 days—hence the term "long-term care."

The Importance of a Long-Term Care Plan

Why should you create a long-term care plan? This is where I want you to pay attention because it's not only about the money, though that's undoubtedly important. It's about protecting the people you love. This aspect of generational knowledge ensures that your family isn't caught off guard by unexpected responsibilities or financial strain. Think about it: who will step up if you need care and don't have a plan? Your spouse? Your kids? Your friends? When someone becomes a caregiver, their entire life changes. As stated earlier, without proper planning, the financial impact can devastate your legacy.

Let me paint a picture for you. Imagine you've saved $500,000 in assets to leave as a legacy for your kids and grandkids. However, an unforeseen extended care need arises, requiring $300,000 for in-home assistance or nursing services. Suddenly, the inheritance you planned to leave for your family is cut down to $200,000. And we're not talking about small amounts here; current costs can reach around $7,000 to $8,000 per month, totaling nearly $100,000 per year. The focus isn't just on losing money but also on the pain of watching your carefully planned generational wealth vanish. How long can your savings sustain that over time?

When we fail to plan for extended care, we not only compromise our own comfort but also fail to protect our family's quality of life. In Episode 8 of *The New Wealth Wave Podcast*[11], Kelly Augspurger, who is an LTC insurance specialist and certified senior advisor working nationwide to help clients and financial advisors plan for extended care, boldly stated:

New Wealth Wave Podcast, EP 8: Kelly Augspurger

"This could force the children or other loved ones to put their lives on hold and become the primary caregivers. Their physical, mental, emotional, and spiritual well-being can be severely impacted, thereby disrupting their careers, straining their marriages, and impacting their ability to build their own financial soft landing. Thus, the very people we're trying to build wealth for could end up sacrificing their financial future to care for us. This isn't the legacy any of us wants to leave."

Generational knowledge involves creating a complete framework that protects both the financial and human elements. It means teaching our children that wealth preservation isn't just a case of smart investments— it's also a matter of strategic protection through vehicles like long-term care insurance, understanding the difference between income and assets, and recognizing that the best time to plan is long before you need it.

Preparing for Your Long-Term Care

The generational transfer of knowledge often starts with communication, as wealth transfer should not be shrouded in secrecy or deferred until a crisis arises. Instead, it requires open discussions with our loved ones about our intentions, preferences, and expectations. Creating a comprehensive plan involves addressing several key elements, including family communication, living arrangements, and financial strategies. You start with having open discussions about your preferences and capabilities. If you're married or have a partner, they need to be part of this conversation. If you have children, don't assume the one living nearby will automatically become your caregiver; that's a massive assumption that could strain relationships, as it is a huge responsibility to place on someone without discussing it first.

What if they have their own family? What if they have a full-time job that demands their time and commitment? They've got their lives to live. Can they be there physically for you? Should they? Most adult children I talk to hope their parents aren't counting on them for physical care, though they might be willing to help coordinate care arrangements. Hands-on caregiving is a different story. Therefore, clarify who will oversee your care. Will it be a professional caregiver? Your spouse? Your kids? Your friends? Also, explain who will make your healthcare decisions if you are unable to do so. These roles should be assigned thoughtfully, ensuring the individuals are capable and willing to carry out your wishes.

Apart from family communication, you have to be realistic about your preferences. Where would you prefer to receive care if needed—at home, in an assisted living facility, or elsewhere? These choices have significant implications for financial planning and emotional readiness. For instance, if you choose to receive care at home, is your home suitable for aging in place? If you have a two-story house, you may need to consider accessibility. Are your doorways wide enough for a wheelchair? Is your bathroom set up for someone with limited mobility? What potential home modifications will be needed? These practical considerations can make a huge difference when care is needed.

Funding Your Long-Term Care

When it comes to paying for care, it's essential to understand your options. I always advise my clients to create a numbered list of the funds they'll use, in order of priority. If you've got a long-term care insurance policy, that's typically at the top of the list. Today, most people aren't buying massive policies; we usually look at something between $3,000 and $6,000 per month for 3-5 years. That means you might need to co-fund your care, but at least you have a foundation from which to work. Choosing which funds to use for paying for care and in what order requires a well-thought-out strategy. To make informed decisions, it's essential first to understand the different ways care can be funded, as each option comes with unique implications for your financial health and long-term plans.

One common approach is self-funding, where you pay care expenses out of pocket using your income and investments. It is the default plan for most people. While this method may seem simple and provide a sense of control, it carries significant risks and drawbacks. For example, self-funding can directly impact your cash flow, potentially limiting your ability to maintain your current lifestyle or achieve other financial goals. Consider this: can you afford an estimated $5,000 or more each month, in addition to your regular expenses? Most people cannot, which is why it is critical to explore other options. Even if you have substantial savings, there may be tax consequences when converting assets to income, particularly when withdrawing funds from retirement accounts. These withdrawals can increase your taxable income and may affect your Social Security benefits and Medicare premiums. Before reaching that point, it is essential to consult with a qualified tax advisor to discuss your specific tax situation. Taking a proactive approach can help you avoid surprises and structure your distributions to support your long-term financial well-being.

Apart from the tax implications of this approach, timing can be everything. The self-funding approach exposes you to market volatility, as you may be forced to liquidate investments during a downturn, locking in losses and jeopardizing your financial stability. Nobody wants to be forced to withdraw money from investments at a loss. Imagine a scenario where you need care during a bear market, a period when investment values, such as stocks, decline by 20% or more and remain depressed for an extended time. This environment can severely hinder wealth growth and disrupt financial plans if assets must be accessed.

Drawing from your investment portfolio under such conditions could deplete the principal quicker than expected, making it more difficult to recover when markets rebound. This approach also forces you to ensure your funds are liquid enough to access when needed. This unpredictability highlights the importance of considering alternatives that offer greater stability and security.

I often recommend a combination approach to my clients—having some insurance as a foundation while self-funding anything above and beyond what the policy covers. So, beyond self-funding, you could be looking at the option of long-term care insurance. You can think of long-term care insurance as leverage—you put in a dollar and get multiple dollars back in benefits. Additionally, these benefits are tax-free, which is a significant advantage. Some states even offer tax credits for having a policy.

An example is New York, which offers a tax credit for premiums paid for long-term care insurance. Additionally, here's something people often overlook: these policies usually include extra benefits, such as care coordination, home modifications, and caregiver training. That care coordination alone can be invaluable when your family is trying to determine the next steps.

In long-term care insurance, there are two main types you need to know about: Traditional policies and hybrid policies. *Traditional policies* are just insurance, pure and simple. They are standalone coverage. These are typically the most cost-effective option, but are also harder to qualify for from a health standpoint. Think of it as car insurance; it's a "use it or lose it" type of policy. *Hybrid policies*, on the other hand, also called linked-benefit or asset-based policies, mean that you're combining long-term care coverage with either a death benefit from life insurance or cash value from an annuity. The significant advantage here is that if you don't need care, there's still something left over for your heirs. Moreover, opting for a hybrid policy incurs a higher price than a traditional policy. However, each state's pricing is different; therefore, it's essential to consult with a financial professional who is well-versed in the laws of your state.

Speaking of life insurance, it's worth noting how the ultra-wealthy have revolutionized their approach to these policies. While standard life insurance policies are straightforward—you pay premiums, and your beneficiaries receive a death benefit—the wealthy have found ways to turn these policies into powerful financial tools. Permanent life insurance, when properly structured, can offer more than just death benefit protection. Depending on the type of policy and how premiums are funded, it may also provide tax-deferred growth, access to accumulated cash value, and liquidity options under certain conditions. Some individuals, especially those with complex financial planning needs, use these policies as part of a broader strategy to meet goals such as legacy planning, business succession, or charitable giving.

Variable life settlements and viatical settlements are prohibited. Any decision regarding a life settlement should only be made after a thorough suitability review and consultation with a licensed financial and tax professional. These tools can be complex and should never be seen as a one-size-fits-all solution, but rather as one potential option within a carefully coordinated financial plan.

Imagine having a life insurance policy with a cash value of $1 million. You could borrow $100,000 against that cash value at a remarkably low interest rate, often lower than what traditional banks offer. This borrowed money can then be invested in higher-yielding opportunities, such as the stock market. This strategy is sometimes referred to as interest rate arbitrage— the idea of borrowing against the cash value of a life insurance policy at a lower rate and investing the borrowed funds at a potentially higher rate of return. For example, if you borrow $100,000 from a policy loan and invest it in the market, and the market achieves a hypothetical return of 7%, while the policy itself continues to earn a hypothetical internal rate of 5% on the full cash value (e.g., $1 million), it may appear that you're benefiting from both growth streams simultaneously.

This creates the potential for a positive spread between the loan interest rate (e.g., 3%) and the external investment return (e.g., 7%). However, it's essential to understand that:

- This is a hypothetical example and does not represent any specific investment or insurance product.
- Rates of return are not guaranteed and will vary based on market performance, policy type, and the terms of the loan.
- The example does not reflect the deduction of any fees, expenses, or insurance charges that may be applicable to either the insurance policy or the investment.
- Policy loans accrue interest and reduce both the death benefit and cash value if not repaid.
- Actual results may vary and are subject to potential impacts from tax implications, market fluctuations, or changes in interest rates.

This strategy is highly complex as it involves multiple risks, including the risk that the investment underperforms or the loan becomes unsustainable over time.

The ultra-wealthy often establish life insurance policies for their children and grandchildren, creating a financial legacy that ensures wealth continues flowing through future generations. This approach to generational wealth-building requires patience and strategic thinking, but the long-term benefits can be substantial. Here's something interesting about policy pricing: Women pay more for long-term care insurance than men of the same age. This is because women typically live longer and tend to go on claim and stay on claim longer than men. It's the opposite of life insurance, where men pay more. Insurance companies must account for this increased risk, which is reflected in the premiums.

In certain circumstances, a life settlement may be considered as part of a broader financial review. A life settlement involves selling an existing, in-force fixed life insurance policy to a third party for a lump sum that is generally greater than the policy's surrender value, but less than the death benefit. This option is typically explored when the policy is no longer needed or affordable, and may be suitable for select clients based on age, health status, and financial objectives.

Life settlements are not suitable for everyone and should be carefully evaluated in consideration of factors such as risk tolerance, tax status, liquidity needs, time horizon, other insurance needs, and the potential impact on beneficiaries. Decisions should be made in consultation with a licensed financial and legal professional. The costs and risks involved can be significant, making professional guidance essential. *Variable life settlements and viatical settlements are prohibited.*

Health Savings Accounts (HSAs) are another valuable tool often overlooked when considering ways to fund long-term care. These accounts are amazing because they offer triple tax advantages: You contribute with pre-tax dollars, the money grows tax-free, and you can withdraw it tax-free for qualified medical expenses. And here's the kicker: You can use HSA funds to pay for long-term care insurance premiums. Additionally, unlike flexible spending accounts, the balance rolls over from year to year, allowing you to build a significant resource over time.

Reverse Mortgages

Let's talk honestly about reverse mortgages.

I'll admit, for a long time, I didn't trust them. And I wasn't alone— reverse mortgages had a reputation, and rightfully so. How they were marketed in the early days often caused confusion, and in some cases, harm. But like many financial tools, they've evolved. And the more I've studied them, especially in the context of how we build and preserve wealth later in life, the more I've come to see their value when used responsibly.

Here's the bottom line: If you're 62 or older and own your home, a reverse mortgage lets you tap into your home's equity and turn it into tax-free cash. You're not selling your house. You're not taking on a monthly payment. You're simply accessing value you've already built, without having to move.

In essence, you can use the money as needed: for medical bills, insurance, daily living expenses, or to support family members. The loan isn't due until you pass away or move out of the home for 12 consecutive months. At that time, the house is usually sold to repay it.

And here's what's changed for the better: Today's reverse mortgages come with protections. You'll never owe more than your home is worth—even if the housing market shifts. And as long as you're keeping up with property taxes, insurance, and basic upkeep, no one can force you out of your home.

It's not the right fit for everyone. However, for many older adults—especially those who wish to age in place—it can be a meaningful way to maintain financial security without liquidating other assets or relying on family support.

We need to stop thinking of equity as something we only pass on to others. Sometimes, it's also something we can *live on*.

Other Programs to Consider

Another way to pay for care is through VA benefits. For veterans, VA benefits might be available, especially if you have service-connected disabilities. The number of benefits you can receive typically depends on means testing—the less income and assets you have, the higher priority you'll have. While I wouldn't recommend relying solely on VA benefits for extended care, they can be a helpful supplement to other funding sources.

Then, there are government programs such as Medicaid. Medicaid is the largest payer of long-term care in the United States; however, it's essential to recognize that this is a safety net, not a comprehensive planning strategy. It's designed for people who have exhausted their resources and are in crisis. While it primarily covers nursing home care, some states do offer waivers for home care, though waiting lists can be extensive.

Medicaid has strict eligibility requirements. In most states, applicants must spend down their assets to qualify. For example, in Ohio, a single applicant typically cannot have more than $2,000 in countable assets. Certain items, such as a primary residence (up to a specific equity limit), one vehicle, and personal belongings, are exempt. Medicaid also enforces a five-year look-back period to review any asset transfers, gifts, or title changes made within five years of the application. If any disqualifying transfers are found, a penalty period may be imposed. They could say, for instance, "We've noticed that just last year you transferred assets to your daughter. As a result, the penalty period will be activated." This penalty period means you're disqualified from applying for Medicaid. They use a formula to figure out how long you have to wait to reapply for Medicaid, which means you're paying out of pocket during that time.

Something many people don't realize about Medicaid is the estate recovery program. After you pass away, Medicaid will try to recover the costs of your care from your estate. This often means they'll put a claim on your home if you still own one. It's their way of getting reimbursed for the care they provide. Assuming they spent thousands, maybe hundreds of thousands of dollars on your care, Medicaid will actively try to recover this cost, often by selling your home. This can completely derail any plans for passing that home down to your children or grandchildren. Let me clear up a common misconception about Medicare. Medicare is health insurance for individuals aged 65 and older, but it is not designed to cover long-term care. I can't tell you how often I've heard people say, "Oh, I've got Medicare, I'm covered." Medicare will only cover skilled nursing care and certain types of rehabilitation. It won't cover the kind of ongoing, non-medical care we're discussing, which includes long-term care needs.

So, talking to your family about your preferences is the "who," the "what," and the "how." *How will I pay for this? What finances do I have? What funds do I have to pay for it? If I have a policy, it will be at the top of the list before others.* Each of these methods has its benefits and limitations.

That being said, your strategy for converting your assets to income must take into consideration the tax consequences. This includes determining which assets to liquidate first, understanding their tax implications, and aligning these decisions with your legacy goals. The key to preparing for successful long-term care and wealth preservation lies in having these plans early and revisiting them often. Life is dynamic, and circumstances evolve, but laying a foundational strategy ensures that even if the exact path deviates from the plan, there's a reliable baseline to guide decisions. This proactive approach protects both your wealth and your family's well-being.

As you plan and have these conversations with your family to develop a comprehensive strategy, it's important to evaluate your current financial situation, understand the costs of care in your area, and weigh the trade-offs of each funding option. A layered approach that combines multiple funding sources may be the most effective solution, offering flexibility, stability, and preparedness. For instance, you could reserve self-funding for initial expenses, rely on long-term care insurance for more substantial needs, and leave government programs as a last resort.

Developing Strategies for Passing Generational Knowledge

Having had these discussions over the years, bringing all this together ensures that everyone is prepared. This is because you would have encouraged your family to ask questions and share their thoughts, building mutual understanding and trust and reducing the likelihood of conflicts or misinterpretations later. In that series of discussions, you should have also talked about the locations of documents. Where is your estate plan? Who is your attorney? Who is your financial advisor? You should dive in deeply. In that way, your family knows who to talk to or where to look when the time comes that you need help. This is not just a single conversation but an ongoing dialogue that adjusts to changes in circumstances, needs, and priorities.

As plans are revisited and refined, they become a living document—a blueprint for action. This is important because even if reality doesn't perfectly align with the written plan, its foundation allows your family to approach decision-making confidently. It enables them to say, "Hey, Mom and Dad already talked about this. We have their plan right here. This is what they wanted." That clarity can alleviate stress and provide a sense of direction during challenging times. Passing on wealth without imparting the accompanying knowledge is like giving someone a GPS with no clear coordinates or an understanding of how to navigate. This is why it's essential to teach your children or heirs not just the value of what they will inherit but how to sustain and grow it. Discuss the principles of financial literacy, the importance of investments, and the significance of making informed decisions. When you embed these lessons into your family's legacy, you'll create a foundation for wealth and wisdom. This wisdom will guide future generations, ensuring they have the resources to preserve and expand upon what they inherit. However, alongside imparting financial knowledge, it's equally important that your comprehensive plan is established with policies tailored to your family's needs, as stated earlier.

This is where we begin to see how all these pieces fit together in the broader context of generational knowledge and wealth transfer. Every decision you make about long-term care or estate plans doesn't just affect you; it creates ripples that impact your entire family's financial future. It's like laying down stepping stones for the next generation to follow or, in some cases, putting down obstacles they'll have to navigate. So, who should consider long-term care insurance? If you're between the ages of 45 and 65, especially as you approach retirement, now is the optimal time to evaluate whether it fits into your financial plan.

Age and health are critical factors—starting while you're younger and healthier expands your options and reduces costs. Waiting until retirement or into your 70s could limit your eligibility, as insurers may decline coverage due to age or pre-existing health conditions. This planning is especially relevant if you are risk-averse, have witnessed family members require extended care, or own a business that could benefit from tax advantages. For instance, C corporations can deduct 100% of long-term care insurance premiums, making it a potentially strategic investment. For most individuals, the optimal time to purchase coverage is around age 50, assuming foundational financial elements such as an emergency fund, savings, and insurance are already in place.

However, it's crucial to prioritize financial stability before purchasing long-term care insurance. If you haven't built a solid emergency fund, established basic savings, or secured life and disability insurance, it may be prudent to focus on these areas first. Likewise, those without a reliable income or those receiving (or likely to receive) Medicaid may find that other strategies better align with their needs. Evaluating your specific circumstances and goals is essential before committing to any policy. Therefore, it's necessary to research, seek professional advice, and assess your financial situation to determine the most effective strategy to meet your short-term needs and long-term goals.

When considering a policy, four primary components merit close attention. First is the benefit amount—the monthly income provided by the insurer, which typically ranges between $3,000 and $6,000 for most individuals. Next is the benefit period, which defines the duration of the benefits, normally spanning three to five years. Inflation protection is another critical element, ensuring your benefits grow over time to counteract rising care costs. Finally, the elimination period, typically set at 90 days, serves as a waiting period before benefits take effect. While more extended elimination periods can reduce premiums, they also increase out-of-pocket costs; therefore, balancing affordability with coverage needs is crucial.

When considering life insurance or annuities, it's important to understand that **insurability isn't guaranteed**. Insurance companies ultimately decide who qualifies for coverage, and factors like your health, occupation, or lifestyle may result in being declined. That's why early planning matters—because waiting until there's a medical concern or significant life change can limit your options.

As you explore coverage, you'll come across something called riders. These are optional add-ons to a base insurance or annuity contract—features that can offer extra protection or flexibility. Some are included automatically, but others come with additional costs, conditions, or limitations. It's crucial to read your contract carefully and ask questions before making a decision.

For couples, especially, shared benefit riders can be an innovative solution. These riders enable both spouses to access a single pool of benefits, providing more flexibility and reducing the need to purchase two separate, higher-cost policies. It's an example of how customized planning can make a meaningful difference, not just in coverage, but also in overall cost efficiency and confidence in the future.

Remember: All guarantees depend on the financial strength and claims-paying ability of the issuing insurance company. Choose wisely, review thoroughly, and build your plan around your needs, not just the products being offered.

The reality is that many of us will likely need some form of care as we age; modern medicine has extended life expectancy, with many people living well into their 80s or beyond. Planning for this eventuality isn't just about finances; it's also about preserving dignity, autonomy, and family relationships. Begin by discussing preferences with your loved ones early on. Where would you prefer to receive care? Who might provide it? How will you pay for it? Document your plan, understanding that it may evolve, and involve your family in these conversations to ensure alignment and clarity.

It's also critical not to delay exploring insurance options until health issues arise. Timing and health status significantly impact eligibility and premiums. One of the first steps I take with clients is to complete a health pre-screen form to determine whether insurance is a viable option. A declined application can make securing coverage with other providers more challenging, so addressing this proactively is vital.

In essence, planning for long-term care isn't just a case of protecting wealth; it's a matter of safeguarding your family from the emotional and financial burdens of unplanned care. A well-thought-out plan ensures that your wealth serves its intended purpose—providing security, opportunities, and a lasting legacy. Families who approach these conversations openly and thoughtfully tend to preserve a greater portion of their wealth across generations. Contrary to popular narratives that focus solely on accumulating wealth, the real power of planning lies in creating options, maintaining control, and aligning financial decisions with family values and goals. It means empowering your family with the ability to handle future uncertainties with confidence and grace.

The Intersection of Legacy and Care

The truth is that generational wealth transfer is as much about values as it is about assets. What principles do you want your family to embody? What story do you want your financial legacy to tell? These are questions that go beyond numbers and require thoughtful reflection. As you work on strategies to preserve your wealth, consider the lessons learned from your financial journey. Perhaps it's the discipline of saving, the courage to invest, or the resilience to recover from setbacks. These are the intangible assets that shape financial outcomes and family character. Always remember that care and legacy are not opposites but complementary forces. We transform the narrative by integrating care planning into our estate through legacy-building efforts. We move from a reactive to a proactive approach, ensuring that preventable struggles do not mar the stories and values we leave behind.

In this sense, the intersection of legacy and care requires balance. It means recognizing that while we cannot control every aspect of the future, we can establish a framework that guides those we leave behind. The focus is on making peace with the inevitability of aging and life's unpredictability while taking steps to ensure our loved ones are prepared to face these challenges without sacrificing the legacy we've worked so hard to create.

This brings us back to the three major phases of life we must plan for: *living too long, dying too soon, and becoming disabled along the way.* It's often the second and third phases that can derail even the most carefully crafted financial plans. Yet, they also offer the greatest opportunity to model financial wisdom for the next generation. By creating a comprehensive plan, you're not just protecting yourself; you're teaching your children and grandchildren valuable lessons about the power of proactive planning over reactive crisis management. You're showing them how to evaluate and guard against significant financial risks, the importance of having challenging but necessary family conversations, the responsibility of caring for both themselves and their loved ones, and how to balance self-reliance with the innovative use of insurance and other financial tools.

This knowledge transfer is vital because we live in a time of significant demographic shifts. Baby Boomers are entering retirement, and Generation X is following closely behind. Each generation faces unique challenges and needs. The solutions that worked for our parents' generation might not work for us, and what works for us might not work for our children.

As we conclude this discussion on building your financial legacy through effective planning for the future, I want you to consider this as just one part of a larger legacy-building process. Everything we've discussed, from understanding the different types of care to exploring various payment options and creating comprehensive plans, is foundational knowledge that needs to be passed down alongside your actual assets.

The next chapter, which focuses on the final stage of the model, will address the concept of generational wealth. For now, remember that everything we've covered from Stage 1 to Stage 6 forms the bedrock for generational wealth. After all, the best plan in the world won't mean much if it gets derailed by unexpected care costs or family conflicts over caregiving responsibilities and inheritance. Creating your financial legacy isn't just a matter of leaving a trail for others to follow; it's a case of blazing a clear path that makes the journey easier for those who come after you. Understanding and addressing extended care needs helps you remove one of the biggest potential obstacles from that path, making it more likely that your family's financial and intellectual wealth will continue to grow and thrive across generations.

To support this process, consider leveraging tools like the Family Roadmap, which I've developed as a guide for extended care planning and end-of-life preparation. This roadmap provides a structured framework to help you consider the essential details. It emphasizes proactive preparation, prompting the user to address critical questions, such as the location of crucial documents, whether an estate plan exists, and identifying key professionals, including attorneys and financial advisors. By creating a centralized reference point, your family can avoid the stress and confusion that often arise in moments of urgency, ensuring that your loved ones have access to clear instructions and critical resources. Additionally, the roadmap encourages you to delve deeper into your long-term care planning by documenting your wishes regarding extended care insurance options, preferred facilities, and financial strategies. This facilitates smoother transitions and reinforces the importance of open communication among family members, supporting an environment of trust and preparedness.

This brings us full circle in the Seven-Stage Generational Wealth Model©. The model emphasizes that generational wealth cannot exist without generational knowledge. While many conversations focus on accumulating wealth, the planning aspect is often overlooked. Stage 6 of the model bridges this gap, encouraging individuals to see planning for the future as a cornerstone of their financial footprints. Ultimately, planning encompasses not only asset management but also the effective transfer of values and purpose. It's also a tool for financial stewardship. When done thoughtfully, it ensures that your legacy will live on, not just in material wealth but also in the wisdom that shapes future generations.

Now, take some time to plan for your future. You're protecting your financial future while creating a blueprint for financial success that will benefit your family for generations to come.

Family Roadmap Worksheet: Extended Care and End-of-Life Planning

This worksheet is designed to help you organize and document essential information for extended care and end-of-life planning. Use it as a guide to ensure your loved ones have clarity and access to critical details when the time comes.

Personal Information

- Full Name: _____

- Date of Birth: _____

- Contact Information: _____
  (Phone, Email, Address)

- Emergency Contact(s):

  - Name: _____

  - Relationship: _____

  - Phone Number: _____

  - Email Address: _____

- Primary Care Physician:

  - Name: _____

  - Phone Number: _____

  - Email Address: _____

Legal and Estate Planning

- Do you have an estate plan? (Yes/No): _____

- Estate Plan Location: _____

- Date Last Updated: _____

- Key Legal Documents:

  - Will or Living Will: _____

  - Trust Documents: _____

  - Power of Attorney: _____

  - Health Care Proxy or Advance Directive: _____

- Attorney Information:

  - Name: _____

  - Phone Number: _____

  - Email Address: _____

Financial Information

- Financial Advisor:

  - Name: _____

  - Phone Number: _____

  - Email Address: _____

- Accounts and Assets:

  - Checking/Savings Accounts: _____

  - Investment Accounts: _____

  - Insurance Policies (Life, Health, Long-Term Care): _____

  - Retirement Plans (401(k), IRA, Pension Plans): _____

- Debts and Obligations:
    - Mortgages, Loans, or Credit Card Details: _____

Long-Term Care Planning

- Long-Term Care Insurance Policy:
    - Provider: _____
    - Policy Number: _____
    - Terms: _____
- Preferred Care Settings:
    - Homecare (Yes/No): _____
    - Assisted Living Facility (Yes/No): _____
    - Nursing Home (Yes/No): _____
    - Other Preferences: _____
- Designated Caregivers:
    - Name: _____
    - Contact Details: _____

Key Document Locations

- Birth Certificate: _____
- Marriage Certificate: _____
- Tax Records: _____
- Property Deeds: _____
- Vehicle Titles: _____

Communication and Preferences

- Funeral Preferences:

    ○ Burial or Cremation: _____

    ○ Prepaid Arrangements? (Yes/No, Details): _____

    ○ Preferred Funeral Home: _____

    ○ Specific Wishes for Ceremony or Memorial: ____

- Obituary Preferences:

    ○

- Family Communication Plan:

    ○ Who Should Be Contacted (Family, Friends, etc.)? _____

    ○ Instructions for Sharing Updates or Plans: _____

Additional Notes

- Use this space for any other important information or preferences:

    ○

    ○

Instructions

This worksheet is a guide for your family and qualified advisors. Keep it updated and stored in a secure but accessible location. Share copies with key individuals, such as your attorney, financial advisor, and immediate family.

FINAL STAGE:

Creating your Financial Footprints (Legacy and Sustainability) - Future

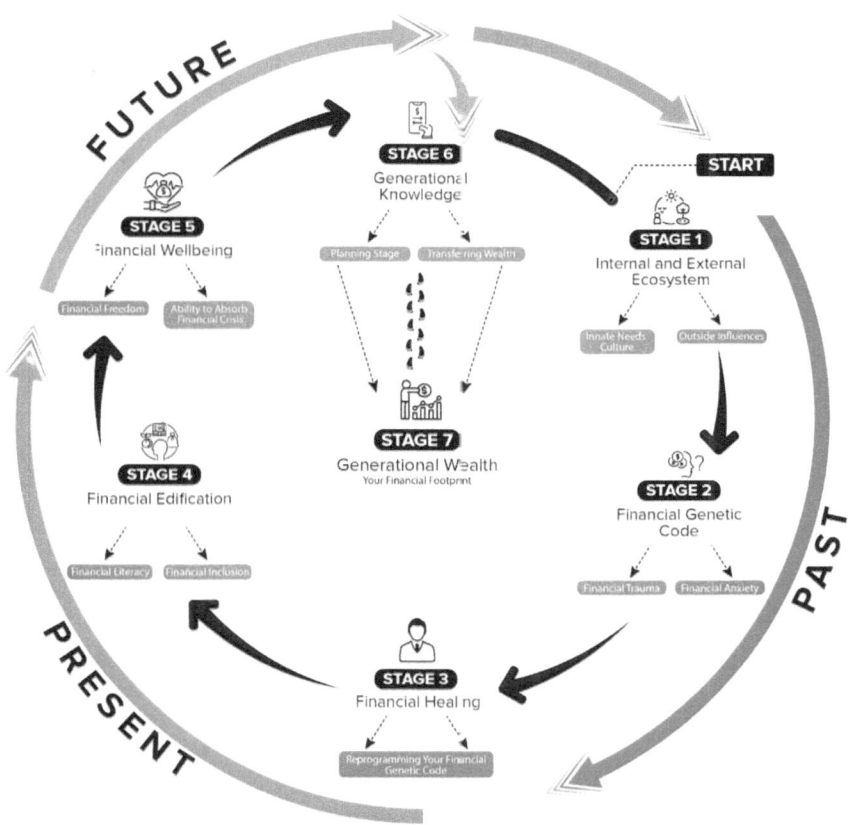

Chapter 7:
Creating Your Financial Footprints

"Wealth is not new. All wealth is diversified from wealth." —John Stuart Mill

Creating generational wealth is a fulfilling journey requiring patience, strategy, and a forward-thinking mindset. It's essential to acknowledge that generational wealth isn't built overnight; it's a process that can span multiple lifetimes. However, even if you're starting with limited resources, you can lay the groundwork for a legacy that benefits your loved ones. A key aspect of generational wealth is shifting from the traditional mindset of simply passing down money through a will. This often results in fleeting gains as it lacks the structure to preserve and grow wealth over time. Instead, the focus should be on establishing a financial ecosystem that empowers future generations to thrive.

As we advance to the seventh and final stage of our model, we turn our focus to the ultimate goal: creating and sustaining generational wealth. This stage builds upon the foundational principles established in the previous six stages to leave a lasting financial legacy that endures through time and transcends generations.

In my opinion, the true strength of the Seven-Stage Generational Wealth Model© lies in its adaptability. What makes it so impactful is its ability to meet individuals exactly where they are at any given moment in their journey. The model is designed to be flexible, allowing individuals to enter at any of the six stages and move fluidly between each stage as their unique needs and circumstances evolve. For instance, someone might need to focus on estate planning while still working on financial healing or literacy. That's perfectly fine—taking the step to establish an estate plan is vital, regardless of where you are in the process.

It's essential to remember that our efforts are not merely about completing paperwork, but about securing a legacy that extends beyond our lifetimes. The focus is on ensuring that the wealth you are working so diligently to build does not dissipate due to poor planning or lack of foresight. This highlights the crucial importance of being equipped with generational knowledge. When we recognize that generational knowledge serves as the foundation for creating generational wealth, we begin to view our plans not as expenses but as investments in the future. This shift in perspective transforms wealth-building from a solitary goal into a holistic mission that prioritizes sustainability, legacy, and the empowerment of future generations.

Stage 7: Generational Wealth

Once you've completed the first six stages of the model, or as you continue working to understand your Financial Genetic Code, heal past wounds, and gain essential knowledge, you now arrive at the summit: creating genuine generational wealth. This isn't the end of your journey; it marks the beginning of something far greater. True generational wealth is not just about what you accumulate but about the enduring impact you create for those who follow.

Stage 7 is where all the pieces start coming together. Remember back in Stage 1 when we discussed your internal and external ecosystems? Now, you're creating a new ecosystem that will outlive you, thanks to the reprogramming of your Financial Genetic Code, which you were introduced to in Stage 3 of the model. Your loved ones won't see money as a trouble to avoid but a tool for empowerment. This is more than just your personal financial success; it creates a lasting financial footprint that paves the way for the next generation. It involves building a legacy that continues to grow long after you're gone.

Yet, I can't tell you how often I've seen families focus solely on accumulating wealth while completely ignoring the human element. We've all read the headlines or witnessed it firsthand: parents obsess over optimizing investment portfolios, negotiating tax strategies, or chasing the next lucrative deal, yet they never pause to teach their children the universal language that money speaks. It's like planting a lush garden and refusing to show the next generation how to water it, prune it, or recognize the weeds that could choke it. Without that knowledge, the garden (no matter how vibrant it may be today) will inevitably wither. Wealth without wisdom is just a ticking clock.

Legacy: The Cycle of Wealth

The real secret to Stage 7 lies in understanding that generational wealth is more than just a concept; it is a living, breathing cycle that can expand, contract, or stagnate depending on the actions of each generation. Now, imagine wealth as a circle passed down through your lineage. When we see generational wealth as a cycle—a continuous loop of inheritance and influence that shapes our financial reality and the legacy we leave behind—we begin to embrace the need for constant nurturing, adaptation, and growth.

"Generational wealth is not just about passing money—it's about multiplying wisdom, values, and opportunity in every life you touch."

Think about the most successful family businesses you know. They didn't survive by accident; they thrived because each generation was prepared to take the reins and add its value to what came before. This goes beyond simply passing down money; it involves the transfer of resources, wisdom, values, and opportunities from one generation to the next, as we explored in Stage 6 of the model.

Just as a small pebble creates ripples in a pond, the wealth (or lack thereof) you inherit will determine the initial size of your circle. However, here's the power of this cycle: You can influence its size, growth, and direction. To illustrate this, let's examine the story of the Ford Motor Company. This successful enterprise has evolved through generations, demonstrating how one family's decisions shaped its trajectory and secured its legacy. Henry Ford founded the company in 1903, a visionary who revolutionized the automotive industry by introducing the assembly line, making cars affordable for the average American family.[1] His leadership laid the foundation for a business that was innovative and financially robust.

As Ford's children and grandchildren inherited the business, they didn't simply rely on the legacy built by their predecessors. Instead, they made their own contributions. For instance, when Henry Ford passed the reins to his son, Edsel Ford, in the 1920s, the company faced new challenges and opportunities. However, Edsel brought a different perspective, emphasizing design and style, which led to the creation of iconic models, such as the Lincoln Zephyr. While his tenure was not without challenges, Edsel's efforts preserved the company's stability, allowing it to weather economic storms.

The legacy continued with Henry Ford II, who inherited the business after Edsel's untimely death following World War II. Through his leadership, Ford recovered from the Great Depression and underwent significant restructuring to modernize its operations. Henry II focused on building a professional management team and reinvested profits into research and development. This shift turned Ford into a global powerhouse, ensuring the family's wealth and influence extended far beyond the United States.

Fast forward to the present, and members of the Ford family remain actively involved in the company. Bill Ford Jr., the great-grandson of Henry Ford, has guided the company into the era of sustainability and electric vehicles, ensuring that Ford Motor Company remains relevant in a rapidly changing market. Each generation built on the previous one's successes while adapting to their era's demands, demonstrating how the generational wealth cycle grows wider and more impactful when nurtured and expanded.

Generational wealth, like a successful business, is a living entity created with a purpose. It extends beyond the rat race of accumulating wealth and striving to maintain it. It needs nurturing, guidance, and periodic reinvention to stay relevant. However, many people tend to stumble here; they think generational wealth involves preserving what they've built. That's a recipe for stagnation.

True generational wealth is constantly evolving. Generational wealth grows, changes, and adapts over time, much like life itself. Your grandparents' idea of wealth might have included owning a home and having a stable pension. Today, wealth may encompass digital assets, intellectual property, or sustainable investments. Staying informed about how money can grow is essential to remaining relevant on this ongoing journey of wealth creation and expansion.

As we consider generational wealth a continuous cycle, in its simplest form, it begins with an initial inheritance, whether it is material wealth, knowledge, or even a lack thereof. As discussed in Stage 1 of the model, everyone begins their financial journey with some "Encoded Financial Behaviors," even if it's a story of scarcity. Your financial past shapes your current mindset, determining your future prospects. Whether you come from wealth, lack, or somewhere in between, your relationship with money has been influenced by the stories and habits passed down to you. That's why when poverty is passed down, we call it *generational poverty*.

In contrast, when wealth and opportunity are transferred, it forms the foundation of *generational wealth*. Therefore, the size of the circle you inherit depends on what was passed to you. The circle starts wide for those who inherit substantial resources, providing more room for growth and influence. However, if a person begins with little to nothing—perhaps just a small dot—it is their responsibility to expand that circle.

Recent studies by the Federal Reserve show that families who receive inheritances are more likely to start businesses, invest in education, and purchase homes, all crucial stepping stones to building lasting wealth.[2] However, the stark reality is that only 30% of American households report ever receiving an inheritance, with the median transfer value among recipients being approximately $83,000.[3] This statistic might seem discouraging. Still, it illuminates an important truth: your starting point doesn't determine your destination. Every financial decision you make today either expands or contracts your circle of influence, regardless of its initial size.

Many people begin their journey with generational poverty, characterized by a lack of wealth, knowledge, or opportunities that have been passed down from previous generations. While it may seem like an insurmountable barrier, it is not an excuse to remain stagnant.

Just because the previous generation didn't prepare well for you is not enough reason to resign yourself to their fate. Instead, it's an opportunity for you to break the cycle of generational poverty and expand your circle, thereby choosing to ensure that your children inherit a larger circle of wealth than you had. This intentional act will empower you to become the starting point of a new lineage of wealth.

Recent research shows that children whose parents are in the bottom 20% of income distribution have only a 7.5% chance of reaching the top

20% in their lifetime.[4] However, those who implement intentional wealth-building strategies, as those shared in previous chapters of this book, regardless of their starting point, can dramatically improve these odds for their children.

The Shift from Wealth Preservation to Expansion

The beauty of legacy, therefore, lies in the "next steps," and perhaps the most important part of this cycle of generational wealth—the shift from preservation to expansion. Each generation builds on the work of the previous one, ensuring the cycle of wealth continues to grow by creating a greater positive impact for future generations.

As we've seen in the previous chapters, preservation often emphasizes risk mitigation—shielding assets from erosion due to inflation, taxes, or poor financial decisions. It is a vital foundation, ensuring that the hard-earned resources of one generation are not squandered in the next. However, history shows us that preserved wealth often stagnates without strategic expansion. Families that fail to embrace opportunities for growth risk losing relevance and purchasing power in a rapidly changing economic landscape.

The transition to wealth expansion begins with adopting a proactive, growth-oriented mindset. While preservation asks, *"How do we keep what we have?"* expansion asks, *"How do we create more and amplify our impact?"* This requires embracing calculated risks, diversifying income streams, and investing in innovation (Stage 4). Expansion is not a case of reckless ambition but a matter of aligning your financial decisions with long-term goals and opportunities. For example, many successful families transition from preservation to expansion by investing in emerging markets, supporting entrepreneurship within the family, or encouraging philanthropic ventures that generate social impact and financial returns. The Rockefeller family, for instance, exemplifies this strategy. Their transition from oil tycoons to pioneers in education, public health, and environmental sustainability highlights how expansion can redefine a family's legacy.

Maintaining this alignment with your family's core values while exploring new frontiers raises yet another challenge. Expansion does not mean abandoning the principles that have guided your family's journey—it means building upon them. For instance, a family rooted in philanthropy might explore impact investing, combining financial returns with measurable social or environmental outcomes. This approach preserves the family's legacy and amplifies its influence across generations.

Additionally, your family must recognize that expansion requires flexibility. The strategies that worked in one era may not suffice in another. Therefore, adapting to new technologies, industries, and societal shifts is essential for sustained growth. Families that embrace a culture of lifelong learning and adaptability are better positioned to thrive in an evolving world. This shift from preservation to expansion is not just a financial strategy but also an act of stewardship. Expansion ensures that wealth not only endures but also flourishes, touching lives far beyond the immediate family.

What about those who choose to direct their wealth outside of familial lines? Philanthropy often plays a significant role in legacy building. Andrew Carnegie's *"Gospel of Wealth"* philosophy advocated for the redistribution of wealth to benefit society at large.[5] Similarly, individuals like Warren Buffett and Mackenzie Scott have donated billions to causes aimed at improving education, health, and economic equity. These actions are not an abandonment of legacy but a redefinition of its scope, extending the circle of wealth beyond family to create a lasting societal impact.[6] The decision to expand the circle beyond one's immediate heirs requires a nuanced understanding of the responsibility that comes with wealth. It underscores that generational wealth is not merely a matter of passing on assets but also a case of creating a legacy of influence and empowerment.

A Personal Role in the Cycle

However, not every generation is guaranteed to add value. Some may contract the circle, limiting the opportunities for those who follow, by either mismanagement, poor decision-making, complacency, or an absence of values and financial literacy passed down alongside the wealth (Stages 1 and 2). We see this manifest in the form of anxiety and trauma (Stage 2), fear of missing out, *keeping up with the Joneses* mentality that is prevalent among Millennials and Gen Z, or in a passive approach to money management, such as avoiding budgeting or financial planning which stem from the belief that one's actions have little impact on financial well-being (Stage 5). In extreme cases, it can lead to neglect of financial health, such as ignoring debts or failing to save for the future.

Studies consistently indicate that 70% of wealthy families lose their wealth by the second generation and 90% by the third—a phenomenon often referred to as "shirtsleeves to shirtsleeves in three generations."[7] This serves as a reminder that no matter how substantial, wealth cannot sustain itself without intentionality and preparation. The active choices of each individual determine whether the circle of wealth will expand or shrink in their time. This is why I always emphasize that your actions today don't just affect you; they influence future generations. To create a lasting impact, you must shift your mindset from merely safeguarding resources to actively expanding them. This shift requires a balance between cautious stewardship and bold innovation, ensuring that your wealth becomes a catalyst for growth rather than a static inheritance.

Passing on wealth to the next generation is not so much about the money as it is about reprogramming a new Financial Genetic Code

(Stage 3) by creating an ecosystem where your family, community, and even society can thrive. Such an ecosystem includes a robust framework of financial edification (Stage 4), shared family values through generational knowledge, and mechanisms for wealth protection, such as trusts, insurance, and estate plans (Stage 6). When done right, this system promotes resilience, adaptability, and a collective commitment to long-term goals that create generational wealth (Stage 7).

The question is not whether you are part of the cycle—it's how you will influence it. Will you expand the circle for future generations or allow it to shrink under your watch?

Whether you inherit a large fortune or begin with nothing but your determination, you are part of the generational wealth cycle. Your starting point reflects the financial foundation influenced by those before you, as we saw in Stage 1 (Internal and External Ecosystem). Yet, your role is essential because the size and direction of the circle in your generation depend entirely on your choices.

If you expand the circle, you leave an inheritance that provides not just material comfort but also the tools and opportunities for future generations to thrive. If you allow it to contract through inaction or mismanagement, you diminish the opportunities for those who come after you. It is your responsibility to recognize this cycle and deliberately choose to influence it in a positive way.

The difference between those who are remembered and those who fade into obscurity is often defined by their willingness to create financial footprints. Through these footprints, their names endure, their legacies live on, and their influence continues to ripple outward, impacting lives far beyond their own, whether within their families, communities, or society at large. This understanding is essential for those born into generational poverty, whose circle might feel nonexistent. Poverty is not an immutable curse; it is a challenge to overcome. Many individuals have broken the cycle of poverty through education, entrepreneurship, and intentional financial planning.

The Five Financial Professionals and Their Roles

Achieving generational wealth requires collaboration with specialized financial professionals who address specific aspects of financial health, growth, and legacy building. Consulting with them will ensure you move seamlessly from internal self-awareness to building lasting generational wealth as you journey into prosperity.

These professionals include *financial therapists, financial educators, financial counselors, financial advisors, and financial planners.* Remember, multiple professionals can work together to address the multifaceted needs of generational wealth and combining their expertise can form a powerful synergy, bridging the gap between preservation and expansion.

The key is ensuring that all parties collaborate effectively with open communication and a shared understanding of your unique vision for wealth. By engaging these professionals, you can unlock the full potential of the seven stages of the generational wealth model. These will empower you to transform financial success into a dynamic, sustainable legacy that uplifts generations and leaves an indelible mark on the world.

Let's break down who these people are, what they do, and how they fit into your journey through the seven stages of the Seven-Stage Generational Wealth Model©:

1. Financial Therapist: Helping You Heal Your Money Mindset

A financial therapist focuses on the emotional and psychological aspects of money, helping individuals address financial anxiety, trauma, and the underlying behavioral patterns influencing their financial decisions. If you struggle with financial anxiety, trauma, or unhealthy money habits, a financial therapist is your go-to professional.

Where They Help:

- **Stage 1: Internal and External Ecosystem**—They guide you in uncovering the roots of your financial behaviors and identifying how internal beliefs and external influences shape your relationship with money.
- **Stage 2: Anxiety and Trauma**—They guide you through overcoming emotional barriers caused by past financial hardships, such as financial fears and trauma.
- **Stage 3: Financial Healing**—They help you reprogram and rewrite your Financial Genetic Code, promoting healthy financial habits and a more positive outlook.

Why They're Important:

Financial therapists play an important role in emotional healing, ensuring individuals and families address their fears and traumas before progressing toward wealth-building and preservation. If you're stuck emotionally, it's hard to move forward. A financial therapist can help you break free from those barriers.

2. Financial Educator: Building Your Knowledge

A financial educator provides foundational knowledge about personal finance, ensuring individuals understand key concepts such as budgeting, saving, investing, and debt management. Financial educators teach you the basics of money management. Their goal is to ensure that you understand the fundamentals.

Where They Help:

- **Stage 2: Anxiety and Trauma**—Educators help you feel empowered through financial literacy, replacing your uncertainty with clarity and confidence.
- **Stage 4: Financial Edification**—They help you understand more advanced concepts, such as investment and wealth-building strategies. They promote inclusivity by educating underserved communities and equipping them with tools to make informed financial decisions.
- **Stage 6: Generational Knowledge**—They create programs and workshops to ensure younger generations grasp essential financial principles. They do this to ensure the next generation is financially literate and ready to build on your legacy.

Why They're Important:

You can't manage what you don't understand. Financial educators make sure you have the tools and knowledge to make informed decisions and move toward long-term financial stability.

3. Financial Counselor: Guiding You Through Immediate Challenges

Financial counselors address short-term challenges, offering practical advice on overcoming debt, managing credit, and stabilizing financial situations.

Where They Help:

- **Stage 3: Financial Healing**—They help you overcome setbacks and rebuild your financial stability by focusing on strategies like debt repayment and credit improvement.
- **Stage 4: Financial Edification**—They create actionable financial plans to help you stay on track with your goals.

- **Stage 5: Financial Well-Being**—They ensure you're financially stable so you can start focusing on growth.

Why They're Important:

Sometimes, you just need immediate help. A financial counselor helps you address your current situation so you can focus on the future.

4. Financial Advisor: Growing Your Wealth

Financial advisors specialize in investment strategies and wealth growth, tailoring plans to align with your specific financial goals and risk tolerance.

Where They Help:

- **Stage 4: Financial Edification**—They introduce you to investment opportunities for diversifying your income.
- **Stage 5: Financial Well-Being**—Their goal is to build an appropriate, personalized portfolio that seeks to optimize returns while helping to maintain financial stability.
- **Stage 7: Generational Wealth**—They design strategies that seek to ensure wealth is not only preserved but also expanded for future generations.

Why They're Important:

Growing wealth requires expertise. A financial advisor helps you make the right moves to expand your financial resources, transitioning smoothly from preservation to expansion.

5. Financial Planner: Mapping Out Your Legacy

A financial planner takes a comprehensive approach, integrating all aspects of your financial life to support long-term sustainability. While they do not provide legal services, they can help coordinate **estate planning strategies**, including discussions around **trust accounts**, by collaborating with legal professionals. Ultimately, they help you create a clear financial roadmap aligned with your values, goals, and legacy priorities.

Where They Help:

- **Stage 5: Financial Well-Being**—They help you create a solid plan to work towards your financial goals systematically.
- **Stage 6: Generational Knowledge**—They facilitate intergenerational discussions by helping to pass financial knowledge to the next generation.
- **Stage 7: Generational Wealth**—They strive to ensure your wealth is preserved, protected, expanded, and successfully passed on.

Why They're Important:

Your legacy won't happen by chance. A financial planner ensures that every piece is in place for generational wealth.

As you decide to take control of your financial destiny, learn, grow, and make informed decisions, you'll be creating your financial footprints. You'll build something that will transcend your lifetime and become part of the story for generations to come.

The key takeaway is simple: You control your financial future, no matter where you started. Your circle doesn't have to stay small, and you have the power to build something lasting. Don't wait for others to change it for you. Start expanding today, and leave behind the kind of legacy that will ensure you're remembered for generations to come. I want you to consider your financial footprint, the mark you'll leave for future generations. Without proper planning, as Martin C. Johnson metaphorically described it in Episode 14 of the podcast:[8]

> "However, with thoughtful planning, collaboration, and the right knowledge, you won't just be passing down assets but wisdom, security, and opportunity."

The time to start this journey is now! Whether you're just starting to build wealth or have already accumulated substantial assets, proper planning ensures your legacy will continue to grow and nurture future generations. That's what creating a meaningful financial footprint is all about: ensuring your hard work keeps working for your family long after you're gone.

Where Do We Go From Here?

As we conclude our journey through the Seven-Stage Generational Wealth Model©, you might wonder: *"What's next?"* The path forward is both personal and practical, and it begins with taking decisive action on what you've learned.

First, take time to reflect on where you are in your journey. Which stage resonates most strongly with your current situation? Remember, there's no wrong place to start. Whether you're still working through understanding your Financial Genetic Code or are ready to implement advanced wealth preservation strategies, every step forward matters.

Your next actions should be both immediate and long-term: Begin by conducting a thorough assessment of your current financial situation. This isn't just a case of numbers; it's also a matter of understanding your relationship with money, identifying patterns inherited from your Financial Genetic Code, and recognizing areas where healing may still be needed. Review the self-reflection exercises from each chapter and use them as guideposts for your continuing journey.

Also, consider becoming a "Future Wealth Builder" by joining *"The New Wealth Wave"* community through our podcast and online platforms. The podcast serves as an ongoing resource where we regularly discuss these concepts in greater depth, featuring insights from experts and stories from individuals on their own wealth-building journeys.

You can find us on Apple Podcasts, Spotify, Amazon, YouTube (@TheNewWealthWavePodcast), or my website (drjwallace.com/podcast).

Take advantage of the resources available through our community. The journey to generational wealth isn't meant to be traveled alone. Connect with others on similar paths, share experiences, and learn from collective wisdom—the principles we've discussed come alive when applied within a supportive community. As part of my ongoing commitment to your journey, I regularly share new insights and resources through my website, podcast, and social media platforms. Stay connected to receive updates on new content, tools, and opportunities to deepen your understanding of generational wealth building.

In addition, start having meaningful conversations about money with your family. If you have children, begin teaching them age-appropriate financial concepts. When working with older generations, open dialogues about legacy planning and wealth transfer are crucial. Remember, Generational Wealth Begins with Generational Knowledge®.

Then, consider working with financial professionals who understand the holistic nature of wealth building. Look for those professionals that we detailed earlier and who appreciate both the technical aspects of wealth management and the psychological dimensions we've explored throughout this book. The right professional partners can help you implement the strategies we've discussed while respecting your unique journey.

Most importantly, remember that creating generational wealth is a marathon, not a sprint. You'll face challenges along the way. Markets will fluctuate, circumstances will change, and you'll have moments of doubt. During these times, return to the principles we've discussed. Let them serve as your North Star, guiding you back to your path when you feel lost.

If you find yourself stuck or needing guidance, remember that the Seven-Stage Model is a cyclical process, not a linear one. Don't hesitate to revisit earlier stages as needed. Sometimes, moving forward requires stepping back to strengthen your foundation.

The end of this book marks not a conclusion but a beginning. You now have the framework, knowledge, and tools to create lasting financial footprints. The question is no longer *"Can I build generational wealth?"* but *"How will I use what I've learned to create a lasting legacy?"*

Remember, every great journey begins with a single step. Your step might be opening that investment account you've been putting off, having that difficult conversation about money with your spouse, or simply committing to breaking free from inherited financial patterns. Whatever that first step is, take it today.

The future of your family's financial legacy begins with you. Make it count.

Creating Your Financial Footprints: Personal Reflection and Action Worksheet

Your Current Financial Ecosystem Assessment

1. Current Wealth Circle Size

   - Estimated Current Net Worth: $_____
   - Inherited Wealth/Resources: $_____
   - Primary Sources of Wealth: [ ] Investments [ ] Business [ ] Real Estate [ ] Other: _____

2. Generational Wealth Inventory Rate each area from 1-10 (1 = Needs Significant Work, 10 = Excellent)

   Financial Knowledge Transfer: ___/10
   Wealth Preservation Strategies: ___/10
   Next Generation Financial Education: ___/10
   Long-Term Investment Planning: ___/10

Estate Planning Completeness: ___/10

Action Planning Worksheet

Personal Wealth Expansion Strategy

1. Short-Term Goals (Next 12 Months) Primary Financial Goal: _____ Specific Action Steps:

   - Step 1: _____
   - Step 2: _____
   - Step 3: _____

2. Medium-Term Goals (1-5 Years) Key Wealth-Building Objective: _____ Critical Milestones:

   - Milestone 1: _____

- Milestone 2: _____
- Milestone 3: _____

3. Long-Term Legacy Objectives (5-20 Years) Generational Impact Goal: _____ Strategic Implementations:

- Implementation 1: _____
- Implementation 2: _____
- Implementation 3: _____

Financial Education Plan for Next Generation

1. Communication Strategy Planned Financial Discussions Frequency: [ ] Monthly [ ] Quarterly [ ] Annually Preferred Discussion Format: [ ] Family Meetings [ ] One-on-One Sessions [ ] Structured Workshops [ ] Other:

   _____

2. Knowledge Transfer Areas Topics to Cover: [ ] Basic Financial Literacy [ ] Investment Strategies [ ] Entrepreneurship [ ] Tax Planning [ ] Risk Management [ ] Ethical Wealth Building [ ] Other: _____

Wealth Preservation Checklist

Critical Documents Status: [ ] Updated Will [ ] Living Trust [ ] Power of Attorney [ ] Healthcare Directive [ ] Comprehensive Insurance Coverage [ ] Retirement Account Beneficiary Designations

Personal Reflection

1. What financial wisdom do I want to pass to the next generation?

_____

_____

2. What are my biggest concerns about generational wealth transfer?

_____

_____

3. How can I make a unique contribution to expanding my family's wealth circle?

_____

_____

Quarterly Review Dates

Review 1: _____ Review 2: _____ Review 3: _____ Review 4: _____

_____

Personal Commitment Statement

I, _____, commit to creating meaningful financial footprints by:

1. _____

2. _____

3. _____

Signature: _____ Date: _____

APPENDIX

Appendix A:
Testimonial Letter from the Economic Round Table

Dear Dr. Wallace,

Thank you for accepting ███████ invitation to, once again, address the Economic Round Table about financial literacy—this time using Maslow's hierarchy of needs to present the data from a much more holistic point of view. Bravo! I was reminded of my own path to financial independence as a negative example of exactly what you were talking about. Oh, how primitive and uninformed I was. I had the same human needs as others but could only see acquisition of real estate as the way to become financially stable. This not only limited the growth of my capital, it caused me to waste my most productive years in being a landlord and maintaining the properties, when I could have used those years in developing my filmmaking business. Yes, there are more passive and less laborious ways to increase one's financial security and, yes, being educated does not insure well-being.

You carefully went over the six stages of awareness from overcoming our "genetic code"—those childhood misconceptions, anxieties, and even trauma, to being able to make informed long-term plans for financial independence. You suggested first taking opportunities offered you such as a deferred tax 401k; regularly investing in diversified mutual funds; and purchasing insurance for protection against economic and medical crises. As we age, we hopefully move up your stages of insight, more capable of identifying our changing needs and risk tolerance. You envision an increase in emotional and intellectual self-awareness and, dare we say, self-actualization.

In closing, I want to say that you are an inspiring communicator who explains difficult concepts with low-key assurance in collegial style. I know I speak for all our members in expressing admiration for your ability to change, not only the lives of your Pruco clients but also, people like us, who are fortunate enough to hear you speak. Finally, I want to extend an invitation to attend any of our Wednesday morning meetings when your schedule permits. You can learn the topic and access the Zoom link from ██████ or our president ███████ ██████████████████████. You will be welcomed warmly.

With all good wishes,
Copy: ███████████████████████

Appendix B:
Generational Wealth Timeline

The Three Phases of Financial Growth and Legacy Building

This appendix outlines a comprehensive timeline for building, preserving, and transferring wealth across the three distinct life phases taught in this book. Readers can develop a strategic approach to achieving long-term financial success and creating generational wealth by understanding these phases and their associated milestones.

Phase 1: Wealth Accumulation (Ages 25-45)

During this foundational phase, the primary focus is on building wealth through career advancement, strategic investments, and financial planning. The decisions made during these years establish the base for future financial security.

Key Milestones:

- **Early Career Development (25-30)**: Focus on advancing your career path, maximizing salary growth opportunities, and developing essential financial literacy skills.
- **Debt Elimination (25-35)**: Systematically reduce high-interest debt, including student loans and credit cards, to improve cash flow and credit standing.
- **Investment Foundation (25-45)**: Maximize contributions to tax-advantaged retirement accounts (401(k), IRAs (Roth or Traditional)) and establish taxable investment accounts with an emphasis on long-term growth.

- **Real Estate Acquisition (30-40)**: Evaluate homeownership as both a lifestyle choice and wealth-building strategy, considering location, appreciation potential, and mortgage terms.
- **Income Diversification (30-45)**: Develop multiple revenue streams through side businesses, passive income vehicles, or strategic real estate investments.
- **Risk Protection (30-45)**: Implement comprehensive risk management through appropriate life insurance, disability coverage, and an emergency fund covering 6-12 months of essential expenses.

Phase 2: Capital Preservation (Ages 45-60)

As wealth accumulates, the focus shifts toward protecting assets while maintaining moderate growth. This phase balances continued accumulation with an increasing focus on preservation strategies.

Key Milestones:

- **Portfolio Rebalancing (45-50)**: Adjust investment allocations from an aggressive growth approach toward a more balanced strategy that incorporates preservation elements.
- **Maximum Contribution Years (45-55)**: Leverage peak earning potential to maximize retirement account contributions, explore Roth conversion strategies, and utilize catch-up contribution allowances.
- **Liability Reduction (50-55)**: Accelerate mortgage payments or eliminate major debts to reduce financial obligations before retirement.
- **Estate Structure Implementation (50-60)**: Establish comprehensive estate planning documents, including wills, trusts, and appropriate powers of attorney.

- **Healthcare Planning (50-60)**: Evaluate long-term healthcare needs, research Medicare options, and consider long-term care insurance policies.
- **Pre-Retirement Assessment (55-60)**: Conduct a thorough retirement readiness analysis, including projected income streams, anticipated expenses, and potential lifestyle adjustments.

Phase 3: Retirement and Legacy Planning (Ages 60 & Beyond)

The final phase transitions from accumulation to distribution, focusing on sustainable withdrawal strategies and meaningful wealth transfer to future generations.

Key Milestones:

- **Income Optimization (60-65)**: Develop strategies for maximizing Social Security benefits, pension distributions, and potential annuity income for sustainable cash flow.
- **Withdrawal Framework (60-70)**: Implement disciplined withdrawal methodologies, such as the 4% rule, to balance current income needs with long-term capital preservation.
- **Philanthropic Strategy (60-75)**: Establish structured giving plans through donor-advised funds, strategic charitable contributions, and family gifting programs.
- **Business Transition (60-75)**: Execute business succession plans, including potential sale or transfer, with careful attention to tax implications and reinvestment strategies.
- **Wealth Transfer Finalization (70+)**: Complete legacy planning initiatives designed to minimize estate taxation while preserving family wealth across generations.

- **Late-Life Care Planning (70-80+):** Prepare financially for potential assisted living requirements, long-term medical care, and end-of-life considerations.

Implementation Framework

The timeline presented above represents an ideal progression through the wealth-building lifecycle. Individual circumstances may necessitate adjustments to specific ages and milestones. The main principle remains consistent: each phase builds upon the previous stage, creating a structured pathway to work towards financial security, generational wealth preservation, and meaningful legacy development.

Appendix C:
20 Essential Inherited Financial Narratives

Narrative Name	Description	Behavioral Impact	Healing Thought
Scar Tissue Narrative	Fear rooted in past financial pain or betrayal.	Avoidance of growth opportunities, skepticism of financial tools.	I am not my past. I can build new outcomes.
No One Taught Me Narrative	Lack of financial literacy is passed down generationally.	Shame, trial-and-error financial habits, and disorganization.	I can learn what I was never taught.
Financial First-Gen Narrative	Being the first in your family to build wealth.	Pressure, fear of failure, and decision paralysis.	I'm pioneering with purpose and grace.
Invisible Retirement Narrative	Belief that retirement isn't possible or relevant.	Lack of planning, delay in retirement savings.	I deserve a secure and joyful future.
Financial Shame Narrative	Guilt or embarrassment from past money mistakes.	Financial self-sabotage, secrecy, and helplessness.	I can reset, reflect, and rise.
All or Nothing Narrative	Belief that small efforts aren't worth it.	Perfectionism, financial extremism, and under-saving.	Small steps create lasting wealth.
Don't Talk About It Narrative	Cultural silence around money conversations.	Poor planning, family tension, and estate confusion.	Talking about money is love in action.
Anchor Guilt Narrative	Guilt from surpassing the family financially.	Self-sabotage, over-giving, under-saving.	I can grow and still honor where I came from.
Financial Martyrdom Narrative	Self-neglect in favor of others' financial well-being.	Burnout, delayed goals, and poor boundaries.	My financial health matters too.
Inherited Scarcity Loop Narrative	Generational fear of running out of money.	Hoarding, underspending, and anxiety with abundance.	There is enough. I am safe to thrive.

Narrative Name	Description	Behavioral Impact	Healing Thought
Self-Insurance Superiority Narrative	Distrust in institutional protection plans.	Underinsured, financially vulnerable.	Protection is a wise and empowering act.
Just Survive, Don't Build Narrative	Mindset focused on survival over legacy.	Low ambition for investment or growth.	I am worthy of building, not just surviving.
Estate Planning is for the Rich Narrative	A belief that planning legacies is for the wealthy.	No will, trust, or clarity in asset transfer.	My family deserves security and a legacy.
Budgeting Means You're Broke Narrative	Stigma that budgeting reflects lack.	Overspending, shame around structure.	Budgeting gives me peace and power.
Success Means Isolation Narrative	Fear that success will create distance from others.	Minimizing achievement, guilt, and hiding wealth.	I can rise and stay connected.
Money Will Always Run Out Narrative	Belief that financial security is temporary.	Overworking, over-saving, scarcity anxiety.	I can rest knowing I am secure.
You Have to Work Twice as Hard Narrative	Cultural pressure to overperform to succeed.	Burnout, fear of slowing down.	I am worthy without proving myself.
Debt is Evil Narrative	Taught that all debt is harmful.	Avoidance of strategic credit use or growth.	I can use debt wisely and confidently.
We Don't Deserve Wealth Narrative	Internalized belief that wealth is for others.	Wealth rejection, undercharging, and underinvesting.	Wealth is my birthright and responsibility.
Money Changes People Narrative	Belief that financial gain corrupts values.	Avoidance of growth, income limits, and self-sabotage.	Money reflects who I already am.

Appendix D:
Revocable vs. Irrevocable Trust Checklist

Checklist Item	Revocable Trust	Irrevocable Trust
Can be changed or revoked	✅ Yes	❌ No
Avoids probate	✅ Yes	✅ Yes
Provides privacy	✅ Yes	✅ Yes
Grantor control over assets	✅ Full control	❌ Limited or none
Used for estate tax reduction	❌ No	✅ Yes
Asset protection from creditors	❌ No	✅ Yes
Medicaid planning benefits	❌ Limited	✅ Significant
Effective upon creation	✅ Yes	✅ Yes
Requires a separate tax ID	❌ No (uses SSN)	✅ Yes
Income taxable to the grantor	✅ Yes	❌ Depends on structure
Cost and complexity	Lower setup cost	Higher setup and maintenance costs
Best for	Estate planning with flexibility	Asset protection, tax, and Medicaid planning

ENDNOTES

Introduction: The Financial Genetic Code Revolution

1. Empower. (2024, February 13). *37% of Americans can't afford an emergency expense over $400, according to Empower research.* https://www.empower.com/press-center/37-americans-cant-afford-emergency-expense-over-400-according-empower-research
2. U.S. Census Bureau. (n.d.). *Median home values: Unadjusted.* U.S. Department of Commerce. https://www2.census.gov/programs-surveys/decennial/tables/time-series/coh-values/values-unadj.txt
3. U.S. Census Bureau. (1952, March 25). *Income of families and persons in the United States: 1950* (Series P-60, No. 9). U.S. Department of Commerce. https://www.census.gov/library/publications/1952/demo/p60-009.html
4. Swaminathan, A. (2025, April 10). *Mortgage rates are down, but it's not about to get cheaper to buy a house.* MarketWatch. https://www.marketwatch.com/story/mortgage-rates-are-down-but-its-not-about-to-get-cheaper-to-buy-a-house-e91423dd
5. U.S. Department of Education, National Center for Education Statistics. (2023). *Digest of education statistics, 2022 (Table 330.10).* https://nces.ed.gov/programs/digest/d22/tables/dt22_330.10.asp
6. Hanson, M. (2024, March 4). *Average cost of college & tuition.* Education Data Initiative.https://educationdata.org/average-cost-of-college
7. Federal Reserve Bank of St. Louis. (Updated 2025, February 7). *Student loans owned and securitized.* https://fred.stlouisfed.org/series/SLOAS
8. Wolff, E. N. (2020). *Household wealth trends in the United States, 1962 to 2019: Median Wealth Rebounds.* National Bureau of Economic Research (NBER). https://www.nber.org/papers/w28383
9. Federal Reserve Board. (Updated 2025, March 21). *Distribution of household wealth in the U.S. since 1989.* https://www.federalreserve.gov/releases/z1/dataviz/dfa/distribute/chart/
10. Chetty, R., Grusky, D., Hell, M., Hendren, N., Manduca, R., & Narang, J. (Revised 2017). *The fading American dream: Trends in absolute income mobility since 1940.* National Bureau of Economic Research. DOI: 10.3386/w22910 https://www.nber.org/papers/w22910
11. U.S. Bureau of Labor Statistics. (2024). *Employee tenure summary.* https://www.bls.gov/news.release/tenure.nr0.htm

12. U.S. Census Bureau. (2024). *Homeownership rates by age of householder: 1994 to present.* (Table 19). https://www.census.gov/housing/hvs/data/histtabs.html

13. Wallace, J. (Host). (Premiered Mar 12, 2024). *Using neuroscience to reprogram your financial genetic code (Part 2) with Dr. Marcia Ruben.* The New Wealth Wave Podcast, episode 9. YouTube, https://youtu.be/yRRtT81tnqU?si=2nT-q0Oesyt_1SU9

14. Wallace, J. (Host). (Premiered Apr 23, 2024). *Generational knowledge and financial blueprints with Saundra Davis.* The New Wealth Wave Podcast, episode 12. YouTube, https://youtu.be/ysM-EDapdvs

15. Wallace, J. (Host). (Premiered Sep 3, 2024). *From poverty to prosperity: Mayor Torrance Harvey's journey to generational wealth.* The New Wealth Wave Podcast, episode 21. YouTube, https://youtu.be/sI82_OHuNYg

Chapter 1: The Roots of Your Money Story

1. Whitebread, D., & Bingham, S. (2013). *Habit formation and learning in young children.* University of Cambridge, commissioned by Money Advice Service. https://altorwealth.com/wp-content/uploads/2024/04/the-money-advice-service-habit-formation-and-learning-in-young-children-may2013.pdf

2. U.S. Securities and Exchange Commission. (2011). *Study on investment advisers and broker-dealers.* https://www.sec.gov/news/studies/2011/913studyfinal.pdf

3. Wallace, J. (Host). (Premiered Aug 20, 2024). *Building generational wealth with Tony Award Winner LaChanze.* The New Wealth Wave Podcast, episode 20. YouTube, https://www.youtube.com/watch?v=gxCGgGuTPiU

4. Chase UK. (2025). *Kakeibo: The Japanese art of budgeting and saving money.* https://www.chase.co.uk/gb/en/hub/kakeibo-saving/

5. Langley, M. (2025, January 6). *Japan's household savings rate hit 1.5% in 2023, marking three years of decline.* FN News Global. https://fnnewsglobal.com/focus/article/446168/

6. Zhu, H., & Xie, Y. (2017). Buying out of familial obligation: The tradeoff between financially supporting versus living with elderly parents in Urban China. *Chinese journal of sociology, 3*(1), 56-73. https://doi.org/10.1177/2057150X16685499

7. GOBankingRates. (2022, April 1). *63% of kids plan to financially support parents' retirement.* Upwave. https://www.upwave.com/presspost/63-of-kids-plan-to-financially-support-parents-retirement-gobankingrates/

8. Bank of America. (2021, August 18). *More than 70% of Hispanic millennials providing financial support to family members – with many increasing their support during the pandemic [Press release].* Business Wire. https://www.businesswire.com/news/home/20210818005404/en/More-Than-70-of-Hispanic-Millennials-Providing-Financial-Support-to-Family-Members-%E2%80%93-With-Many-Increasing-Their-Support-During-the-Pandemic

9. Federal Deposit Insurance Corporation (FDIC). (2022, October). *2021 FDIC National survey of unbanked and underbanked households.* https://www.fdic.gov/analysis/household-survey/2021report.pdf

10. Center for Responsible Lending. (2020, November). *Payday and vehicle title lending disproportionately harm communities of color, exploiting and perpetuating the racial wealth gap.* https://www.responsiblelending.org/sites/default/files/nodes/files/research-publication/crl-payday-cartitle-comm-of-color-nov2020.pdf

11. Looney, A., & Yannelis, C. (2024, September 17). *What went wrong with federal student loans?* Brookings Institution. https://www.brookings.edu/articles/what-went-wrong-with-federal-student-loans/Brookings+4

12. Lindblom, C. (2018). The science of "muddling through". In *Classic readings in urban planning* (pp. 31-40). Routledge.https://doi.org/10.2307/973677

13. Himmelstein, D. U., Lawless, R. M., Thorne, D., Foohey, P., & Woolhandler, S. (2019). Medical bankruptcy: still common despite the Affordable Care Act. *American Journal of Public Health*, *109*(3), 431-433. https://doi.org/10.2105/AJPH.2018.304901

14. Gray, M. (2024, June 28). *California high schools will require personal finance course for graduation under new bill*. California Department of Education. https://newsroom.ocde.us/california-high-schools-will-require-personal-finance-course-for-graduation-under-new-bill/

15. Council for Economic Education (CEE). (2024). *2024 Survey of the states.* https://www.councilforeconed.org/survey-of-the-states/

16. S&P Global. (2015). *S&P Global FinLit survey: Financial literacy around the world*. https://gflec.org/initiatives/sp-global-finlit-survey/

17. Board of Governors of the Federal Reserve System. (2021). *Report on the economic well-being of U.S. households in 2020.* https://www.federalreserve.gov/publications/files/2020-report-economic-well-being-us-households-202105.pdf

18. Malmendier, U., & Nagel, S. (2011). Depression babies: do macroeconomic experiences affect risk taking? *The Quarterly Journal of Economics*, *126*(1), 373-416. ttps://doi.org/10.1093/qje/qjq004

19. Chetty, R., Hendren, N., Kline, P., & Saez, E. (2014). Where is the land of opportunity? The geography of intergenerational mobility in the United States. *The Quarterly Journal of Economics, 129*(4), 1553-1623. https://doi.org/10.1093/qje/qju022

20. Bronfenbrenner, U. (1979). *The ecology of human development: Experiments by nature and design.* Harvard University Press. https://www.hup.harvard.edu/catalog.php?isbn=9780674224575

21. Wilson, W. J. (1996). *When work disappears: The world of the new urban poor.* New York: Alfred A. Knopf.

22. Maslow, A., & Lewis, K. J. (1987). Maslow's hierarchy of needs. *Salenger Incorporated, 14*(17), 987-990. https://www.researchhistory.org/2012/06/16/maslows-hierarchy-of-needs/?print=1

23. Seligman, M. E. (1972). Learned helplessness. *Annual Review of Medicine, 23*(1), 407-412. https://doi.org/10.1146/annurev.me.23.020172.002203

Chapter 2: Decoding Your Financial Genetic Code

1. Gladstone, J. J., Jachimowicz, J. M., Greenberg, A. E., & Galinsky, A. D. (2021). Financial shame spirals: How shame intensifies financial hardship. *Organizational Behavior and Human Decision Processes, 167*, 42-56. https://doi.org/10.1016/j.obhdp.2021.06.002

2. Wendy. (2025, January). *The cycle of financial trauma and shame.* Whole Person Finance. https://wholeperson.finance/the-cycle-of-financial-trauma-and-shame/

3. Davis, A. Y. (1983). *Women, race, & class.* Vintage Books.

4. Angelou, M. (1994). *Wouldn't take nothing for my journey now.* Bantam.

5. Wallace, J. (Host). (Premiered Mar 10, 2024). *Neuroscience and reprogramming Your Financial Genetic Code with Dr. Marcia Ruben.* The New Wealth Wave Podcast, episode 5. YouTube, https://youtu.be/JBMWgO6dQ-o?si=JOHq17Y5dujl6Ah8

6. Brad Klontz. (2009). *Mind over money: Overcoming the money disorders that threaten our financial health.* Crown Currency.

7. LeDoux, J.E. (2000). Emotion Circuits in the Brain. *Annual Review of Neuroscience, 23, 155–184.* https://stanford.edu/~knutson/ans/ledoux00.pdf

8. Kahneman, D. (2011). *Thinking, fast and slow.* Farrar, Straus and Giroux.

9. Kahneman, D., & Tversky, A. (1979). Prospect theory: An analysis of decision under risk. *Econometrica, 47(2), 263–292.* https://doi.org/10.2307/1914185

10. Otuteye, E., & Siddiquee, M. (2019). Underperformance of active managed portfolios: Some behavioral insights. *Journal of Behavioral Finance*, 21(3), 284-300. https://www.tandfonline.com/doi/full/10.1080/15427560.2019.1692210

11. Wallace, J. (Host). (Premiered June 18, 2024). *Building Wealth From The Inside Out With Dr. Michael Thomas, Jr.* The New Wealth Wave Podcast, episode 16. YouTube, https://www.youtube.com/watch?v=fUDvHpDeBJg

12. Wallace, J. (Host). (Premiered May 7, 2024). *The Power of Financial Literacy, Independence, and Education with Brian L Thomas.* The New Wealth Wave Podcast, episode 13. YouTube, https://www.youtube.com/watch?v=zgKA2MzJUiM

13. Wallace, J. (Host). (Premiered Mar 10, 2024). *Navigating Our Internal and External Ecosystems For Lasting Wealth with Tiffany Grant, AFC®.* The New Wealth Wave Podcast, episode 7. YouTube, https://www.youtube.com/watch?v=MOJ3IRNIPhg

14. American Psychological Association. (2022). *Stress in America: Money, inflation, war pile on to nation stuck in COVID-19 survival mode.* https://www.apa.org/news/press/releases/stress/2022/march-2022-survival-mode

15. Coan, J. A., & Sbarra, D. A. (2015). Social Baseline Theory: The social regulation of risk and effort. *Current Opinion in Psychology*, 1, 87–91. https://doi.org/10.1016/j.copsyc.2014.12.021

16. Klontz, B., Britt, S. L., Mentzer, J., & Klontz, T. (2011). Money beliefs and financial behaviors: Development of the Klontz money script inventory. *Journal of Financial Therapy*, 2 (1) 1 http://newprairiepress.org/jft/vol2/iss1/1

17. Edwards, K. (2022). *Most Black Americans say they can meet basic needs financially, but many still experience economic insecurity.* Pew Research Center. https://www.pewresearch.org/short-reads/2022/02/23/most-black-americans-say-they-can-meet-basic-needs-financially-but-many-still-experience-economic-insecurity/

18. Oliver, B. (2019). *The hidden 'black tax' that some professionals of color struggle with.* Fast Company. https://www.fastcompany.com/90296371/the-hidden-black-tax-that-some-professionals-of-color-struggle-with

19. Jackson, R., Hamilton, D., Darity, W. (2015). *Community development issue brief. Low wealth and economic insecurity among middle-class blacks in Boston.* Federal Reserve Bank of Boston. https://www.bostonfed.org/-/media/Documents/Community-Development-Issue-Briefs/cdbrief32015.pdf

20. Wallace, J. (Host). (Premiered Apr 9, 2024). *Unpacking Financial Trauma and Literacy with Rahkim Sabree, AFC®*. The New Wealth Wave Podcast, episode 11. YouTube, https://youtu.be/xyHIrUweu-U?si=_QPbRdsd1JJSi8N2

21. Podoshen, J. S., Andrzejewski, S. A., & Hunt, J. M. (2014). Materialism, Conspicuous Consumption, and American Hip-Hop Subculture. *Journal of International Consumer Marketing, 26*(4), 271–283. https://doi.org/10.1080/08961530.2014.900469

22. Ariel Investments & Charles Schwab. (2022, April). *2022 Black investor survey: Report of findings.* Charles Schwab. https://content.schwab.com/web/retail/public/about-schwab/Ariel-Schwab_Black_Investor_Survey_2022_findings.pdf

23. Klontz, B., & Klontz, T. (2009). *Mind over money: Overcoming the money disorders that threaten our financial health.* Crown Currency.

24. Thaler, R. (1985). Mental accounting and consumer choice. *Marketing Science, 4*(3), 199-214. https://doi.org/10.1287/mksc.4.3.199

Chapter 3: The Path to Financial Healing

1. Kahneman, D., & Tversky, A. (1979). Prospect theory: An analysis of decision under risk. *Econometrica, 47(2), 263–292.* https://doi.org/10.2307/1914185

2. Yehuda, R., Daskalakis, N. P., Bierer, L. M., Bader, H. N., Klengel, T., Holsboer, F., & Binder, E. B. (2015) Holocaust exposure induced intergenerational effects on FKBP5 methylation. *Biological Psychiatry,* 80(5), 372–380. https://doi.org/10.1016/j.biopsych.2015.08.005

3. Wallace, J. (Host). (Premiered Apr 9, 2024). *Unpacking Financial Trauma and Literacy with Rahkim Sabree, AFC®*. The New Wealth Wave Podcast, episode 11. YouTube, https://youtu.be/xyHIrUweu-U?si=_QPbRdsd1JJSi8N2

4. Wallace, J. (Host). (Premiered Nov 12, 2024). *The Psychology of Money Mindset and Wealth Building With Dr. Wendy Ashley.* The New Wealth Wave Podcast, episode 26. YouTube, https://www.youtube.com/watch?v=1tdLynG8Xro

5. Bandura, A. (1977). *Social Learning Theory.* Prentice Hall.Bandura, A. (1977). *Social learning theory.* Englewood Cliffs, NJ: Prentice Hall.

6. Wallace, J. (Host). (Premiered July 30, 2024). *Empowering Underserved Communities Through Financial Literacy with Louis Barajas.* The New Wealth Wave Podcast, episode 19. YouTube, https://www.youtube.com/watch?v=ys5G6oVfe9o

7. Heen, M. (2009) Ending Jim Crow life insurance rates, *Nw. JL & Soc. Pol'y*, 4, 360. https://scholarlycommons.law.northwestern.edu/njlsp/vol4/iss2/3

8. Wallace, J. (Host). (Premiered Oct 15, 2024). *Closing The Racial Wealth Gap with Brian Seymour.* The New Wealth Wave Podcast, episode 24. YouTube, https://www.youtube.com/watch?v=l3cs1oI76-c

9. Wallace, J. (Host). (Premiered Oct 1, 2024). *Financial Trauma, Anxiety, and Healing with Nate Astle.* The New Wealth Wave Podcast, episode 23. YouTube, https://www.youtube.com/watch?v=PhN5xS32Mgo

10. Wallace, J. (Host). (Premiered Mar 10, 2024). *Building Wealth Through Financial Literacy with Jasper Smith.* The New Wealth Wave Podcast, episode 6. YouTube, https://www.youtube.com/watch?v=xRppiN18KYU

11. Porges, S. W. (2011). *The Polyvagal Theory: Neurophysiological Foundations of Emotions, Attachment, Communication, and Self-regulation.* W. W. Norton & Company.

12. Rock, D. (2008). SCARF: A brain-based model for collaborating with and influencing others. NeuroLeadership Journal, 1(1), 44-52. https://membership.neuroleadership.com/material/scarf-a-brain-based-model-for-collaborating-with-and-influencing-others-vol-1/

13. Wallace, J. (Host). (Premiered Mar 10, 2024). *Neuroscience and reprogramming your financial genetic code with Dr. Marcia Ruben.* The New Wealth Wave Podcast, episode 05. YouTube, https://youtu.be/JBMWgO6dQ-o?si=68tAG1jM-nVBjv5W

14. Fowler, James H., & Christakis, Nicholas A. (2008). Dynamic spread of happiness in a large social network: Longitudinal analysis over 20 years in the Framingham heart study. *BMJ, 337,* a2338. https://doi.org/10.1136/bmj.a2338

15. Kandel, Eric R. (2006). *In search of memory: The emergence of a new science of mind.* W.W. Norton & Company.

16. Hebb, D. O. (1949). *The organization of behavior: A neuropsychological theory.* New York: Wiley.

Chapter 4: Building Financial Intelligence

1. Peterson, R. L. (2011). *Inside the investor's brain: The power of mind over money.* Wiley.

2. Thaler, R. H., & Sunstein, C. R. (2009). *Nudge: Improving decisions about health, wealth, and happiness.* Penguin Books.

3. Lind, T., Ahmed, A., Skagerlund, K., Strömbäck, C., Väställ, D., & Tinghög, G. (2020). Competence, confidence, and gender: The role of objective and subjective financial knowledge in household finance. *Journal*

of Family and Economic Issues, 41(2), 626–638. https://doi.org/10.1007/s10834-020-09678-9

4. Wallace, J. (Host). (Premiered Oct 1, 2024). *Financial Trauma, Anxiety, and Healing with Nate Astle.* The New Wealth Wave Podcast, episode 23. YouTube, https://www.youtube.com/watch?v=PhN5xS32Mgo

5. Schwartz, J. M., & Begley, S. (2003). *The mind and the brain: Neuroplasticity and the power of mental force.* Harper Perennial.

6. Kaiser, T., & Menkhoff, L. (2017). Does financial education impact financial literacy and financial behavior, and if so, when? *The World Bank Economic Review, 31*(3), 611-630. https://doi.org/10.1093/wber/lhx018

7. Wallace, J. (Host). (Premiered Mar 10, 2024). *Building Wealth Through Financial Literacy with Jasper Smith.* The New Wealth Wave Podcast, episode 6. YouTube, https://www.youtube.com/watch?v=xRppiN18KYU

8. National Endowment for Financial Education. (2025, April 9). *Poll: Adults in multigenerational households average $500 per month in familial support; 73% make financial sacrifices to offer support.* https://www.nefe.org/news/2025/04/financial-well-being-of-multigenerational-households.aspx

9. Bandura, A. (1997). *Self-efficacy: The exercise of control.* W. H. Freeman. https://www.academia.edu/28274869/Albert_Bandura_Self_Efficacy_The_Exercise_of_Control_W_H_Freeman_and_Co_1997_pdf

10. Warnock, R. (2023). *Senator Reverend Warnock, colleagues urge review of Navy Federal Credit Union after reported racial disparities in mortgage lending.* https://www.warnock.senate.gov/newsroom/press-releases/senator-reverend-warnock-colleagues-urge-review-of-navy-federal-credit-union-after-reported-racial-disparities-in-mortgage-lending/

11. Bhutta, N., Hizmo, A., & Ringo, D. (2024, March). *How much does racial bias affect mortgage lending? Evidence from human and algorithmic credit decisions* (Working Paper No. 24-09). Federal Reserve Bank of Philadelphia. https://www.philadelphiafed.org/consumer-finance/mortgage-markets/how-much-does-racial-bias-affect-mortgage-lending-evidence-human-algorithmic-credit-decisions

12. Aaronson, D., Hartley, D., & Mazumder, B. (2021). The effects of the 1930s HOLC "redlining" maps. *American Economic Journal: Economic Policy, 13*(4), 355-392. https://doi.org/10.1257/pol.20190414

13. Mani, A., Mullainathan, S., Shafir, E., & Zhao, J. (2013). Poverty impedes cognitive function. *Science, 341*(6149), 976–980. https://doi.org/10.1126/science.1238041

14. Huijsmans, I., Ma, I., Micheli, L., Civai, C., Stallen, M., & Sanfey, A. G. (2019). A scarcity mindset alters neural processing underlying consumer

decision making. *Proceedings of the National Academy of Sciences,* 116(24), 11699–11704. https://doi.org/10.1073/pnas.1818572116

15. Constantine, L., Farahi, Y. (2025, February). *Down the drain: Payday lenders take $2.4 billion in fees from borrowers.* Center for Responsible Lending. https://www.responsiblelending.org/sites/default/files/nodes/files/researc h-publication/crl-down-the-drain-paydayloanfees-feb2025.pdf

16. Dahl, G. B., & Lochner, L. (2012). *The impact of family income on child achievement: Evidence from the Earned Income Tax Credit. NBER working paper series.* National Bureau of Economic Research. https://doi.org/10.3386/w14599

17. Wallace, J. (Host). (Premiered Oct 29, 2024). *Unpacking The Emotions of Trading, Investing, and Growing Wealth with Anmol Singh.* The New Wealth Wave Podcast, episode 25. YouTube, https://www.youtube.com/watch?v=nFeVvlDJVuw

18. Shanks, T. R. W., & Robinson, C. (2013). Assets, economic opportunity and toxic stress: A framework for understanding child and educational outcomes. *Economics of Education Review, 33,* 154-170. https://doi.org/10.1016/j.econedurev.2012.11.002

19. National Endowment for Financial Education. (2012). *The effect of financial literacy and financial education on downstream financial behaviors.* https://www.nefe.org/_images/research/Effect-of-Financial-Literacy-on-Financial-Behaviors/Effect-of-Financial-Education-on-Financial-Behaviors-Final-Report.pdf

20. Aliche, T. (2021). *Get good with money: Ten simple steps to becoming financially whole.* Rodale Books.

21. Lusardi, A., & Mitchell, O. S. (2014). The economic importance of financial literacy: Theory and evidence. *Journal of Economic Literature,* 52(1), 5-44. https://www.aeaweb.org/articles?id=10.1257/jel.52.1.5

22. Yakoboski, P. J., Lusardi, A., & Hasler, A. (2022). *How financial literacy varies among U.S. adults: The 2022 TIAA Institute-GFLEC Personal Finance Index.* TIAA Institute. https://www.tiaa.org/content/dam/tiaa/institute/pdf/research-report/2022-04/tiaa-institute-gflec-2022-personal-finance-p-fin-index-ti-yakoboski-april-2022.pdf

23. NewHedge. (n.d.). *Bitcoin volatility index.* https://newhedge.io/bitcoin/volatility-index

24. Klebnikov, S., Gara, A. (Updated 2022, June 16). *20-year-old Robinhood customer dies by suicide after seeing a $730,000 negative balance.* Forbes. https://www.forbes.com/sites/sergeiklebnikov/2020/06/17/20-year-old-

robinhood-customer-dies-by-suicide-after-seeing-a-730000-negative-balance/

25. Banerji, G. & Chung, J. (Updated 2021, January 27). GameStop Mania Reveals Power Shift on Wall Street—and the Pros Are Reeling. *Wall Street Journal*. https://www.wsj.com/articles/gamestop-mania-reveals-power-shift-on-wall-streetand-the-pros-are-reeling-11611774663

26. Mitchell, C. (2025, March 11). *Historical average stock market returns for S&P 500: 5-year up to 150-year averages.* Trade That Swing. https://tradethatswing.com/average-historical-stock-market-returns-for-sp-500-5-year-up-to-150-year-averages/

27. D'Acunto, F. (2015). *Tear down this wall street: The effect of anti-market ideology on investment decisions.* SSRN. https://dx.doi.org/10.2139/ssrn.2705545

28. McMenamin, J. (2024, September 9). *Motivation vs. consistency: What matters for building wealth?* LinkedIn. https://www.linkedin.com/pulse/motivation-vs-consistency-what-matters-building-wealth-mcmenamin-q53we

29. Finlay, M., & Zorn, J. (2023, February). *Cost averaging: Invest now or temporarily hold your cash?* Vanguard. https://corporate.vanguard.com/content/dam/corp/research/pdf/cost_averaging_invest_now_or_temporarily_hold_your_cash.pdf.

30. U.S. Bureau of Labor Statistics. (n.d). *CPI Inflation Calculator.* https://www.bls.gov/data/inflation_calculator.htm

31. S&P Dow Jones Indices LLC. (Updated 2025, May 27). S&P CoreLogic Case-Shiller U.S. National Home Price Index [Data set]. Federal Reserve Bank of St. Louis. https://fred.stlouisfed.org/series/CSUSHPINSA

32. U.S. Bureau of Labor Statistics. (2024, January 3). *Baby boomers born from 1957 and 1964 held an average of 12.7 jobs from the ages of 18 to 56.* TED: The Economics Daily. https://www.bls.gov/opub/ted/2024/baby-boomers-born-from-1957-to-1964-held-an-average-of-12-7-jobs-from-ages-18-to-56.htm

33. SBA Office of Advocacy. (2010, July). *Small Business Access to Capital: Critical to Economic Recovery.* https://www.uschamber.com/assets/archived/images/legacy/reports/1007_sb_accesstocapital.pdf

34. Corley, T. C. (2025). *Rich habits: The routines millionaires use daily that will help you build wealth* (2nd ed.). Entrepreneur Press.

35. Life Insurance Marketing and Research Association (LIMRA). (2021). *2021 Insurance barometer study reveals common misconceptions that prevent Americans from getting life insurance they know they need.* https://www.limra.com/en/newsroom/news-releases/2021/2021-

insurance-barometer-study-reveals-common-misconceptions-that-prevent-americans-from-getting-life-insurance-they-know-they-need/

36. Maleh, J., Bosley, T. (2023). *Disability and death probability tables for insured workers born in 2003.* Social Security Administration. https://www.ssa.gov/oact/NOTES/ran6/an2023-6.pdf

37. Insurance Information Institute. (2023). Facts + statistics: Homeowners and renters insurance. https://www.iii.org/fact-statistic/facts-statistics-homeowners-and-renters-insurance

38. Federal Emergency Management Agency. (n.d.). *When disaster strikes: Preparation, response and recovery for your business.*https://www.iii.org/article/when-disaster-strikes-preparation-response-and-recovery

39. Johnson, R. (2019). *What is the Lifetime Risk of Needing and Receiving Long-Term Services and Supports?* Urban Institute. https://www.urban.org/research/publication/what-lifetime-risk-needing-and-receiving-long-term-services-and-supports

40. LIMRA Secure Retirement Institute. (2019). *10 Myths/Misconceptions That Can Threaten Retirement Security.* https://www.limra.com/siteassets/research/research-abstracts/2019/10-myths-misconceptions-that-can-threaten-retirement-security/2019_09_sri-retirement-myths.pdf

41. Lankford, K. (Updated 2024, March 6). *5 Things you should know about annuities.* AARP. https://www.aarp.org/money/retirement/learn-about-annuities/

42. Employee Benefit Research Institute & Greenwald Research. (2024). *2024 Retirement confidence survey.* https://www.ebri.org/docs/default-source/rcs/2024-rcs/2024-rcs-release-report.pdf

43. National Library of Medicine. (2024). Mortality in the United States, 2023. National Center for Health Statistics. https://www.ncbi.nlm.nih.gov/books/NBK611296/#:~:text=In%202023%2C%20a%20total%20of,2022%20to%2049%2C932%20in%202023.

44. Federal Reserve Board. (2024, May). *Report of economic well-being of U.S. households in 2023.* https://www.federalreserve.gov/publications/2024-economic-well-being-of-us-households-in-2023-retirement-investments.htm

45. Employee Benefit Research Institute & Greenwald Research. (2024). *2024 Retirement confidence survey.* https://www.ebri.org/docs/default-source/rcs/2024-rcs/rcs_24-fs-1_confid.pdf

46. Toosi, M., Torpey, E. (2017, May). *Older workers: Labor force trends and career options.* Bureau of Labor Statistics. https://www.bls.gov/careeroutlook/2017/article/older-workers.htm

47. TransAmerica Institute. (2013, February). *10,000 Baby boomers turn 65 every day.* Transamerica Center for Retirement Studies. https://www.transamericainstitute.org/research/publications/details/10000-baby-boomers-turn-65-every-day-nfographic

48. Boivie, I., Rhee, N. (2015, March). *The continuing retirement savings crisis.* National Institute on Retirement Security. https://www.nirsonline.org/reports/the-continuing-retirement-savings-crisis/

49. Employee Benefit Research Institute & Greenwald & Associates. (2020). *Retirement and financial attitudes.* https://www.ebri.org/docs/default-source/rcs/2020-rcs/rcs_20-fs-8_rf.pdf.

50. Wallace, J. (Host). (Premiered Oct 15, 2024). *Closing The Racial Wealth Gap with Brian Seymour. The New Wealth Wave Podcast.* The New Wealth Wave Podcast, episode 24. YouTube, https://www.youtube.com/watch?v=l3cs1oI76-c

Chapter 5: Your Soft Landing

1. Pfeffer, J., & Sutton, R. I. (2000). *The knowing-doing gap: How smart companies turn knowledge into action.* The Harvard Business School Press.

2. Global Financial Literacy Excellence Center (GFLEC). (2025). *The TIAA-Institute GFLEC personal finance index (P-FIN Index).* https://gflec.org/initiatives/personal-finance-index/

3. Bleich, S. N., Bennett, W. L., Gudzune, K. A., & Cooper, L. A. (2012). Impact of physician BMI on obesity care and beliefs. *Obesity,* 20(5), 999-1005. https://doi.org/10.1038/oby.2011.402

4. Seneca. (2014). *Letters from a Stoic (R. Campbell, Trans.).* Penguin Classics.

5. Brüggen, E. C., Hogreve, J., Holmlund, M., Kabadayi, S., & Löfgren, M. (2017). Financial well-being: A conceptualization and research agenda. *Journal of Business Research,* 79, 228–237. https://doi.org/10.1016/j.jbusres.2017.03.013

6. Wallace, J. (Host). (Premiered June 4, 2024). *Finding Financial Freedom, Wellness, and Lasting Wealth with Dasarte Yarnway.* The New Wealth Wave Podcast. The New Wealth Wave Podcast, episode 15. YouTube, https://www.youtube.com/watch?v=RJM9WQ5-NyU

7. Consumer Financial Protection Bureau. (2015, January). *Financial well-being: The goal of financial education.* https://files.consumerfinance.gov/f/201501_cfpb_report_financial-well-

being.pdf

8. Duhigg, C. (2012). *The power of habit: Why we do what we do in life and business*. Random House Trade Paperbacks.

9. Board of Governors of the Federal Reserve System. (2023, May). *Economic well-being of U.S. households in 2022*. https://www.federalreserve.gov/publications/files/2022-report-economic-well-being-us-households-202305.pdf

10. Certified Financial Planner Board of Standards, Inc. (2019, January 24). *New survey shows consumers, no matter their income or assets, need support with spending and household budgeting*. https://www.cfp.net/news/2019/01/new-survey-shows-consumers-no-matter-their-income-or-assets-need-support-with-spending-household

11. National Foundation for Credit Counseling. (2024, April 2). *Survey: Financial anxiety soars as Americans doubt ability to reach goals*. https://www.nfcc.org/press_release/survey-financial-anxiety-soars-as-americans-doubt-ability-to-reach-goals/

12. National Foundation for Credit Counseling. (n.d.). *Client impact: Sharpen your financial focus program*. https://www.nfcc.org/client-impact

13. National Foundation for Credit Counseling. (2018). *Evaluation of outcomes: The NFCC's sharpen your financial focus program (Executive summary)*. https://www.nfcc.org/wp-content/uploads/2019/04/NFCC-Sharpen-Exec-Summary-2018-update.pdf

14. Warren, E., & Tyagi, A. W. (2005). *All your worth: The ultimate lifetime money plan*. Free Press.

15. Wallace, J. (Host). (Premiered Apr 23, 2024). *Finding Financial Healing with Saundra D. Davis, MSFP, APFC®, MCC, FBS®, CSC*. The New Wealth Wave Podcast, episode 12. YouTube, https://www.youtube.com/watch?v=ysM-EDapdvs

Chapter 6: Building Your Legacy Through Thoughtful Planning

1. Chernow, R. (1998). *Titan: The life of John D. Rockefeller, Sr.* Vintage.
2. Williams, R., & Preisser, V. (2010). *Preparing heirs: Five steps to a successful transition of family wealth and values*. Robert D. Reed Publishers.
3. Wallace, J. (Host). (Premiered Mar. 10, 2024). *Generational Wealth With Martin C. Johnson, ESQ*. The New Wealth Wave Podcast, episode 4. YouTube, https://www.youtube.com/watch?v=Ri2QYOfLKas

4. Lustbader, R. (Updated 2025, March 31). *2024 Wills and estate planning study*. Caring. https://www.caring.com/resources/2024-wills-survey/
5. Burtka, J. (Updated 2025, February 5). *Probate lawyers' fees and billing*. Nolo. https://www.nolo.com/legal-encyclopedia/probate-lawyers-fees-billing.html
6. White, E. (2023, July 5). *Aretha Franklin's sons battle over handwritten wills 5 years after her death*. Associated Press. https://apnews.com/article/aretha-franklin-will-dispute-f7d4569021754cdba88dc5f2149b2ec9
7. Wallace, J. (Host). (Premiered May 21, 2024). *Building and Protecting Generational Wealth with Estate Planner Martin C. Johnson, Esq.* The New Wealth Wave Podcast, episode 14. YouTube, https://www.youtube.com/watch?v=PjEctcZXJR4
8. Wallace, J. (Host). (Premiered Mar. 10, 2024). *Generational Wealth With Martin C. Johnson, ESQ*. The New Wealth Wave Podcast, episode 4. YouTube, https://www.youtube.com/watch?v=Ri2QYOfLKas
9. Adams, M., Vittayarukskul, L. (n.d.). *The realities of aging and gaps in long-term care planning*. Caregiver Action Network. https://www.caregiveraction.org/gaps-long-term-care-planning
10. Schoch, D. (Updated 2022, July 15). *Study shows 1 in 5 Americans provide unpaid family care*. AARP. https://www.aarp.org/caregiving/basics/info-2020/unpaid-family-caregivers-report.html
11. Wallace, J. (Host). (Premiered Mar. 10, 2024). *Generational Knowledge and Long-Term Care Planning with Kelly Augspurger, CLTC®, CSA*. The New Wealth Wave Podcast, episode 8. YouTube, https://www.youtube.com/watch?v=JE3gH_p5PYM

Chapter 7: Creating Your Financial Footprints

1. Brinkley, D. (2003). *Wheels for the world: Henry Ford, his company, and a century of progress*. Penguin Books.
2. Bhutta, N., Chang, A.C., Dettling, L.J., & Hsu, J.W. (2020, September 28). *Disparities in wealth by race and ethnicity in the 2019 survey of consumer finances*. Board of Governors of the Federal Reserve System. https://www.federalreserve.gov/econres/notes/feds-notes/disparities-in-wealth-by-race-and-ethnicity-in-the-2019-survey-of-consumer-finances-20200928.html
3. Wolff, E. N., & Gittleman, M. (2014). Inheritances and the distribution of wealth or whatever happened to the great inheritance boom? *The Journal of Economic Inequality*, 12(4), 439-468. https://doi.org/10.1007/s10888-013-9261-8

4. Chetty, R., Hendren, N., Kline, P., & Saez, E. (2014). Where is the land of opportunity? The geography of intergenerational mobility in the United States. *The Quarterly Journal of Economics, 129*(4), 1553-1623. https://doi.org/10.1093/qje/qju022

5. Carnegie, A. (1906). The gospel of wealth. *The North American Review,* 183(599), 526–537. http://www.jstor.org/stable/25105641

6. Ostrower, F. (1995). *Why the wealthy give: The culture of elite philanthropy.* Princeton University Press.

7. Williams, R., & Preisser, V. (2003). *Preparing heirs: Five steps to a successful transition of family wealth and values.* Robert D. Reed Publishers.

8. Wallace, J. (Host). (Premiered May 21, 2024). *Building and Protecting Generational Wealth with Estate Planner Martin C. Johnson, Esq.* The New Wealth Wave Podcast, episode 14. YouTube, https://www.youtube.com/watch?v=PjEctcZXJR4

www.ingramcontent.com/pod-product-compliance
Lightning Source LLC
Chambersburg PA
CBHW021705120626
46545CB00004B/1414